Front cover pictures Academy classes

1940   1940s 1954   1958
1959   1963   1971   1973
1974   1974   1978   1979
        1984 1986 2016

At the Academy:

NJ State   NJ State   NJ State
Archives   Archives   Archives

  1954   1954   1993
    1954   1993 2002

The Best Job in the World:
Learning the Job

Additional books by author:

Firehouse Fraternity Oral History Series:
Volume I: Becoming a Firefighter
Volume II: Life Between Alarms
Volume III: Equipment
Volume IV: Responding
Volume V: Riots to Renaissance
Volume VI: Changing the NFD

The Newark Riots: A View from the Firehouse

An Eerie Silence: An Oral History of Newark
Firefighters at the WTC

First Days/First Nights: The Beginnings of Newark
Fire Department Careers

Remembrances of Newark

Hervey's Boys: New Jersey's First Chinese Community
1870-1886 (And What Happened After That)

Fiction:
The Firebox Stalker
The Hand Life Dealt you
A-zou: A Woman Living in Interesting Times

Children's Fiction:
A Hundred Battles (YA)
A Broken Glass (YA)
Balancing Act (Middle Grade)

The Best Job in the World: Learning the Job

An Oral History of the Newark Fire Department
1940 - 2016

Neal Stoffers

Springfield and Hunterdon Publishing
Copyright 2022
www.newarkfireoralhistory.com

First Printing: 2022

ISBN: 978-1-970034-34-9

Springfield and Hunterdon Publishing
East Brunswick, NJ 08816-5852

Dedicated to past, present, and future generations of Newark firefighters, and especially to the 67 firefighters who made the ultimate sacrifice upholding their oath to protect the lives and property of Newark's citizens.

"Ain't a bad job kid. You'll wind up getting a house out of it and you'll get a pension, so you won't starve to death when you retire." (Said to Deputy Chief James McCormack 1949)

_____

Contents

Acknowledgements

First, I must again acknowledge my long-suffering wife Miaoli who has put up with my obsession to preserve the history of the Newark Fire Department for more than thirty years. I anticipate at least another three books will come from the interviews I have already conducted, so her sacrifice has not yet ended. My sister Dorothy took the time to read through the manuscript and point out all the typos, omissions, and repetitions I had inserted while transcribing. And finally, my brother Mark made the cover possible. Of course, in the end I am responsible for the final product.

The credit for much of this book goes to the members of the Newark Fire Department who gave so generously of their time to take part in my oral history project. The hours of recorded conversations they contributed will help preserve the history of Newark's fire department and of Newark itself. A list of those interviewed appears at the end of the book. This is their story. I am honored to tell it.

Foreword

The Best Job in the World: Learning the Job introduces the reader to how people became part of the Newark Fire Department. It is the first of a series of four books based on an oral history project I began in 1991. The book is divided into four parts. My original intention was to have nine chapters, but the final product would have been a tome of a thousand or more pages. Anyone who has sat around a firehouse kitchen table knows that firefighters can be verbose if given a chance. My purpose all along was to give them that chance and use their words to preserve the history of the NFD. In order the make this book more reasonable in length, I added a fourth book title to the original three and spread the subjects out to make each volume a little more focused on more specific topics.

In *Learning the Job*, I have focused on the how and why of becoming a firefighter. Part Four *Hours and Salary* begins to frame out the occupation itself. As the quote after the dedication says, "Ain't a bad job, kid." But no one becomes a firefighter to get rich. The reasons vary between individuals and are deeply humane.

Why a Firefighter

Conville: Well, I graduated Rutgers University. It was the beginning of the Depression. It was very difficult to get jobs. I got laid off. But in the fire department, you could get a job in the fire department and for the next twenty-five years you would receive a pay and then you would also receive a pension when you retired. That was the main reason. It was a security job. Just keep your nose clean; do the time; you come out; you got a pension. Very few companies had pensions. You would never be laid off. There would be no more depression for you.

Ryan: My brother was a fireman. He was on the fire department before me. I guess he was appointed around '43, during the war. He was on that way. So, I figured I'd go on the fire department, same as him. I knew plenty of people on the fire department. My neighbors up and down the street were firemen, Captain Olohan from Eight Truck, Patty Haybrin from Eight Truck. Across the street was Elmer Tefoder from Eight Truck. Chris Cula from Sixteen Engine. There was a couple of more in the neighborhood. So, go on there is just any other job. Had the old Irish Civil Service. You had a pension and you had a steady job. So, you did good.

Conover: Well, for security mostly. I got out of service in July of 1945. I didn't want to go back to my old job. I was a shipping clerk in a paper mill in Bogota, New Jersey. The Robert Dare Company was the name of the company. They were a big outfit, but I didn't want to go back there even though I heard from the union and everybody else. I just didn't want that job. So, I went to work for the federal government in the office of Dependency Benefits. They used to issue the dependency checks. After a year they closed up shop in Newark and the entire agency moved to Saint Louis, Missouri. My wife didn't want to go to Missouri. So, I had to bow out. I went to work in East Orange for a lock joint pipe company. They were a pretty big pipe manufacturer. They had plants in Norton, New Jersey, Kenilworth, and East Orange, where I worked. The home office was there too. I started as a clerk in the payroll department and in a year and a half time, I was assistant department head in the payroll department. But I wanted more security. So, my father-in-law, Gene Hurle, was in the fire department and an uncle, Ed Vine. They kept extolling the advantages. When you're in civil service, you were always led to believe that about the only way that you could be discharged would be for the conviction of a felony. So, you had security.

J. Doherty: After I got out of the Army, I took all the civil service tests there were. My first job was a Port Authority Policeman. I was there for about two years and I wasn't cut out to be a cop. So, when the fire list came out in 1949, I took the fire department in December of '49 which was the institution of the fifty-six-hour week. Fifty or so of us were sworn in and I was assigned to Twenty-three Engine up on Mount Prospect Avenue. In a day or so I reported into Twenty-three Engine. I didn't know anything about the fire department. Mid-morning a little red pick-up truck pulls up with a big package in brown wrapping paper, Fireman Doherty on it. So, I get it. I open it up, sheets and pillow cases. I said, "Wow, this is a job." I was only in three hours and here's your sheets and pillow case. I said, "Okay" So, that's how I came into the fire department. I had a few friends that I knew were in the fire department, but I didn't know anything about it at that time.

Gibson: I became a fireman because I didn't like the cops and I was in trouble all the time. The old timers on the police department, they were just chintzy people. Like I got into the Traffic Division and they were so cheap. Of course, in those days you drank for nothing if you were a cop. I got into the Traffic Division and these guys, they'd have two blocks like on Mulberry Street or Raymond Boulevard or Commerce Street, didn't need a nickel for the meter for the eight hours. Paid forty cents, put it in their pocket and let you park there all day for nothing. I hated this shit. I had trouble when I first went into the cops. I got suspended and I had to pay money to the people that I had the trouble with. They wouldn't let me into the PBA or anything. So, I just went along. My father really didn't want me to be a cop. He was a cop. I was a son of a bitch when I was young. Then I put into the fire department.

G. Alfano: I had all these friends on the job. They said come on the job. I took the police and fire exams and I got knocked down for the police because I wasn't tall enough. I think the cops were five eight at the time and the firemen were five seven. When he measured me for the fire department he said, "You shouldn't have got that crew cut, kiddo." I just made it. Why the fire department? Helping people for one thing and I figured I'd like it. Outside of that I don't know why I became a fireman. At the time that I took it, I think security was one of the things we were looking for, a job where you wouldn't get laid off. I had a job and I was on sympathy strike most of the time. You know, not for myself, but for somebody else. I got kind of sick of that. When it came up, my boss said to me, "Take it George and if you don't like it, I'll take you back." When I took it, I said to a very good friend of mine who was on the fire department, "I really don't know why I took it because I was making twice the amount of money and I was working half the hours. I got to be crazy." He said to me, "Stay here for three months. Tell me you'll stay for three months and if you don't like it, we'll have a big party for you." So, I said you got a deal. I took it and you couldn't get me out with a bulldozer. I loved the job. I enjoyed every minute of it. I put thirty-six and a half years in.

D.C. Griggs: Well, it was actually an accident. I was out of the service, out of the Navy, not too long. When Bobby Dorsier, we went to Benedict's together in high school, his father-in-law, knew my dad on the police department. Bobby had already taken Newark's police exam and when he was in the company of Bobby he said, "Is Johnny Griggs out of the Navy yet?" And he said, "I think he is." He says, "Well, you're getting an application for the fire department. You get him one." So, Bobby called me up and said would I be interested in taking it. I have an application. I said sure and in doing so I ended up down on Washington Street where the old Salvage company was, nosing around to see if they had a school going which they did.

I called Bobby up, he was working midnights down at Ballantine checking freight cars loading the beer into them. I was at the Sherwin Williams paint company and I said a certain night that they had the schooling. It was a dollar a night to go there. And he said, "I'm interested." So, we would meet and go and then he would go to work and I'd go home. That was the beginning. Then I took it upon myself to go down to the public library and dig out every Arco book that I could find that was left. All the new ones were gone. I was getting the old ones because everybody else is digging. I went over that stuff because four years in the service, you're not keeping up with things. So, I did that and I started working out because I found out you had to take a performance test. I would spend weekends in Bayonne Park or any other park, in Branch Brook with my young daughter and my wife. They'd be sitting on my legs and I'd be doing sit-ups. That was the beginning.

Duerr: At the time I came out of the service in the mid-50s and there weren't too many jobs available. I got a job at Public Service as a lineman and I didn't think there was a future climbing poles because I had seen a lot of guys cut out. So, I decided to take civil service tests. I figured there was a good future there. The pay was good. I took the New Jersey State Police, the Newark Police, and Newark Fire Department exams. Came out high on all three and said, "Well whoever calls me first has got me." The fire department called me first. That's how I got on the fire department. Now while I was trying to take the fire department exam, I met

Jimmy Donlon, Chief Donlon, and he was running a class and I went to his class. He was very instrumental in me becoming a fireman. I got a very high mark, higher in the fire department than I did with the State Police and the police department. That's how I got on and my father was an auxiliary during the war. He used to operate out of Ten Engine. He used to tell me all these sea stories and so I said, "Hey that's a good job." Got a chance to save lives and property. and the pay wasn't that good because we were working fifty-six hours. I started at forty-two hundred a year. I had been making five thousand with P.S. But I just liked the job. I thought it was going to be beneficial to me.

Schoemer: My father talked me into it. Good hours, the pay wasn't so bad. It was exciting. I had ridden with him a few times, with him being in the fire department, and I had ridden on the apparatus. I'd ridden with him to a couple of jobs. I knew it was exciting.

A. Prachar: Tradition. It passed down from the family. I was the fourth generation in my family to be a Newark firefighter. My son John, who came on the job later, became the fifth and final member of the Newark Fire Department. My great-great-great-grandfather was the seventh man killed in the line of duty on the Newark Fire Department. My mother received an award for dragging a man out of a burning building. So, fires are all I ever knew. And then on my wife's side of the family, my brother-in-law was a fire captain, my father-in-law was a Newark fireman, so between my wife and I, we're surrounded by the Newark Fire Department.

Bitter: Why'd I become a fireman? 1957, I had never been in the firehouse in my life. I knew nothing about the fire department. Myself, Chris Larson, Eddy Cassidy, and Richie Guski, Richie was in Eleven Truck, he was taking classes on Court Street given by the police sergeant. I believe his name was Reilly. And he was running a course to pass the police exam. The fire exam happened to be on the same day. I think we took our written in Barringer. I believe Barringer and when you got done with the police exam, you walked down the hall and took the fire test. And I took the fire test. Just happened to be the same day. Had no interest what so ever. I don't know why I wanted to be a cop. Thank God I never became a cop.

Cardillo: Well, I was working in the warehouse and I was number one in the warehouse. But they needed a driver in the warehouse, so they asked me, "Do I want to drive a truck?" I didn't, but I took that job, it was a little bit more pay. I didn't know I was the last on the truck and I was the first guy to get laid off. I can't do this. This is Westinghouse I'm working for. If they're on strike in California, you go out too. I was walking on the picket line. On my break, I went to City Hall and took the test for fireman and cop. I come out as a cop. They're the first to call me. I went down there and they took the prints and all. Then I went back to work for Westinghouse. All of the sudden, I'm at my brother-in-law's house which I used to give as my address at that time. So, the doorbell rings and a guy yells, "Is Cardillo up there?" "Yeah." It's the fire department and I had to go get a physical. So, I said, whoever takes me first I'll go to. And sure enough, the fire department called me first. So, I went there. I was over the age, but they took my service years away. So that's why I got on the job.

Elward: From my area, I'm going to say from Fifth Street down to about First Street. It's just a geographical territory. It just seemed like on the south side from Fourteenth Street and the north side from Fourteenth Street down to about Sixth Street. Don't ask me why. Andy Masterson, all of us were firemen. John Reiss, fireman, Vinney McGrath, fireman. I can't think of somebody who broke what we called the color line. The color line, that means the cops and firemen. So, I'm trying to think, previous to me coming on the fire department, the '59 list had already been started. I come on in '62. I think I come on with Billy Carragher, Chief

Carragher, that list. You got me thinking. I think out of our group in my neighborhood, with all the people. We used to hang on Roseville Avenue in bars, the Clipper Ship, the Annex, the Wonder Bar. Anyway, it just seems that when the '59 list started, I used to ask people, "When the hell do you work?" I can't tell. One night I went down to Seven Engine. John Hughes was a good friend of mine. And I was working in Liquid Carbonics, crazy hours on the trucks. And I said, "You get off in the morning." He said, "You go home for three days." I said, "Go home for three days. You don't have to come back?" And he says, "Yeah." Then they started explaining. I had no inkling at all that I was going to become a fireman.

Schofield: Why'd I become a fireman? At the time I didn't know about it. Because I was married and had a family and I needed something so I had an income. At the beginning it was not involved with benefits. The family comes first and everything. After I got on the job, I found out it was the only one I could say I really loved. I couldn't wait to get to the firehouse.

Cosby: I really had no intension of becoming a firefighter. A friend of mine, Laurence Shepard, convinced me to take the test. I was working at Lockheed Electronics. I had plans on going into the electronics field. Back then I was doing circuit boards for space ships. I liked it pretty well, but I thought I'd go to I.T.&T after I finished my schooling and my training program. I took the test and lo and behold they call me. He said, "Go on down and try." So, I did. I tried it. While I was on the job, I got a five thousand dollar raise. So, I decided I'd stay. That's when I got my first house, that first year. I enjoyed it. I liked it. I continued to stay where I was. I'm in Twelve Engine, Five Truck the last twenty-nine years. So, I enjoyed it. It's been good. It's a-okay.

Dalton: The main reason I became a fireman, I was fascinated. Living down the street from Engine Seventeen on West Runyon Street, I used to love to see them coming back and forth, back and forth. Then on hot summer days they would open up the fire hydrant for us and I thought that was really nice. As I got older, I went into the service. I got firefighter training in the Navy and I'm thinking maybe I'd like to do this. So, when I came out, I went to work with the Western Electric in Kearny. I became a paymaster over there in the financial department and the test for the fire department came up. So, I took it. I came out seventeen, but that was with the veterans' status.

Gaynor: My father suggested it. At the time I was working for General Motors and he thought the security of civil service would be a good thing. So, in 1964, I took the exam.

Perez: Because I wanted my summers off. I was a cop and I couldn't get summers. As a cop your vacation time was in the winter as a rookie. I wanted summers off, so I switched over to the fire department. I came out of the service and I was with a couple of my buddies who were cops. The last day to file they said, "Why don't you become a cop?" We were all under the weather. The last application was taken to the Third Precinct front door by four drunken people. It had to be post marked by twelve o'clock midnight. One of my buddies was a cop. Had it postmarked before twelve.

I just never even thought of becoming a fireman. George Pianka, Six Engine, he was a friend of mine at the time and he wanted somebody to take the exam and the physical. He was afraid to go up there and do it by himself. George and I went and took the exam at Barringer. it was good because George wanted to be a fireman. About ten months later I get a phone call from a guy in the Arson Squad, "You're on the list. You're thirty-seven on the list. You want to become a fireman?" I'm a cop. I thought about it a little bit, vacations, between winter and summer. I had to become a fireman. If not for George Pianka going to take the exam, would never have become a fireman. I would have stayed a cop.

Calvetti: It was an accident. I was a mailman and I was delivering mail in the Weequahic section. I stopped in the firehouse on Lehigh and Bergen. I had mail for the firehouse. I stopped in to drop the mail off and the guy in the firehouse said to me, "Hey you want an application for the fire department." I said, "Yeah, why not. Give me an application." Got the application; went home; filled it out; sent it in. Not even three months later. I'm on the job.

I knew people on the job, but I never gave it any thought, coming on the fire department. I knew Angelo Ricca. He was on the job. I knew Richie Giovenco. He was on the job. I never hung around with Ricca. He was older than I am. The same with Richie Giovenco. I never hung around with either one of them. So, I didn't know anything about the fire department. Oh, and I knew Sally Marino. I knew Sally. In fact I saw Sally before I took the test for the fire department. I was driving a bus before I became a mailman. I was driving the 51 Park Avenue and I was coming from East Orange into Newark. Guy gets on my bus. It's Sal. He says, "Hey Frankie how you doing?" I says, "Not bad. What are you doing?" He says, "I'm a fireman". "A fireman?" "Yeah, I'm a fireman in Newark. You ought to take the test. You'd love the job." I said, "Yeah, yeah, yeah. Okay." I forgot all about it until I stopped in the firehouse. They gave me the application. And I took the test like I said, came out, and here I am on the fire department. Did twenty-five and left.

Lawless: I had just got married and I was actually looking for security, benefits. I knew nothing about the department actually.

Benderoth: Well, I was a Newark volunteer auxiliary fireman in 1950 and I thought it was a good job at the time. I got married and took the test.

Miller: I became a fireman actually for something to do on a Saturday morning. I wound up filing for the exam with my brother-in-law, who became a

Newark cop. He was married to my fiancé's sister. I think it was a weekday night, I said I wanted to go take the fire and police exam, it was at the Training Academy on Eighteenth Avenue. We went over there one night and I thought we were just going to sign up for it. I was working as an inventory accountant in Garwood at the time. I figured I was going to take the exam, but really it was a starting up of classes to study for the exam. But at that first class you filled out the application to take the exam and they forwarded them. So, I signed up for a combination exam, police and fire. I was living in the Ivy Hill Apartments at the time. I got up on a Saturday morning and saw that it was the date for the exam and the physical which were held at Barringer High School. I didn't have anything going until twelve o'clock that day, so I went down and I took the exam. My uncle was a career fireman in Newark, but I was very happy being an accountant.

Weber: My dad was on the job and he talked me into it. I had no intention growing up of ever being a fireman. I didn't know exactly what I wanted to do, but I was working in construction and the examination came up. My dad talked me into taking it.

Saccone: Because first of all, at the time I was getting married and I thought that the fire department was the best opportunity for me to support my family if I did get married. It was a steady job. At that time, I was driving trucks, going to different places for jobs. The main reason why I took the test is because of the steady job. That's what I wanted. You see you're getting married to a woman. It's nice to have that check there. I took the test and the rest is history.

Daudelin: Well, actually I started with the Newark Police Department. I knew a lot of fireman and cops at that time. Where I grew up on Grafton and Summer, it was either you became a criminal or you went into police and fire, so first I went into the police department and then I transferred over and became a firefighter.

Marcell: I needed a job. My wife and I had one baby and I think we had another baby on the way. I was working at the Mexi Can Company at night. I was a fulltime student in the daytime. And I didn't have real good benefits. My Uncle Andy was a fireman. He said to me, "Why don't you take the test for fireman?" I said, "I don't know." I was reluctant to take the test because when I was fifteen years old, we lived on 78 North Sixth Street, a four-story brick H shaped apartment building on the fourth floor. And at 5:30 in the morning we had a fire. The apartment next door to us caught on fire. We lived pretty close to Eleven Engine. Sixth Street wasn't that far from where Eleven Engine was and I had visited my uncle a couple of times. Whenever he would go up the street, when the sirens were going off, he would do like a yell. So, we knew he was on the back step, whatever hour it was. This time we hear the fire engine and we go to the window to see maybe my uncle's on there. And all of the sudden the smoke was coming up through the radiators, around the wall, and stuff. My dad said "Uh-oh, this building's on fire."

It was the next-door apartment. The guy's air conditioner caught on fire and the whole apartment caught on fire. I checked it out in the books later on from Four Engine. Four Engine did go to that fire, but anyway, my brother, my sister and myself, my brother was a baby. We all went to the front door. The smoke was from the floor all the way up to the ceiling in the hallway. We had to escape through the fire escape. And unfortunately, my dad left the door open and we lost everything that we had. So having that experience with a fire, I was a little bit hesitant. I was still remember going down the fire escape and the firemen breaking the glass and it shattering down on the fire escape as we came down. My mother being helped by a fireman. And then my uncle gave us some furniture to replace the furniture that we had and we got things, clothes from our relatives. Stuff to just replace what we lost.

So, when my uncle said do you want to be a fireman, I wasn't too crazy about being a fireman. Plus, right around that time there were the riots and I knew the firemen were doing a lot of work. I'd seen on the news where there were many multiple buildings on fire. I said, "But I really need a job bad. I'm going to try and take this job. I took the test and I did alright. I came out I think twenty-one on the list. I was the first or second non-vet on the list.

I got called and went down to City Hall and got put on with a bunch of guys, maybe twenty-five guys. And they promoted some guys; they promoted Jack Hall and Tenpenny the same day that I went on. That was June first, 1970.

P. Doherty: Well, my cousin Danny was a fireman. My cousin Peter was a fireman. They talked me into taking the test in July of 1970. I went and took the test and became a fireman in October of 1970.

Dainty: I had finished my time in the Marine Corps in February 1970 and I was working for an electrical contractor. I really wasn't happy, even though that was my trade. So, I was sitting in the truck in the morning having some coffee and I had the Star Ledger. They had this full-page ad for the City of Newark hiring cops and firemen. I said, "I ended up being shot at in Nam and I really don't care to do that again." So, I decided, let me try the fireman route. It was just that. I didn't know any firemen. I didn't know any cops. It was something that sounded like it might be interesting.

Kelly: Well, my father was a fireman and I always respected him. I looked up to him. He never encouraged me. He wanted at least one of his kids to go to college because he felt like that would make him very happy. So, I happened to be the one he sent to college. I wanted to quit because it just wasn't my cup of tea. I couldn't see sitting in an office somewhere. I said, "Listen, I'm going to take the test to be a fireman. I want to be a fireman." So, he said, "Go ahead. Go be a fireman. But you know, still get the degree. You can always fall back on it." So that's what I did. I took the test. Tommy Grehl and I studied together when we came on the job.

We had those Arco books I think it was and we aced the test. We were in great shape then too. We came on the job and we both gradated college; never used a lick of it. I saw how happy my father was with the job. He'd come home with funny stories all the time. So, I said, "You know, the hours were good. You'll never be rich, but you'll never be poor."

I deferred. I could have come on in '70, but with college they let you defer the year. So that's what Tommy Grehl and I did. Cause we were good friends then. If it wasn't for Chief Grehl we would never have even got on the job because they had three lists at the time and they stopped with our list. They weren't moving anybody off our list and it was almost dead. They just happened to put him in as the chief of the department for a week when the chief was on vacation. He said, "We need eleven guys." They put eleven guys on. We just got in. Really it was just a stroke of luck. Otherwise, we weren't making it.

Romano: I guess I became a fireman because I was unhappy with what I was doing at the time. I was working in the Post Office in Newark, downtown Newark at the main Post Office. My hours were six in the evening to two-thirty, three o'clock in the morning five nights a week. And my days off were Monday and Tuesday. At that time, I think I was making about eight thousand five hundred, maybe nine thousand dollars a year. I knew a couple of people on the fire department, Bobby Gaynor being one of them, who I used to see in one of the South Orange Avenue saloons. I got to talking with him about the fire department one night and I liked what I heard. Next time the test came up I studied for it. I don't even know if those books are still in existence. I used to go to the library, get the library books, and I studied for the test. I think I took the test in '71 and much to my surprise I came out near the top. Due to my veteran status, I was third on that list. This was in '70 or '71 and I was hired in February of '72. I really had no family history of anybody else on the fire department. It wasn't as though I was following in anybody's footsteps. I really knew nothing about the fire department other than what the couple of people that I knew told me about it. I would see them in the street from time to time. I worked at a small Post Office substation on Bergen Street for a while. And it seemed like every morning that I went to work in the Post Office there'd be a few more buildings missing in smoldering ruins. And I would see the firemen there. That was my knowledge of the fire department.

Rosamilia: Before I was a fireman I worked at the monastery on Thirteenth Avenue, St. Dominic's, Thirteenth Avenue and Eighth Street. I worked there for about six months. I used to do maintenance inside the building, chauffeuring. Anyway, I was only nineteen years old. After about six months, when they sent me out, I wouldn't hurry back too much. Finally, the sister says, "We like you a lot and we're happy with your work, but we think that you need to be a little older for this job." Basically, it was inside. They really didn't do much and they took good care of you. It's just that being shut in a monastery with about thirty or forty nuns all day, I didn't last. I was unemployed and the test came up for cadet. That's how I started out, put in an application, went down to One Lincoln Avenue. They were running some practice runs there, a little bit of written, tutoring kind of stuff. I went down there, participated in that. Took the test and I got the call.

My brother brought me the application and he did influence me, but I wasn't thinking about being a fireman at that point. I was nineteen and I was thinking about other stuff. Maybe going to school, finding something to do, make a few bucks. I wasn't thinking about a long term, career type thing. And then lightning struck and I loved it.

Burkhardt: My father brought home the application for me. At the time the fire department was offering a cadet program. It put me through college and paid half the fire department salary. I wanted to be a cop. I didn't want to be a fireman, but I took the test. I came out like third in the test and thirty-two years later here I am. The best job I ever had. The only job I ever had also. I had a lot of crumby part time jobs, but as I tell the new kids coming on the job now. All you have to do is show up for work and it's not a bad job. Where else do you start off with a coffee break and end with a coffee break?

Stoffers: Why did I become a fireman? Good question. Because I had come back from Albuquerque and my Uncle Carl said, "Here's the test." So, I took the cadet test, not the fireman's test. It was cadets, Fire Cadets and they were sending you to school for an Associate's Degree in fire science. They were going to make everybody smarter, a better fireman, a smarter fireman. That's why I took the test. It didn't work out the way they thought.

Morgan: No particular reason why. I was looking for a job. A guy I did some work for had an in, suggested I take the test for the cadet program back in 1971. Took the test, came in the top twenty and there I was.

Brownlee: Why'd I become a fireman? My uncle who was a captain on the fire department came to my house. He handed me an application and he said, "Fill this out and mail it." And then he said, "No, fill it out and I will mail it." And that's how I became a fireman.

Coale: It's probably something I always wanted to do. I was a volunteer before. The test that they ran was the only one that was open to the whole state. I lived in Bergen County at the time. I saw a full-page ad and I said, "Boy this sounds interesting. If I'm doing this for nothing I might as well do it and get paid." There must have been twenty-five or thirty different towns and when you took the test it was for all of them or you could select what you wanted. So, I might as well go to Newark cause it's the biggest and the best. So that's how it happened. It was the best twenty-five cents I ever invested on a Sunday paper. It was the inside of the Star Ledger that had the advertisement. And it just went from there.

Banta: Well, I took the test when I came out of the Marines in '72. I wasn't a Newark resident. Our test in '73 was open to all state residents. I took it because I was born and raised in Paterson and I lived a block from a firehouse. I had it in my blood from that point. I used to hang in the Paterson firehouse and I was the gopher for the guys. Run to the store for cigarettes, run to the store and get this, run to the store and get something else. And my reward for working like that in the firehouse for the guys was the ten-cent soda machine. I'd get a bottle of Yoo-hoo out of them. That was basically where I had it. I had it in my blood from the time I could walk. My father had friends that were in the fire department. He would take me over to Engine 6 in Paterson on Market Street where a friend of his worked. They bounced me all over the fire truck. I remember being in the firehouse one day with the door closed and they had an old FWD rig. I reached down and I pressed the siren button right as a guy walked in front of the fire engine. He almost died because of the noise. That was it. I've always enjoyed it.

Killeen: For crying out loud, my father was a fireman and I recall the old days when they had the cotton jacketed hose. It would get an odor in it. It would get a smell. I remember going to the firehouse visiting him and getting that smell. You'd smell a little bit of the apparatus, but that mildewy, that damp, mildewy smell was always around. I guess I was always attracted to the smell.

I guess it was a romantic thing. My dad was first a fireman down in Fort Lauderdale, Florida when he came out of the Navy. The first time I recall being on a fire engine was on a hook and ladder in the tiller seat. I thought we were going out on a run. Actually, the engine was going on an engine only run and I'm a little kid sitting in the seat. I'm thinking I have to steer this thing. They're breaking my balls, but having a good time. But there was a romantic thing there, the size of it, the sound, people hanging on to it. That was a big thing and the smell, but also that you were doing something. There was a physical nature about it. I don't know if it's romantic, but it was very appealing.

I was living with my mother and stepfather in Florida and I said I wanted to live with my father. I used to spend summers up here, but I came up here and I did my last two years of high school up here. I ended up at Ten Engine because my dad was studying with Captain Joe Miller. He was a fireman at Six Truck and he made Captain. They put him at Ten Engine. So, now Joe Miller's there and I ended up going to Ten Engine because my father studied with Joe Miller. My father came down once or twice and after that I knew how to get to Ten Engine. He really didn't know the extent of what was going on with my life down there. He had an idea and he figured nobody would let me get hurt, but I figured that he let me grow up a little bit. Instead of hanging on the corner with guys and doing whatever, I was going down there and hanging with older guys and doing shit. But that actually opened up my eyes to what firefighting was pretty much like.

I had all my own gear. One Christmas my father took me out and bought me a leather helmet. I still have the helmet. I had my own filter mask. They weren't even SCBAs then. It was still a filter mask. I had my own filter mask; one of his coats; and that was it. There were three guys. There was myself. I was like the young kid. Jack Theabolt, who has since passed away. He was there. He became a New York City fireman. And Al Gerjanowitz, Albert was in the Navy. He would come home on leave and stay at Ten Engine for the weekend. Go back down to, I guess, he was at Norfolk. And we were the three buffs down at Ten Engine. There were more there. Some weekends there were so many guys there from Bound Brook that you couldn't get a spot on the rig. You'd be riding the hose bed on the pumper, because it was two-piece. That was pretty much my baptism of fire of getting into fires.

Camasta: I came on the fire department to build a career, in general. My father was on the job in Linden. I could see it; my father was riding on the fire engine. So, that established my interest. Between flunking out of college, needing a job, and the background I had from my family I took the job. I worked at getting on the fire department job. I wasn't one of the guys that his friend was going to take the test and he tagged along. I worked at taking it because in 1972 they did away with the residency requirement and you were allowed to the test for cities throughout the state. So, I competitively took all the examinations in 1972 for every city throughout the state, as many cities as I could. I had a previous interest in firefighting and salary-wise wasn't important. I just wanted to ride on a fire truck.

In that time frame they couldn't get enough people to take the fire department job. That was one of the things that established the statewide ability to take the test. They couldn't get people to take the job. Newark had no choice but to go out of the city to find people to take the job. Newark was the big city. That's where all the fires were. I wanted to go to fires. And throughout the state probably coming on the job in '74, Newark was one of the first ones that I was certified for. There were a couple of small towns. I think I might have been certified for like Glasgow or something down south Jersey. I felt that was too far, so I passed on that one. I was hoping for Newark or Jersey City and fortunately Jersey City didn't come along. Jersey City was very competitive at that time because I worked really hard for the Jersey City list and come out two hundred and something. Where the Newark list, I either came out eighty-four and got a ninety-five or came out ninety-five and got an eighty-four, literally something like that.

Security had nothing to do with it at the time. That wasn't even conceived. At that time there wasn't a layoff in any department. Security was a given for this job. It was nothing that you even thought about. And I think the majority of the guys I came on with, salary wasn't a question either because guys took cuts in pay. In fact, the class that I come on with was the first completely non-vet class. It was the guys that had the top scores throughout the state at the time.

Partridge: My father was a volunteer. He was the chaplain of the Glen Rock fire department which is the town where I grew up. So, I just grew up with it. So many guys grew up with it in Newark. Their fathers were on the job in Newark. In my case it was with the volunteer department and I grew up always thinking I'd be a volunteer. I never thought I'd be a career firefighter. It just wasn't on my radar. I just never thought about it, not that I wouldn't have done it, it was just something I felt like other people have that job. I'm going to do whatever I'm going to do and be a volunteer.

When I turned eighteen my parents wanted to get me some kind of fire related gift because at age eighteen, I was joining the volunteer fire department. I had a catalog lying around the house from this guy EJ Thomas who was a deputy chief in Bloomfield that sold text books. At the time he was the main source for everybody that was studying for promotion. They saw the catalog lying around which I didn't leave around as a hint, but they found it. And they actually took a ride to this guy one day and bought me a copy of the Fire Chief's Handbook. In the process, he was asking about me. They said, "Well, you know, he's going to join the volunteer fire department." And Thomas said, "Well, has he ever thought about making it a career?" And they were like, "I don't know. We never - - ." He said, "Well, I'll tell you what. They just changed the residency law. You don't have to be the resident of a city to get on the job. And right now they're having filings for a test for a whole bunch of cities. Let me give you a name for him to call. This is a Paterson Captain who helps guys study to get on the job. If he's interested, this will get him on the road."

So, my parents came back, and on my birthday, they gave me the Fire Chief's Handbook. And they also gave me the phone number and told me the whole story. It was also about that time the book came out, *Report from Engine Eighty-two* which I read and which everybody in my generation read. I thought it was cool. When my parents told me what Thomas had said to them, I felt like, "Of course." A light bulb went on. "Of course, this solves all the issues."

So, I called the guy in Paterson and he was running prep classes for the exam. I got involved in that. And I took the test. Actually, at that time, Newark wasn't on the list. Paterson, Union City, a whole bunch of places were on the list. I check off

Paterson, Union City, a few other places. Figuring Paterson would be my choice out of those cities. And then one day this guy whose name was John Marrow from Paterson called me up and said, "Hey, Newark just reopened filing. They had some kind of problem and now they have to reopen the filing, so now if you want you can also apply to Newark. I thought, "Perfect. Biggest, busiest city in the state, I'll get that application right in." It turned out that I did well enough to get made. I wasn't a veteran, so there were several classes put on from the list before they got to me, but luckily, they got to me.

Straile: It's something I always wanted to do and I always like the idea, see firemen helping people. Thought it would be a great career to be able to be out there to help people. And it was really something I wanted to do. I wanted to make something out of myself with my life.

J. Prachar: A couple of reasons, one it seemed the right thing to do at the time. I was going to college. I was in NJIT. My dad brought the application home from work. Said, "You want to take the test?" "Yeah, I'll take the test." Took the written, aced the written. Took the physical. I dropped out of school in May of '77. The fire department came along. At the time it was sort of "Well, I'll do this until something better comes along." Not knowing that all along that's what I wanted to do.

I'm fifth generation on my dad's side on the job and in a roundabout way, third generation on my mom's side. My mom's dad was a fireman. My mom's brother-in-law, my uncle, through marriage was a fireman. So I guess in a roundabout way, you can say three generations. But we go back to Daniel McGee. 1883 he died; third paid fireman to die in the line of duty. Trampled by the horses.

Mitchell: Why'd I become a fireman? Because I liked the excitement of the job. I like working physically. And my father and uncle were firemen too.

Daly: Knew the job. All my friends were fireman. My brother was a fireman, Joe D'Alise , Jack Donavan, Kevin Dowd, Bernie Dowd. I had two captains on my block, Bill Edelman and Dan Dolak and Bob Bart. So firemen were all around me all the time. Down the street was another fireman, Chief Boyle. I hung out with his son. So I got to meet a lot of firemen. Jimmy Mooney is my cousin. He wanted me to become a fireman in 1971 when I graduated from high school. They had the cadet program. I was intent on going to college and that's when Donavan and Dowd came on. Later on down the road when I was twenty-six I took the firemen's test and the police department test and the State Troopers' test all at the same time. I passed all three. When it came down to which job I was going to take, I went down to the State Troopers at Sea Girt and they looked like Marines. The psychiatrist looked at me. He goes, "You have a problem with this?" I said, "No." I said to myself, I have a problem with jumping up, standing at attention, and getting my hair cut. Here I am with a beard and long hair. Then I go to the fire department. They're up in there up on Eighteenth Avenue. I said "What do I get?" The guy jokingly said, "Two sheets and a pillow case." I said, "How could you beat that?" So, I basically did it because my friends and my brother and people around the neighborhood being firemen.

Zieser: Why'd I become a fireman? I guess because of a family tradition. My grandfather was a fireman, of course my father, my uncle. When we were kids growing up, my brother Artie, he was the one who always wanted to be the fireman. He would chase fire engines. I liked it a little bit, but I wasn't crazy about it. Then I took the test and I got really excited about becoming a fireman. Like all those memories I guess from my grandfather and my father. I said, "We've been in the department forever it seemed." When I was a kid, I was going to the FMBA picnics and I always grew up around fire department activities, the memorial mass, things like that. So, to me it just became a great stick. It was where I was supposed to be. Something I didn't realize maybe when I was younger.

Hopkins: Why'd I become a fireman? Let's see, my father, my grandfather, my great grandfather was a cop and the other two were firemen. Took the test, had nothing else to do. Ricky Zieser and I took the test and there you go. That was it. My father was, "Here, take this test. You'll like the job." I said, "Okay." I didn't want to become a teacher after college.

Sandella: I became a fireman; it was more by chance than anything else. My neighbor walking by my house handed me the application. He said take the test. I did and I came on.

Witte: Well, my brother Ray gave me this. He said, "Here sign up." I said, "Okay." I was going to college at the time. I thought, okay, I'll give it a shot. So, I signed. Then I got on the job.

Brown: I became a firefighter for financial reasons, for the salary and the security of the job. I was working at the water department. The superintendent Tom Ewing was a fire buff who couldn't pass the test. He told me about all the opportunities with being a fireman. I felt I could make a difference. I expected a good salary and a rewarding job. I felt that people would look up to me as one of the pillars of the community. I knew it was going to be challenging and demanding. And I felt I could do it, actually, I felt that I could do the job and would be able to help people.

When I came out of the service, I took the test for the police department and the fire department. And I came out number three on the police department and number forty-one on the fire department exam. I took the fire department because I said in order to be a cop, I felt I had to be a jerk off when I woke up in the morning and maintain that attitude all day, so I became a fireman.

Kormash: My brother was going out with Chief Marinucci's daughter. I think it was around Christmas time. We were up at his house on Isabella Avenue for dinner. I was taking the police exam and he kind of talked me into wanting to be a fireman. He talked me into being a fireman and I took the exam.

Reiss: I think I always wanted to be a fireman. From when I was a little kid, I really enjoyed firemen. My uncle was a paid fireman in South Orange and you know it was just something I was very interested in, a fireman or an EMT.

Caufield: Why an operator? It was supposed to be firefighter. When I was in the Navy, I got a pretty bad head injury and a s a result I started having seizures. Seizures could come at dinner table. It could happen at three in the morning. It could happen when I'm on the third floor of a burning building and that was no place to put myself or my coworkers in. My father, who was a firefighter, came to me and said "Why don't you take the operator's test?" I was just out of the Navy pretty much and I was full of piss and vinegar and the last thing I wanted to do was be a dispatcher. I wanted to fight fires. I wanted to do all the good stuff. There's a lot of firefighters at a fire. You're one of the guys and it's a team work thing and everything else. That's the thing that led me towards the fire department in the first place, the team work. The team work lifestyle that I was used to from the service. I have no regrets. I have none what so ever. I kind of miss that I didn't get my chance to do that, but it happened. It happened. So, you take your pair of deuces and you try and make a flush out of it.

Almaguer: Why did I become a fireman? I never thought of becoming a fireman. It just happened. What happened was my father used to hang around Sixteen Engine or knew some guys that lived on Hawkins Street that were firefighters. I'm pretty sure those individuals told my father, "Hey, you know, the fire department is looking for firefighters. You've got good kids." this and that.

Plus, across the street from Sixteen Engine was Joyce's Tavern. Joyce's Tavern happens to be Tommy Joyce's father and uncle that owned that tavern and we were part of that tavern. I guess that's how my father found out about the Newark Fire Department and gave me the application.

I was working at Saint James Hospital at that time. I was an orthopedic technician, emergency room tech, O.R. tech, and in charge of the morgue. So, my father comes back to visit me a week after he gave me the application and he said, "Did you fill out the application? Did you mail it out?" I said, "No, it's right there on the table." He said a couple of things to me and then we filled out the application together and he mailed it out. My father paid attention to me and my brother.

But we went to Saint Alowyous Parish and I guess my father knew those firemen that lived on Hawkins Street. We lived on Vincent Street. We were all from the same parish and I would say the main circle that kept us all together, don't forget we're Latino and these guys were Irish, was Joyce's Tavern. At the time I had no inclination of what I was doing. I mean, to me I was just twenty years old and it was very political. You got to realize that there was a lot of drama going on. There's no Latinos on the job. A lot of that stuff was going on. After I got on the job and realized what was going down, I was pissed off because I should have been on that class in 1978.

F. Bellina: I got out of the Marines in 1980. My brother always wanted to be a fireman. I was home one or two days and my brother said to me, "What are you going to do now?" I said, "I don't know. I'm looking at my options." He goes, "Well they're giving a fire test in the City of Newark." Now me growing up in Newark on 15th Avenue during the riots and after the riots, we didn't move to Vailsburg until 1970. I wanted nothing to do with the fire department. I was scared. I was seeing burning buildings and fire trucks. When a fire truck would go by with its siren going, I would have stomach cramps. He said, "Just fill the application out." I fill the application out. I was in such good shape. I get teamed up with a good friend of mine, Scott Gerow, and we go down to practice sessions and I do well. I come out on the list and I go to the Academy. It wasn't like a lifetime dream of mine. It was my brother's dream. He always wanted to be a fireman. It turns out I get on the job four years before he does and he really wanted the job.

Wapples: Well, after getting out of school I didn't know which direction or where I had wanted to go. And I decided to move to California. I was living in Englewood and the Los Angeles fire department had decided on giving a test at that time. I waited until the last minute. I had an Englewood driver's license and when I went to apply, I didn't live in LA city limits so I wasn't eligible to take their test. So, I came back to Jersey. This was like '80 and they were in the process of giving their test. That's what made me decide to go for this particular job because I had an interest when I was out there. Plus, I had a child and it provided job security and benefits. That's what made me have somewhat of a desire to make a step toward the firefighting career.

I ran into a lady I knew as a child and she was just reminiscing back on my childhood, telling me I always had a desire to be a fireman. I used to live over on Watson Avenue between Badger and Ridgewood. I remember one incident; there was a fire up above Ridgewood Avenue. The firemen left an axe and one of my friends and I found this particular axe after they left the scene. We took it back to the firehouse with our parents. And we got a tour of the firehouse on Bergen and Lehigh. It's some coincidence that now I am there as an officer at that particular firehouse. So that and just hearing the sirens as all children do and having that desire to be on a truck. It definitely left some type of impression to want to be in the fire service.

Griffith: I worked at Sacred Heart while I was going to high school and I worked with Barney Baldino and Tony Detroia. I had a lot of conversations with them and they got me interested. Actually, Tony gave me the application for the

25

job. Living in Vailsburg, there were a lot of police and fire that lived in the neighborhood. So, you were very familiar. The Boy Scouts, we actually met at the old training academy on Eighteenth Avenue. That's where we had our meetings. I was taught first aid by the fire department through the Boy Scouts. So, you become familiar with these men that are in town. Everything that you did, you were there. As a kid you're excited about it, but then as you get older and look into it as a career. Working with these men, it seemed like the right thing to do. I don't regret it for a minute.

Arce: Well, I loved the job. I loved the idea of putting my life on the line, just saving people, putting fires out. It's kind of an action job. I love that whole thought of it. The feeling that you get when you're inside a burning building is amazing. When you can see flame all around you and you're putting it out. And you're going through places that you've never been through or even heard about or people wouldn't even go into. It's just amazing. It's the best feeling in the world. Believe it or not, living in Newark, the fires either would follow me or because I'm in Newark there were fires all around me. So that's what happened. I became fireman. It's just an exciting job.

Nasta: Basically, it was kind of by accident. I had my focus over the years; I was going to be a truck driver. I went into business with my dad and started driving for him. I had a couple of buddies that were on the fire department. And I would spend a lot of time on the road. I had no benefits, no medical benefits, no retirement. My buddies kept telling me, "Why don't you do this? Why don't you do this?" My dad had been a volunteer fireman, so I kind of started taking the test. I did it mainly because of the benefits and I liked the schedule. Back then they worked tens and fourteens, as they were known and I liked that. I figured I'd have medical benefits and I'd have a retirement and a steady salary. And that's how pretty much it went in that direction.

Weidele: I always wanted to be a fireman since I was in kindergarten. I always told my mom I wanted to be a fireman. When I lived in Newark, there was a small fire in the street and I saw the firemen show up. It just made me want to be a fireman. Just to see how they put out the fire, ever since I can remember.

Johnson: I was just like all the young kids; they want to be a police officer or a fireman. What changed my life is there was a fire in 1979 at 144 Fairmont Avenue. It was a fire involving my grandmother's house, a three-story frame. It was a bad fire and my father and I went there. We lived across town in the South Ward. We got there. It was heavily involved with fire. She was on the first floor and they couldn't get her out. We got there when the firemen weren't there yet. It was heavily involved on all floors and I saw the firemen pushing in. They did a valiant effort, tried to save her, but she died in the fire. After that, I respected the profession and one day I said, "You know, maybe I was interested." I was actually involved with the youth organization around the corner here, IYO, International Youth Organization. Mr. James Wallace, who was involved with Community Relations, told us, "You guys should take the test to become a fireman." I was, "Listen I have a beard. I don't want to shave. Who wants to lose their beard?" He said, "Yeah it's not a job, it's a career." So, me along with Herb Harris and Fateem Ziyad, we took the test, as well as Derek Hunter because he lived down the street as well. So, Herb Harris and I came on together. Fateem followed. He became the Director. Once I came on it was exciting. I had a lot to learn. Things you never knew about, how the functions of the fire department worked. Very, very informative and educational.

DeCuester: I got out of the Navy, I was six and a half years in the Navy and I didn't like to sit around. I didn't want to sit on unemployment, so I got a fluke job working in New York at an investment banking firm, a Wall Street firm. I worked there four years. I was working on the trading desk. I moved up, got my broker's license. It was a private firm and they were selling. General Electric was going to buy them because now corporations could hire their own banking and Wall Street operations. General Electric was buying us out and I just didn't see a future. So I'm sitting in a bar in Hoboken and Billy Murnane, Captain Newark fire department goes, "Hey, Stevie, they're giving a test for the fire department." So I'm not a person that all my life wanted to be a fireman or anything. I've seen firemen. I admired them, but it wasn't my thing in life to do that, but found out it was the best thing that ever happened to me.

Giordano: Well, friends of mine in a tavern I owned at the time, the Three Twenty-two Club, were firemen and one of my friends, Greg Salvato asked me to take the test. The next thing I knew I was taking the test for the Newark Fire Department. That was in 1982 or '83.

Lee: It was a good opportunity. Growing up in the city, I saw firemen. I initially wanted to be a police officer, but I didn't score as high as I did on the fire department exam, So I ended up being a fireman and have not regret my choice at this point in my career.

Sorace: I had a uncle that was a fireman in Washington, DC. I remember when I was a small kid, like maybe four or five years old going to his firehouse often, visiting. I didn't know anything really about it.

Masters: I grew up in a household with my dad being a fireman and I knew a lot of the firemen on the job, the captains, the chiefs. He used to take me to the firehouse on payday. Just the atmosphere, being around the men, the camaraderie, fooling around, I actually saw quite a few fires living in Newark on Avon and Farley Avenues, so it kind of stayed with me. In fact, I first got called to be a

Newark police officer in '85. I took that. Went right up to be sworn in then Newark fire called and I deferred them twice. I just couldn't be happier with my decision. It's in your blood.

Goetchius: Well, I saw in the paper, it surely wasn't the salary. Surely had nothing to do with that. It's more like my father coercing me that it's a good job. He was a fireman. His father before him was a fireman. And he really said to me that, "Go for it. If you make it, fine. You can get on the job, okay if you don't like it go." He really left it to me, my choice. He really helped me in ways to get on but I really didn't know anything about the fire department. I have memories of visiting Bergen Street, climbing on the fire trucks and stuff like that. Seeing the poles and everything. I never really saw a fire, just a few times when we were living up in Vailsburg.

N. Bellina: The biggest thing was when my father's father died. We lived on the third floor. My aunt lived on the second floor, my father's sister, and my grandmother and grandfather lived on the first floor, three story frame, three apartments. It was around '64 when he passed away. I heard yelling. My father ran out the kitchen door. I stayed upstairs. We all stayed upstairs, my mother and my brother. I hear sirens and the first thing that pulled up was the Police Emergency truck. They pulled up and then the Rescue pulled up, Rescue One. So, I said, "What's going on?" So, after we found out he passed away, that was that. That whole thing really that set me up right there. Just to hear the sirens and coming to my house. So, I always wanted to know where they were going.

Then around 1966 I was living on Fifteenth Avenue Nineteenth Street. One of the friends I had there was a little older than me. In '66 I would have been eleven. So, he was maybe fourteen. His last name was Wasnicki and he lived in Irvington. I was at Fifteenth Avenue between Nineteenth and Twentieth. Twentieth was the line. So, he lived at Twenty-first and Fifteenth Avenue in Irvington. His name was Dennis Wasnicki, Polish kid. I was never in his apartment on the second floor. So, one day he invited me over there. We went into his room and we're in his room for a little while and he turns this radio on. I said, "What's that?" He goes, "Oh, my uncle's a dispatcher on the Newark Fire Department. I listen to the fire calls and I write them down in this note pad." I said, "Really?" He would write these alarms down. So we're sitting there and an alarm came in and he wrote it down. He had it logged in in such a way that he had the location first, the box number, the battalion, the engine, just like the running card.

Now, if I heard sirens, I got a little anxious because there were a lot of fires in the area. Well, I left there and that was pretty interesting. I said, "Wow I can know where they're going now." So, I went home and I was on my mother's case. I need one of these radios. It wasn't really a scanner at the time. It was a police band radio. It had AM FM. It had a couple of other things on it, but it had the police band and the fire band. You would adjust it down to one five four point one three and you'd pick it up. So, my mother said okay. We went down to Lafayette Electronics on Central Avenue almost at Broad. I got the radio and brought it home. Got my spiral pad, I did it just like he did and I started writing the alarms down. I started listening to the radio and that was it. And I used to ride my bike if they got close, in the beginning if they got close, Eighteenth Street, Sixteenth Avenue, Nineteenth Street, I was there. I was on it. The bike was out in the backyard and I was gone. So, I started catching fires and I started catching the units. That was the start of it; that was all how it went down; and that was the beginning actually.

My mother's father was a fireman in Fort Monmouth. But I didn't find out until years later when we moved to Vailsburg. Actually, when he passed away in the early '70s is when I found out about it, but I was already on my way to wanting to be a fireman.

Chief J. Centanni: I think it was my childhood dream. I had family and some neighborhood friends that I saw as firefighters. Our neighborhood was active with fires as a kid growing up in the North Ward of Newark, the Garside Street area. As long as I can remember I wanted to be a firefighter. We had a fire on Garside Street in our house. I'll tell you two experiences I had as a kid, many fires in our neighborhood, but two very close ones. Once we had a fire in our house and it was all family. I think my aunt and my mother were coming over. They would have late coffee at my grandmother's house. And when they got in the house there was smoke in the house. The way we remember it, someone stuffed something underneath the siding on the side of the house and lit the siding of the house up. The whole outside was burning. Funny part of that story at the time, Danny Coppola, Mr. Coppola who was our Little League coach was a fireman. They were there. They knew our family. They knew us from Little League. And they removed us from the house and overhauled on the wall. I remember my aunt's wall was all ripped down on the first floor looking for the fire. So that was one experience. A more frightening experience which wasn't our house, was right on the corner of Bloomfield Avenue and Mount Prospect. There were several two story duplex tenements and they were fully involved. And on the angle of where we lived our backyard looked like the sun was crashing in the yard. The windows cracked on our houses. My father, my uncle, they were on the roofs knocking off embers and we were actually evacuated from the house. But that was a major event where the street was filled with people and we all were taken from the houses on that side of the street and went over to my grandmother's and our aunt's.

It must have just been something in me. From a little kid I used to ask my older cousins when I would hear sirens and we would see smoke. I was Garside and Bloomfield Avenue. At that time what we call Third Battalion, Cutler Street, Summer Avenue area, Seventh Avenue was very busy. So, this is the '70's. Almost every night or day there was a fire in our area. And I would always ask them give me a ride when they were a little older or take a walk with me because I wasn't allowed to go too far off the block to see these fires. So, I was always attracted to it. And I never was really afraid of it and it was just something that I was drawn to.

Ziyad: I became a firefighter for a couple of reasons. One because I had relatives, my brother, my cousins, four of them, and my uncle were firefighters. Seeing them literally getting on the job. It seemed to be a life change that I would be interested in. My cousin and uncle had encouraged me just to apply. I was hesitant initially and didn't put in an effort. Eventually, when I saw the quality of life they had, I decided to make a serious effort.

Herb Harris is my brother. My cousin, Jackie Jones, was the first female firefighter in the city of Newark. One of the first female firefighters in the tri-state area. My uncle, Ernie Smith was an arson detective, the first African-American arson detective. My cousin Arnum Wapples, retired as a battalion chief. We're first cousins. His mom and my mom are sisters. And Courtney Ruffner is also my cousin. My mother's sister also. So, I had a number of family on the job prior to me coming on. They all urged me to join. Once I saw what they were doing, it inspired me to want to join the fire department.

Coming in the job at twenty-nine as opposed to a lot of guys coming in their early twenties right out of high school or straight from the military at twenty-two, twenty-three years old. It was a little different for me. I was more mature, more focused. That made me goal oriented because I had a family and I had already seen what the real world had to offer. So, I came in the door with the aspiration/inspiration to do better and to be in management because that was, you know, more so my background. I wasn't looking to be a firefighter. I was looking to be an officer. And actually, I walked in the door with the aspiration to be the fire chief or fire director.

Alexander I: As a child growing up in the city of Newark, in the '60s and '70s, I would constantly see fire trucks, constantly rolling, constantly moving, as a kid it just fascinated me. That one day I would definitely love to do what they're doing. I just always thought that firefighters were the greatest people in the world.

I graduated from Weequahic High in '79 and then from there I went on to college in North Carolina, Fayetteville State University. My first year there I lost my father. He was fifty-five at the time. He died of a massive heart attack. It kind of bothered me, but I was still trying to hang in there. So, after I completed my second year, I came back home. Tried to just figure out what I wanted to do. I already had a cousin who's on the fire department, Calvin Hunt. Myself and his brother Kent, we were like glued at the hip. So, he talked us into wanting to take the test. He said you guys always talk about how much you like it. He said take the test. So, he encouraged us to take the test and that's where it all began for us

Maresca: I guess it as in my family blood. My father was a fireman. My uncle was a fireman. I grew up with it.

DeLeon: It started back in '84, '86 around there. Gil Colon used to stop by my dad's business and the applications were going out. And he would like say fill it out, fill it out, send it. I said, "What am I going to do? I don't know much about this career." I'm glad he did because I come on in May of '88. And then from there forward, loved it, loved it. I told him he should have kicked me in the teeth and asked me sooner. I gave him such a hard time and I don't regret it. I love it. I'm first generation. None of my family is firemen. So, I'm a one and done, unless my son takes it. He's in the military right now. When he gets out, if he wants to take it. But he said something about wanting to be a police officer. He'll go right in. He's got veteran status.

Taylor: I became a firefighter because I got laid off from my teaching job. Then I fell in love with the job. I was a teacher in the Elizabeth Public Schools. That was the year the mayor in Elizabeth ripped a bunch of teachers, firemen, and cops and I didn't have tenure so I got laid off. I had already taken the test. Arnum Wapples and Charlie Crenshaw I grew up with and they were already on the job. More so Wapples than Charlie, encouraged me to take the test and come on the job.

Griggs: Why'd I become a fireman? It sounded like an interesting profession. Actually, it's a boring story. I was out of work at the time. God's honest truth, my father was always pushing me to take the exam. "Take the test. Take the test. Take the test." And basically, I took it to pacify him, to get him off my back. I took it a few times and this time to turns around to be pay dirt. I got the certification and I gave it a whirl. And it turned out to be the best thing I ever did. Unfortunately, I should have listened to him years earlier than I did. But it worked out great for me.

Greene: I guess it was something always in the back of my mind, but it wasn't my first choice for an occupation. Actually, I was just walking down the street one day and I saw a poster. It was something almost like the Uncle Sam poster. Become a Newark fireman. And I was kind of ambivalent at that time, but for some reason I decided to fill out the application and take the test.

Sperli: I always wanted to be a fireman since I was a little kid. I was always amazed with the siren and the excitement of it. There was no question of anything else. Newark was the biggest department in Jersey. So, I figured, if you're going to do it, you might as well do it with the biggest and the best.

Alvarez: I wanted to be a cop at first. I was working carpentry and I decided there had to be something better. And I always kind of had this interest in being a cop. When I finally made my decision to be a cop, I filled out the paperwork to become a US citizen and eventually I became a US citizen. Then I was waiting for the police application. I enquired about the process of it and I found out you had to wait for the applications to come out. I waited for the applications and in the process of waiting for the applications to come out, I saw this retired fireman that I knew as a kid. He asked me, "Hey, what are you doing?" And I said, "Oh, nothing. I was just going up here to visit a friend of mine." He goes, "No, no what are you doing with your life?" And I said, "Well, I'm working construction right now, but I'm waiting for the application for the police to come out." And he goes, "You don't want to be a cop." And I said, "Yeah." And he goes, "No, you want to be a fireman. The applications are out now." Then he spoke to me a little bit and he said, "Why don't you be a fireman? Listen, at least you'll have time in with the city. Then you fill out the police application and just jump over. But trust me; you're not going to want to jump over." So, I filled out the application for the fire department. I sent it in and about a block and a half from my house where I grew up at 260 Ferry Street there was a firehouse, Engine Eight. So, I went over there to pick up an application and the captain that handed me the application, Gene Anderson was there. When he handed me the application, he started talking to me. That night we spoke for about an hour and a half and I just was all ears. Kind of like at that moment I said, "You know what? I think this is what I want to be. I want to be a fireman not a cop." Then I went back to visit him. I knew how his schedule worked. He told me about it. I went back to visit him and now I went inside the firehouse and met a few of the other guys. When I was passing by the firehouse, I spoke to other guys who were outside the firehouse. I said, "Oh, hey, you know I met Captain Anderson. I was talking to him. I filled out the application." And those guys were friendly. Now they started talking to me. So, eventually I met all the tours. Then they asked me if I wanted to come over for dinner every once in a while. I did. In the process of waiting for the test and I got to meet all the guys and I got very friendly with them. At that point I knew that's what I wanted to be. I wanted to be a fireman. And in the process of waiting to take the test, the application for the police department came up and I never even filled out the application because I said, "I don't want to be a cop. I want to be a fireman."

I knew at that point after I met those guys and I saw the camaraderie and how they spoke to me. Their passion about the job and Captain Anderson at the time, he was over sixty and he had well over thirty years. And he stayed on and he still loved this job. I was working construction for just about two years and I hated it. And I was like, this guy's doing it for thirty-plus years and he loved it. There's got to be something to this. When I went and told my father, I remember the respect he had for firemen in Cuba and how he looked up to them. And I said yes, this is it. This is it for me.

Cordasco: From when I was a little kid, I wanted to be a cop and Newark fireman. So, what happened was in '82 I took the police test. In '83 I took the fire test. The police called me first. Gibson was still the mayor. We got investigated; background check, and the medical and they didn't call us for two and a half years. In the meantime, I took the fire test; I did well; and I got investigated fully again. I was left number one on the list. So, two months after that I found out my uncle was good friends with Caufield. "What are you doing?" I said, "Ah, I took the police and fire tests." "Ah, Caufield's my buddy." But by then it was too late, so I went on the police because they finally wound up calling two and a half years later, in '85. I went in the Police Academy and I like being a cop, but the hours were horrible. So, Wayne Linfante and I said, "You know what, we'll take the fire test again." So, we took the fire test and we decided it would be a better move to switch over. It worked out for the best. So that's why, but it was between police and fire growing up and I knew that from a young age. So, I did have some relatives on the police, some on the fire. I had both.

Daniels: I didn't have a job. I was about twenty-two or twenty-three at the time. I had been walking downtown just looking for a job, out of high school. Back and forth trying to find something stable and a guy came up to me and said, "Hey, you want to be a Newark fireman?" This guy was Gary Holmes. I didn't know him from a hill of beans. And I said, "Sure, where do I get the application?" He gave me the application. He said, "When you finish this application, just go straight up to City Hall and follow through." Right. I filled it out. He said, "Don't worry about how much it costs." I think it cost like twenty-five dollars or thirty dollars at the time for the application. I put it in and I forgot about it. The next thing I know they started calling me about the prep course on Jersey Street. Midge Harris and Shack were there. Shack comes in when you get there. He said, "The first thing you need to know is you need to put all your information down on the application. I don't care what you did, put it on there because if you don't, they're going to find out. You're going to be disqualified." So, I put all my information down. I got in some trouble when I was younger. I said, let me put it down anyway because I did exactly what they said and I kind of put it away and just kept looking for a job and working hard and trying to improve my life. The next thing you know, I get the phone call and they started investigating me. I was just overwhelmed, good thing I wasn't the kind of person that moved around. I had a stable home. And that's how it happened. I'm not like those guys where they knew about the job and they really wanted the position. I wanted the position, but I wanted the position out of necessity. I always go to the point where I prayed. It was like I just want to do something significant, something that would make a difference in my community and just in the city. I didn't know what that was, but that was what I wanted to do. This came along and that was the driving point. I had no idea that this was what it was. But that's what made me want to get the job.

No one's ever been a firefighter in my family. I remember being younger and always seeing firefighters and going to watch fires and seeing what you guys were doing, just amazing. I used to live right on Sixteenth Avenue, two buildings right on Sixteenth Avenue, right behind the firehouse right there on Hunterdon. You go over where the firehouse is and I remember just running to see any kind of fire. You guys were fighting a fire one day that was so hot that all the bricks were turning red on the building, stacked up three or four story brick building. And I was just amazed. So when I became a firefighter, when the opportunity came around and I actually got the job it was just a proud moment for me and my family.

LaPenta: Why did I become a fireman? Well, when I was younger the father of my best friend who lived behind me was a fireman in East Orange. So, he used to take us to the firehouse when we were kids. I was put on the fire truck and that stuck with me for a while. It was just something that I wanted to do from a very young age. Then that show was on TV, Emergency, we used to watch that as a kid. I remember there was a fire up the street from me. I happened to be out with my neighbor, my best friend whose father was a fireman in East Orange. We were riding bikes and we watched the firemen put this fire out. I think that was really what kind of led me into this career. This is something that I've always wanted to do. I'm actually one of those people that wanted to be a fireman when he was a kid and became one. So, not many people can say that. Living the dream.

Tarantino: The guy who lived next door to me, his name is Joe Lardiere, used to work at Thirteen Engine. I was going to school at NJIT during the day and stocking shelves at Shoprite at night. And he would see me kind of come and go all the time. I guess the applications came out. So, he saw me. He waved to me one day and he said, "Listen," he goes. "I'm a fireman. There's an application coming out for the fire department. I see you run all over the place all the time. I know you're working, stocking shelves at night. Join the fire department." I was like, I have no desire to join the fire department at all. He goes, "Listen it's a good job. You know you could go to school part time." I didn't even think of that at all. I thought about it and he's being a nice guy and I said, "How about you give me like ten of them. I'll bring them to my friends on the corner." I'll hand out a bunch of applications. So, he got me ten applications. When I went to the corner a night or two afterwards, I walk up with these ten applications and I start to hand them out to all my friends. They're like, "We filled it out already." I'm like, "What do you mean filled it out already?" "We filled it out already. We knew about it." "Well, why didn't you tell me?" "You're going to school. We didn't think you wanted to."

I wasn't going to take the job. I took the test because I just wanted to do it to beat everybody. And then my mother says, "Are you out of your mind? Take the job. You can go to school part time and you get a pension. You get a salary. You get health care." Best move I ever made though.

West: I'm not really sure of the answer. I was a volunteer firefighter before I came here. I did have family members who were firemen. I sort of gravitated toward it because family members were firemen. I didn't have on my side of the family. It was on my wife's side of the family.

Pierson: I needed a job. I was working for a fireman and he had a whole crew of guys working in a paint company. He'd be in the firehouse, had about six or seven of us working. I said, "Not a bad gig. I might be able to pull this off." I had no clue though what it entailed. He knew I was dumb enough, just sign the paper.

Petrone: My dad was a fireman. That was always something I wanted to do. I looked up to him. I enjoyed the camaraderie of it. He always had a lot of good friends. He really enjoyed it. I know he made so many good lifelong friends. It seemed like something I really wanted to do.

Castelluccio: I kind of fell into it. I had friends of mine on the job. They wanted me to take the test. I kept telling them nope because I was making a lot more money in the carpenters' union. Then things got kind of slow, so I decided to take the exam. First my father-in-law who was a deputy chief of police in Newark wouldn't give me an application for the police department. He said, "No way." So, I became a fireman.

Snyder: My dad was telling me what to do. I saw growing up, what my father did and I liked it. It looked like a thing that I wanted to do. I can't say I had a big master plan for it, but once I got on I enjoyed it.

Bartelloni: The reason I originally was interested in it was because I was playing softball and a number of friends on my team were firemen. At that time, I was out of college working in the real world and the economy was kind of sagging. They kept telling me, "Take the test. Take the test." A lot of the North Ward friends of mine were taking it already. So we ended up training together. And I said, "Hey, what's the worst that could happen? Let me take the test and if I finish and it works out that way, maybe I'll be interested in the job. It'll be an opportunity. Thank God I took advantage of that.

Gail: I became a fireman by chance. I was in college and I worked a part-time job as a roofer. All the guys I worked with part time were all firefighters. They gave me an application, set me up with instructions on how to become a firefighter. I did well on the test and the month after I graduated college, they called me for the job. So, I took it. It was the path of least resistance and the easiest route. I ended up loving it.

Osterstag: I was a volunteer for a short time in Scotch Plains and I always wanted to become a paid fireman. I found the job to be very exciting. I wanted more action. I wanted to find a bigger city to do it in. I happened to be in Newark one night eating dinner in the Ironbound section. Believe it or not I stopped in at

Engine Eight to see if there are any applications available. Captain Anderson was there. He says, "Well, there's a test coming out, but I can't help you right now. We don't have any applications here." I'm on my way out the door, John Kunze stops me. "Hey, hey, hold up a minute. I got somebody who's recruiting, Orlando Alvarez. Give this guy a call." Next day I called up Orlando Alvarez. He says, "Yeah, we're looking for guys." So, he kind of told me what was involved and I actually moved into the city. I lived on Hawkins Street and I lived on East Kinney Street. I went through the right way to do it, the proper channels. I took the test, came out pretty high and got hired in the second round in 1994. That's how it all started.

Ramos: Why'd I become a fireman? To be honest with you I became a fireman because I had a dream one night. I had a dream I was a firefighter back in 1991. At that time, I was actually going to school for computer drafting. Something happened. I was upset that night. I had a dream I was a firefighter. I woke up that morning and I made the call. I called the city of Newark and I said, "Are there any openings on the fire department?" And they said the test is coming out in April. I had to file in December. And it went from there. I took the test and it went from there.

Richardson: Bob Frey lived down the street from me and he told me, "Go take the test, become a fireman." I was like, "Why would I want to do that? I don't want to go into a burning building." He says, "No, you'll love the job. You'll love the job." I had a high school education. That was about all, kind of a dead-end job. I got married and I moved into a town west of here and I joined the volunteer fire department to meet some guys in the town. That year we had three house fires which was very unusual for a small town. I went to Bob, I says. "Bob, this is the best job around. That was great. How do I get this job?" He says, "Well, move into Newark. Get an apartment. Take the test. It's coming up." So, I did that. I moved in on South Street. Took the test and then went over onto Paterson Street, finally got appointed. And the rest is history. Twenty-two years later I'm still here. But it was because of Bob Frey telling me.

Jackson: Actually, I didn't want to become a firefighter. I was given an application by a member of the Vulcan pioneers in 1991. After filling out the application, taking the test, and getting accepted as a new recruit coming on the job, I went into the academy and I fell in love with this career. I can remember living on Dewey Street as a kid and seeing this fire truck go down the street. The guys are standing on the back step. The water's just dripping down the street and the guys are drenched.

But I never thought back then that I would be in this profession. I mean I was a small boy. Another encounter is when we did have fires in the neighborhood, everybody from the neighborhood, and I'm a small kid, they would grab the little kids' hands and they would walk to the fires. They would stand back on the sidewalk and watch the firefighters fight the fires. Then fast forward to high school, it never really dawned on me that this was a profession. You know I never really saw or paid that much attention to this profession.

Y. Pierre: Well, coincidence, it was like this opportunity that I had seen at the moment when I had decided I wanted to become a police officer and I took the test at the same time I took the test for the fire department. Fortunately, the fire department called me first. And I was just leaving the Marine Corps and coming back out of there, I know I didn't want to really bother using any guns chasing anybody down. I'd rather be doing something firemen did that would actually help the people instead of something where you're going to injure someone. That was the main reason why I joined the fire department. I figured I'd be more helpful to the city and as far as dealing with the people that we work with, it's just a great thing for me. I enjoy working with the people.

Willis: Two reasons, one was I wanted to be a fireman. I enjoyed watching them going in and out of the house. I was born and raised in Newark. The other reason is the finances. It's a stable job. Those are the two of the main reasons why.

I worked in Port Newark. I worked a lot of hours down there. My family were all longshoremen. My dad recommended that I get out of there before it turned. So, my brothers became police officers. One was the head of maintenance for the Newark Board of Education. I figured, you know what, it's time to make a move. And I really was always looking at the fire department. I took a shot. I would never be a cop, watching my brothers, how miserable they were. And that was it.

Farrell: I was born and raised on this job, pretty much. My father did thirty years. I never really thought I would be a fireman growing up because my father obviously worked in the decades when this was one of the busiest fire departments in the country, the '60s, '70s, and '80s. I was a kid. Like every other kid, especially if your father's a fireman, you want to gravitate toward that. Oh, I want to be a fireman. You're my hero, the whole bit. And my father swore, "You're never going to do this job. You're bound for something much better than that. You're going to go to school. You're going to do this. You're going to do that. You're going to play baseball for a living." Whatever it is. He didn't want me to be on this job. But like anything else, there's the job. He saw the changing times of the job. It certainly wasn't as dangerous. It still was a dangerous job, but it wasn't as crazy as it was when he was on. In his thirty years it was nuts. When I was twenty-two years old and just ready to get out of college, I was just leaving school, Rutgers. I played baseball there and what I had to decide was what do I do. At the time I was engaged. My wife's begging me, please don't take the job. Had I taken it at twenty-three, I'd be looking at retirement right now. But I didn't. Got divorced six years later and decided to take the job. My father said, "Take the test. See how you do." Best move I ever made in my life. I worked for ten years as a buyer for a lumber company. Doing that seven to four grind every day, six days a week, it was tough.

This is a different kind of tough. The hours, obviously different and the job, when you catch a job, it's brutal. It's rough, but it's the most rewarding job you could ever have. If you're not afraid of going in that fire building, this is the job for you. You'd don't realize it sometimes until you do it and you sit there and say, you know what, I have found my calling. I truly have. I never considered this a job. Number one, it's a career and number two for me it's a way of life. You know, my father always taught me even growing up, you're never not a fireman. We're driving on vacation somewhere, you see something. You're compelled. He did numerous times I remember him stopping for different things. You're never not a fireman. After a while it's gets drilled in your head. It got drilled into my head at an early age, but then on the job you just realize it. That's the way you are. You only do twenty-four hours on the job and you do three days off. But those three days off, you really don't get de-programed, you know. You still have that twenty-four-hour mentality. I'm sure some of the guys on the job can block it out and leave the job here when they leave. I'm quite sure there's got to be guys like that, but most of us, especially if you grew up on the job, you'll never not be a fireman. I have a feeling when I retire, I'll still be a fireman in some way shape or form. So, it's a great job. I love it dearly. I was just away for three weeks. And people think, "Oh, you got to go back to work, that's got to be horrible." No, it's not. I love going away. I love spending time with my son and going on vacation. But I also love coming back. I couldn't wait to get back to work this morning. Today's my first day back after three weeks out and I look forward to it. I look forward to coming in with the crew. Especially if you have a good crew. You're in a good house and a good crew, really. You got the world by the you know what.

Roberson: Because I enjoyed helping people, helping my community, and being a public servant. I'm from a family of public servants and so that's why I decided to become a Newark firefighter.

My mom was a corrections officer. My dad worked for the Newark Housing Authority, but we always did community service in Newark. So, for years my whole life has been dedicated to public service.

After I graduated high school I went into the service, Air Force reserves. I was an air medical technician which pretty much means you can turn an airplane into a flying hospital to take care of patients on a plane. In peace time we actually transported military and civilians back and forth from overseas. So, before I was twenty years old, I'd been to Madrid. I was going to Germany every other month. I was going to Portugal every month. I've been to England. I've been to Iceland. You name it, all over the states. So, I did that and also, I was in school. I went to Mercer County College which I transferred over to Essex County College. And my field was television production and radio. So, Cable Vision, the public station they have right now, we were the first graduating class in 1987, to develop that station.

After that I worked in recreation for the City of Newark because I want to be in public service. At that time, I ran into one of my classmates from Saint Vinny's named Shawn Norwood. He was a fireman. He had been on for four years. He was like, "Come on man, come on over. Man, you'll like it." I said, "Man I'm happy where I'm at. I like working with young people with recreation." And so, I stayed in Recreation for about eight years. After that it was time for a career change because there was no advancement in that field for me. I needed extra money to take care of my family. I was young. I had a family; had a wife and a baby and next thing you know the opportunity came to me to become a firefighter again. So I took the test. At that time, I was having my second baby and she was born two weeks before I went into the Academy. So, every year she turns a year older, that's how many years I've been on the job.

Meier: Why'd I become a fireman? My father was an Irvington fireman. And growing up those guys were like a bunch of uncles to me. It was very comforting. It was a great job. But I didn't get to see him often because between him working part time work and the fire department schedule, we didn't have a close relationship. But the times we spent going to firemen's picnics and stuff, it was a great time. My father always pressed me to become a fireman or when I was going through high school always pressed me, take the test, take the test, take the test. I wanted to live life a little bit before I made that commitment to the fire department. So, ultimately, I didn't get on until I was twenty-seven. It took me a little while to come around to it, but then once I came around to it and I was interested, that's all I could think about.

Rodrigues: Why? Well, it comes from my father and my grandfather in Puerto Rico. Back in the day, they used to have the Civil Defense which is kind of volunteer. I just became part of it and ever since I loved the job. And that's the reason why I became a fireman. I loved the job. It's one of the greatest jobs in the world.

Montalvo: I had an uncle that was pushing me to take the job for years and I never took it. Finally, one day I decided to check it out and see what it was all about. I went to a practice exam for the physical. I just saw a bunch of the older guys helping out the new guys and teaching them how to go about this. I thought that was kind of cool, how these guys were helping out the younger guys on what it took to become a fireman. It kind of intrigued me, the camaraderie I saw out there. These guys just helping us take the test.

Freese: I think, personally, every childhood dream is to be a cop or a fireman. It's what you play growing up. It's what you want to be. It's what you mind. It's what you stop for as a kid when you see the fire truck or police car zooming by with the lights and siren. I was blessed to have the opportunity to take test. That was the main reason why. I did about twelve different jobs before I became a fireman, waiting and taking the test and working out. I was never happy until I got to the fire department. But it was a childhood dream.

Highsmith: I just happened to be walking downtown and firefighter Thaddeus just happened to look at me and said, "You look like you're in shape. You want to be a fireman?" I said, "Oh, what the hell." I went home, filled out the application, and when they called us back for the first meeting and they explained the job to us, climbing buildings and roofs and jumping trees, I said, "That's my kind of thing." That's when I took the job seriously.

My cousin's on the job. I met him at a family reunion. This was before the job came along. Once I got to the investigation stage then I had my uncle call him up. He called me back, He said, "You've already done the work on your own. You just have to get through the investigation stage and I'll make sure all that goes good for you. I'll make sure everything is done right." And that's what happened.

Carr: First of all, I'd like to say that this job has basically been taking care of me most of my life. My father was a fireman. He used this job to take care of his family, assisted me. And then it became a station in my household for the most part. I saw a lot of the camaraderie that he had with his friends. Those guys would come by the house. Shadow (the firehouse dog) would come by the house every now and then. Shadow has come to Underwood Street and he would hang out with us and then he would go to work the next day with daddy when he went to work. But I pretty much admired the camaraderie.

How I'd see my dada getting up in the morning and shaving and getting his stuff. Getting ready to go to work, leaving the house at 6:50 to be to work by like 7 o'clock because he was on Central Avenue. But I just liked the atmosphere that it presented for me. It presented a great option for me to be able to move forward and take care of my family the way it took care of me. I think that's what made it so attractive for me. To be able to move on and move forward to doing that. To be able to provide for myself and be able to spend the amount of time that I had with my family. You know it allows me to do that.

Rosario: Actually, I dealt with the fire department twice as a young kid. On Park Avenue and Ninth Street, there was a fire and we lived in the building. We were on the top floor and we were the last family to get out. We actually didn't get out and Ladder Seven, Engine Fifteen came to our rescue and pulled our whole family out from the top floor with the aerial. I was about five or six. Another time I had my hand stuck in a garage door on Lake Street right across from the Tony hotdogs. They came down, got my hand out, and then gave me a ride in the fire truck and that's it. Fell in love with the service. Had to be about ten. I actually came from another fire department, the Harrison Fire Department, before coming here. I ended up going into the military for a couple of years and then coming out. And all I did was work towards becoming a fireman.

I actually got hired in Harrison as soon as the list was published. And back then you could take a job in another city and remain on the list. Now you can't. If you take an appointment somewhere else, you're removed from the list, but back then you were able to do that. So, I did that. I wanted to be a fireman, so I went over there for two years. It actually took Newark over two years before they hired anyone. And then once they hired, I went through their process and then switched right over.

Jenkins: To make a difference, I put in for the job, but it really became effective for me when nine eleven happened. I was working at the Frelinghuysen Avenue Post Office and next door was the firehouse actually. I had rapport with the guys that were in the house. I was talking to them and it made me want to join the fire department to see.

Kupko: First impressions are everything. Your parents are your number one influences. My father had this job. My mother was a school teacher. I was in school studying to be a phys ed teacher when I took the test. My father said, "Keep your options open." Graduated from school. Got a teaching job. Four months later the fire department called and for me at the time, it seemed to be an easy decision. I made the switch.

Mickels: I became a fireman because I wanted to help people. I had a desire in my heart to help individuals that were in danger. Those who weren't able to help themselves, more so in the physical sense from danger. Local danger as in a fire, a car accident, some type of contaminants in the atmosphere, I wanted to be able to help those that needed the help. I wanted to provide that service. I always thought there was a need for first responders. There was always something going on in Newark, buildings catching on fire, whether it was vacant or occupied. Criminal activities, so I felt Newark needed to be handled. It needed to be controlled and well taken care of. That's what I was there for, to assist in helping with public safety.

Gaddy: One night we had a fire in my house in 1991. It was just me and my little sister. I heard glass break. And we had a building right next door, next door to my own family house. Someone threw a Molotov cocktail through the bathroom window. Me being a kid, I tried to investigate, to find out what was going on. My aunt was in the house at the time. I didn't know she was just coming in there and putting bottles for my little cousin in the refrigerator. She also dropped off my little cousin inside the room that was next to the fire. So I was investigating. I go in and look. No one is in there and I hear some crackling noise. I open the door. My hands get burnt a little and I close the door. The fire jumps out on me and I close the door. It was just my instinct. That saved my sister's life. It saved my cousin's life. And it saved my life.

What I did then was I told my little sister to go downstairs and tell everybody we had a fire. I didn't know my little cousin was in the house at the time. That's when I was going to the windows and trying to tell everyone we had a fire in the house. We had just come back from a family reunion down South. So my whole family was outside. I couldn't get anyone's attention. I guess everybody thought I was bullshitting. So, I had to curse to get their attention. Once I cursed to get their attention, they ran upstairs and we tried to put the fire out. And then I was told my little cousin was in the house. I ran and got my little cousin, handed her to my aunt or my grandmother at the time. That was like an instinct. I didn't know what I was doing at the time.

When I was in high school, I passed every test there was from Conrail all the way up to State Police. I didn't know that being a fireman would be this rewarding. The neighborhood that I came from where you could be looked at as a real hero instead of somebody that's playing basketball. I wouldn't expect to give back to the community like I'm doing now. So in essence, I mean I was pretty much picked. Instead of me picking this job, I was already picked. That's how I explain that. When I got the opportunity to take the test, my uncle Larry Berfet came and gave me the application.

Figuereq: Just as a kid, I kind of looked up to the fire department. As I got older, I realized it was something that I wanted to do. And job security, actually was another reason. I had kids and I was working in IT, but in that field, you're God today and they lay you off the next day. And I saw it happen. The opportunity came, I took it.

Medina: It was a good opportunity. I lived right across the street from Engine Thirteen and I grew up watching them coming in and out when I was growing up. That's what I wanted to do. I wasn't too sure yet. I became a mechanic. I was doing different jobs. I became a mailman. Then I took the civil service test. I always like the fire department. Actually, the Corrections Department called me. I didn't want it. The police department called me. I didn't want it. And then I filled out an application for the fire department. That's what I want. That's what I really wanted. Something that felt right.

Dugan: Because it's always what I wanted to do since I was a little kid. Saw my grandfather, my father, what life that gave them. Once I came up to the firehouse I was hooked. I liked everything that comes along with the job. The time it gives you with your family is very key to me because I always wanted to have a big family which I do now. I like to help people and I like the rush of going into a fire too. I'm a little bit of an adrenalin junkie. I was a paratrooper in the Army, so this is right up my alley.

K. Alfano: Because my father's a firefighter. It was just growing up; I saw my father. He was a fireman. He loved the job. So, I figured I'd give it a shot

M. Bellina: I was trying to become a police officer and then my father suggested taking the test out of nowhere. That's how it happened. So I took the test and I did well. Then I went to the academy and I love it.

B. Maresca: I got out of the Marine Corps. I didn't know what I wanted to do and my dad said take the test so that's what I did.

G. Centanni: My father was a fireman. He inspired me to take the test and become a fireman.

G. Pierre: I became a fireman because I liked the life style. My father and my uncles being firefighters already, I got an opportunity to see it firsthand. It was an opportunity for me to help, make a decent living, honorable living. And it kind of meshed with how my family and how I was brought up. And I like helping people. It's a cool job.

Rawa: Because I didn't want to be a cop. I come from a family of cops and it was kind of written in the stars already that that is where I was going be headed to. I took the test and I got on, but I didn't take it. Dad wasn't happy, but figured I'd hold out. Took the test for the fire department a couple of years later, didn't get called. Took it once again after that, finally got called. I think it took about six years total.

J. Centanni: My father was a fireman. I grew up around it and he always took me to work to hang out. And it was something I always wanted to do.

Garay: My husband always wanted to be a firefighter. He kept trying and in 2009 he tried for the third time. When he went to the orientation, he heard a captain inviting girls to just take the test. My husband came home that day and told me, "Veronica, they're welcoming women to take the test." I said, "Oh, yeah." And he said, "I'm going to sign you up." And I said, "Okay." He had signed me up for other stuff. I didn't think much of it until I started training for the physical aspect. I started watching videos and everything. I said to my husband, "You know what? I could see myself doing this." I was speaking to a colleague of mine; she made a comment which reminded of something that happened years before. She said there are people that are meant to go into the fire and there are people that are meant to run away from the fire. I remember when I was younger; I was about thirteen, fourteen years old. It was a summer afternoon. I was taking a nap. I used to live with my grandmother. And I heard the screams of this lady, a very young mom, "Oh, fire, fire, fire. My baby's in the house." I woke up, ran into the apartment to get the baby. It was really smoky and everything. And it brought me back to that. I said, "Well, I guess there's something in it." The more I got involved with fire scenes, it changed my heart. I became passionate about it. So, I prayed every day until I got in because I loved it.

Fortunato: It's something I've always wanted to do since I was a little kid. I was around it. Met a few people, they let me hang out in the firehouse and it kind of grew from there. Took the test, got called a few years later, ended up having the best job in the world.

Earp: My senior year in high school, the fire department came to a job fair and they were explaining the whole career, the brotherhood, the rich history of the fire department. I knew right from there I wanted to join. Plus, I wanted to have a career I could be proud of and my family could be proud of as well. Right after high school I went to college, but when I finished school, I took the exam and from there that's what got me here.

Corales: I wanted to help. I wanted to be part of the community in some sort of way. It was just something I always wanted to do growing up and just wanted to help the community.

Alexander II: Tradition. It's funny too, because when I was younger, he always told me not to be a fireman. He always told me, "I did it so you didn't have to." He was trying to get me to be an athlete or a doctor, something else. But as I got older, the economy's not so good. He kind of pushed me into it a little bit. You might want to look at this. Then I got to come around as I was older and saw the camaraderie with the guys and how the job was. I thought maybe this might be something for me, especially coming from an athletic background. It's a team sport. That's really what the job is. It's a team sport, so I fit right in. I love it.

Cruz: When I was in the second grade, they asked us, "Why do you want to be a firefighter?" I said, "Because I want to be able to drive the firetruck." Then I was working for the city of Newark and I saw the test come out. I would work out and I'm like, "I know I can do this." There are not a lot of females on the job, but I want to be a female that can actually do this job. And I have to show these guys that I can actually become a firefighter, to be a firefighter. I set out to prove something. I have no family on the fire department. I also want to be a role model. I want kids to see anything is possible. So, I worked for the city of Newark, too, for several years.

I worked for the Business Administrator and then I worked for the Inspector General's office investigating corruption. I was a civilian there, but I would assist in doing the reports. I would be doing the statistics and reports on any investigation. If there was anything, they would have to go to the mayor for press releases. That was me, memorandums, directives that would come from me. I'm happy being a firefighter. I don't want administrative work. I did enough of that. I want to be in the field.

Entrance test

Conville (1940): I took whatever test they were giving, a written and a practical. With my lifestyle, I'm an athlete, I had no problem. I can get a hundred and fifty percent in any physical. The written, you could study from Delancey or one of those books. But it wasn't that difficult to get in the fire department. Your size and what you were, color, race, all that was important. There was a limit of weight, height. I remember one fellow in Six Engine that became a friend, he was like a half inch shorter. We tried to hang him up by his feet so he would get a half inch longer when he went for the practical. He got the job, and he was one of the best firemen Six Engine had.

Conover (1948): There was a physical part. I remember climbing rope and other things like how high you can jump above your reach. You had to reach and then you'd jump up to see if you jumped twenty inches beyond your reach from a flat position. I can't remember whether there were sit-ups or not. I think there was. It was a general physical exam. You had to be in halfway decent shape to pass it.

Ryan (1948): There was a physical and a written. I think there were about a hundred and fifty questions on the entrance written. And there were ten performances in the physical exam. Sit-ups, had to climb a rope, run an obstacle course, push-ups, squat jumps and a couple of other things. Then the written was a hundred and fifty and they were general questions. Nothing related that much to the fire department in the test. It was current affairs and what you learned in high school subjects, easy math questions. Most people who graduated high school should have passed the test. It wasn't that hard. I think it was more or less a test to test your reading more than anything else.

J. Doherty (1949): Oh, I can't remember. I took so many of them, but one of the few gifts that I have is I generally ace all kinds of exams. I was a high school dropout. I went to work at sixteen years old on a tugboat in the harbor. And then when I turned eighteen, I enlisted in the Army Air Corps. I was a navigation cadet. When I had the DIQ test in the Army I know what it was, a hundred and thirty-eight. You needed to have a hundred and thirty-five in order to make West Point. They sent me to five months of college training in the University of Alabama, but the point is I was good on written exams.

The physical was pushups, sit-ups, I think it was pretty much all the same. I mean it's a physical. How high can you jump?

G. Alfano (1953): I took a written and I took a physical and a medical too. The written had subjects like phosgene, I remember one answer was phosgene gas. It was chemicals and they asked a few first aids and different questions like this, but no basic fire questions. Mostly things you would get in high school. And that's another thing, you had to have two years high school, later on it was a high school diploma.

The physical test was a broad jump, a run where you carried a weight under a ping-pong table. You dragged it through and then they did kazatskies. They had them. I had a very good physical because I was in really good physical shape at the time. But two weeks later don't you think I got pinned between a truck and a car. The bones came out here, here, and here. And on this arm too. I wasn't on the job then. This is my other job. I would have been on a lot sooner, but Tenore was the doctor. He wouldn't let me come on. He said, "Well you just have to wait and when you heal." So maybe a year and a half later he called me back and he gave me an exam and he put me on.

D.C. Griggs (1956): Basically, it was a hundred questions towards the mechanical end of it. And a couple of rates were put in there. They wanted to know which was the higher rate ranking in a fire department. Was it Lieutenant, Captain, Battalion Chief, or Deputy Chief? What a conflagration was and a pyromaniac. The rest was like mechanical with autos, driving, and construction. I was able to finish in time, go back over my test, and I felt pretty good about it.

After that I was waiting for notification and you had to go to the Elizabeth Armory for the physical. I thought I had prepared myself pretty well. When I got notified, I was already on the Essex County Park Police, and I was down here at Seagirt going to school. I was going into my last week when the fire department notified me that I had three days to clean up my act and come aboard. I had to go down to City Hall on a weekend. During the week I couldn't go to get fingerprinted because I was in Seagirt. They wouldn't let you out of there because you couldn't leave the base all week. You had to stay on the base. The Troopers ran the show. When I came home, I went down to City Hall on a Saturday or Sunday and got fingerprinted. My wife had to come with me to sign the insurance and everything else. Somebody did come to the house while I was in Sea Girt to check on me. That was the beginning there.

The physical test I can give you just about every step of the way. You were down in the basement in the Elizabeth Armory. You would start off with pushups, sit-ups, sitting rope climb, hand grip, a vertical jump, a run that included hurdles up and down the armory with snatching a dummy at one end and dragging it across a line. That was timed. The broad jump and then the back lift and then the kazatskies. That was the whole thing.

Duerr (1958): Back then they had the old test which was questions and then they had four answers. You had to pick one of the four answers. Multiple choice I guess you would call it and then after that they had a physical. You had to do so many pushups, so many sit-ups, so many kazatskies, and then they would take the two marks and that's where you came out on the list.

A. Prachar (1959): What kind of test? General knowledge as far as I recall. I took both tests at the same time, Newark fire and Newark police. And Newark fire called first. I was a Newark firefighter for about two months when I got called for the police department. Bobby Griffith who was a fire alarm operator, his father was a lieutenant in the police department, talked to me for almost two hours telling why I should stay a fireman and not become a cop. And I followed his advice.

Bitter (1959) It was one physical for the police and fire. Never having been involved in anything to do with civil service, I didn't realize at the time that when you took this physical exam it was competitive. So, you needed twelve chin ups, I give it twelve chin ups. I just did basics. I never realized that it was competitive scoring. I figured you did it, you got the job. And that was in '57 sometime. I took the last exam that only requires two years of high school. I went to Bloomfield Tech. I left school around April when I was fifteen. I had more important things to do like go to Florida. When the test came up you needed two years of high school. I went back to Bloomfield Tech and asked, "Did I pass my second year of high school?" And he said, "You're going into the third year on condition." I said, "That's all I wanted to know."

Schoemer (1959): It was a regular, general knowledge test. My brother-in-law took the test. He came out eleventh on the list and I came out twenty-first. There were about five thousand because that's when the forty-two hours went into effect. A lot of people taking that test.

The physical had pushups, jumping jacks, then you had to run an obstacle course and carry a heavy thing when you were running. I think they held the physical up in Barringer. You had to be five foot six tall.

Elward (1962): I almost didn't take the written. I was going to work and I had crazy hours. We used to go into New York. Leave Belleville at eight o'clock at night and come back the next day at twelve, delivering dry ice. That night I was getting ready to go to work. Fortunately, I stopped at the Clipper Ship. And I had a little something to eat before I went up to Belleville. As I walked in, the bartender said, "The guys are waiting for you." I completely forgot that the written exam was that night in the school I graduated from, Barringer. I looked up and the guy was saying, "We got about an hour to get ready. We're supposed to be at Barringer at seven o'clock." I said, Oh my God." I had the card, reporting date for the exam, but you got to remember I was working man killing hours. So, I went to Barringer. As it turned out, I passed that. I think we were notified in the mail that you passed; you didn't know you're final standing until you took the physical.

Then we took the physical, could be three four months after we got our cards. It was at the Sussex Avenue Armory. I had a wing dinger and then I almost missed the physical. Fortunately, I was living at home. I came home around three o'clock in the morning. I had to go down to take the physical at nine sharp at Sussex Avenue. So, I did a minimum on every station or I would have had a stroke. The thing I'll always remember about the physical, the last station was the kazatskies. The guy wanted to show us an example and guess who the guy picked to demonstrate it. You got all these guys and he said, "Alright, this is the way I want the thing done. Otherwise, you don't get credit. I'm all sweated up and I'm the first guy he looks at. This will count for you if you do it right. So, he says, "Follow me." And he did it and I did it. Up, down, I think you had to do for some odd ball reason, twenty-three. After that they had these stairs that you went down to change your clothes, down in a locker room. I came down like that and I felt like these were jelly. I had nothing left. I didn't even have a pulse. So, I finished that and got the results later. This is the card was saying that I passed. I went down to Miami Beach. This was the first time I took off in a year and a half with that crazy schedule I was working. While I was in Miami Beach, thank God I left my mother the phone number because something got let through. I had to take an immediate physical to go on. It was a Thursday. I had to go on the job Monday. So, I have a gin and tonic down in Miami Beach, life is good and then I had to go home. I can't get a break here.

Schofield (1963): General knowledge at the time for the entrance exam and then a physical. For the physical, I worked out at the academy, the old Academy on Eighteenth Avenue, a couple of nights a week doing sit-ups and pull ups, all kinds of sprints and everything. My brother-in-law, Johnny Hoffman, he was a captain at Six Engine. He took me in there. You had to go with somebody.

After you passed the written, back then you had to have a certain score, you took the physical in the Sussex Avenue Armory. Had to be a hundred and some odd guys, took the whole test. Also, you had a medical at the time. I was working two different jobs doing some directly physical stuff. The doctor took me on the side, called my name out, and asked me some questions. I started to get nervous. And his response was that he had to check me out because I was in such great physical shape. The last thing I had to do was the kazatskies, the deep knee bends. In the armory, you had to go down maybe twenty steps to the locker room. The rise on the step is usually about seven, eight inches. These were only about four. After doing the kazatskies there, I went down so fast I bounced off the wall because my legs were so shaky.

Gaynor (1965): Basically, it was an IQ test. At the time you could also take the police test at the same time for an additional maybe twenty questions. I came out on both lists. The police was never a consideration. It was only the fire that I would be interested in.

There was a physical component to the test. It may have been six or so features, chin-ups pushups, a shuttle, what they call kazatskies. I can't remember what the others might have been. But there were actually six different exercises. I didn't prepare for it. I walked in.

Perez (1965): It was a written and a physical. A written first, then if you passed that you were alright to get into the physical. If you passed that they let you know in about three months. I just skated right through. There had to be a couple of thousand guys who took the exam. I didn't do anything, no effort, nothing and I came out like thirty-eighth. I took the exam at Barringer. I went right through the exam and that same day if they marked you passed, you take the physical. I went to take the physical and I asked the guy to tell me if I got at least a seventy, so I can change clothes.

Calvetti (1966): Back then it was a written test, and a physical test, and a medical. You had three things. First was the written then you went for a medical then you went for the physical. It was pretty easy. I was in shape then. I was only twenty-five years old, so I was in good shape. That's why I came out so high. I came out fifth, so I came on right away. The physical was pushups, pull-ups, a run, sit-ups, and these things they call kazatskies where you jump up and down. It was five things, I think. Let's see the run, push-ups, pull-ups, sit-ups, and the kazatskies. They were the five things. Wasn't bad.

Lawless (1966): There was a written portion. You took everything at the same time. You took a written portion then you took a physical. It was for both police and fire. I took both tests the same day in Barringer.

Benderoth (1967): Well, it was written. The test was I guess a hundred and twenty-five questions, true or false. We took it at Barringer High School on a Saturday morning. I think out of the guys that took the test in Newark there were like fifty that passed. I was the next to last group that appointed from it. Four fellows, we were appointed the same day.

Weber (1969): The testing that they gave to us at the time, if you wanted to be a policeman or a fireman; you took exactly the same test. It reminded me very much of the type of test that you got when you joined the military. And it wasn't anything to do with firefighting. The test was strictly basic knowledge as far as a Q and A test. And then there was the physical performance test which I excelled in which is why I did as well as I did. But it was a mechanical type test and just basic knowledge.

Miller (1969): It was general knowledge. You had some math in there, but a lot to do with the State government, questions like that. Nothing really hard that I remember, a couple of very light, very light police questions. Nothing that you had to know any really heavy detail for.

The physical was pretty strenuous. I was in pretty good shape at the time. I thought I could do everything really quick. Actually, I had a date with my fiancé at 12:30 and I wanted to get out of there. So, they were letting you do the squat thrusts and the dashes and the piling up of the blocks on top of each other and the push-ups and the pull-ups. They're letting you do that with breaks in between, but

I just jumped. I started doing them all right away because I had to get out of there. And I remember doing the squat thrusts and I forget how many we had to do, but I didn't realize they took this much. As young as I was and as good shape as I was in, I almost didn't finish it because I took it all right away and as fast as I could.

I think I was number twenty-two on the police list. And I was number fourteen on the fire list. And I was either first or second non-vet on the fire list. Cause Billy Weber was just in front of me. He was appointed off of the same list, the end of '68 I believe. I was appointed February tenth of '69.

Saccone (1969): The testing procedure was different. You had like a hundred questions. If you had a decent education, you try to answer to the best of your ability. And I had an idea that when I went in to take this written test, you could take a police and a fire test if you wanted to. And I'm pretty sure I took both. I remember taking the physical and we had to do certain exercises, like squats and things like that. But taking the written test for the fire department, I would say without any exaggeration it looked like to me it was two thousand guys were going. I guess people knew it was a good job at the time. It was either that or the Post Office and the Post Office didn't pay too much. The fire department paid a little bit more, I guess. After the test was over, I just put it in my mind. I blocked out that I would ever be on the fire department. I just said, "Well, I'm just going to be a regular guy. Just you know getting a job in a factory or just doing what I was doing." When I came out after that test, I just said, "Well that's it." There were individual monitors at the door at Barringer High School where I took the test, the old Barringer High School, which was across the street from where the cathedral at that time. And at that time, they called your number. And as they called the numbers the crowd was dispersing because people would go, "Oh I failed." While I was walking away, I heard the magic number one seventy-two and that's what I couldn't believe it.

There were a lot of people then. There were a lot of people from Civil Service there, they had monitors at doors, things like that. And there were a lot of people that took this test. So, I remember, it was just a number. I can't forget that number one seventy-two because that changed my life, that one seventy-two.

Daudelin (1970): Oh, the test was general knowledge questions. Basically, they had the whole gamut in those days, multiple choice, general questions on aptitude. I think seventy percent of your score was based on your written exam and thirty percent was on the physical at that time which only consisted of pushups, sit-ups. They had a shuttle run. Pull ups, that was basically the physical part of the test.

P. Doherty (1970): Multiple choice and the physical. The physical consisted of pull-ups, pushups, standing broad jump, run and get the hockey pucks out of the circle and the kazatskies, flat jump and that was it.

Dainty (1970): It was at Barringer High School. They gave the police candidates their test, the fire candidates their test, and there was a third test that was a combination, police and fire. You could file for either or job. I wasn't interested in the cop job so I just filed for the fire job. The other thing that was very different was they did everything there right at the school and they did it all in one day. Versus how they do it today with multiple sites and times. So, you went in. You had to verify your identity. You went into a classroom. They gave you an aptitude test, basically the same as what the military gives you. If I remember correctly there were a lot of mechanical questions, some with hydraulics but just general mechanics. When you finished you gave your test to the monitor, you left, and went outside. Civil Service graded the papers right there.

So, you hung around outside, you couldn't really leave because you didn't know when they were going to come out and call your name. So, I don't know how long later, maybe an hour, an hour and a half, they came out and started calling off names. They were the candidates who had passed the written. Then they get you in a group and they say okay we're going to do the next part of the test. The next part of the test was seeing the doctor. All the doctor was interested in was you had a heartbeat, you could tell colors, and you could read the eye chart. They didn't want you to die taking the physical. Then you went outside, waited again. They called your name and told you whether you're going to the third phase or not.

The guys who passed went inside and took the physical agility test. That was basically pull ups, sit-ups, lunges, squats, and then running, you ran down a certain distance, came back around, and you were timed. It wasn't a long distance, it wasn't a mile or anything like that, and you left. And you waited and you waited. It depends on how interested you were in the job whether you were on pins and needles or whether you just waited. I think in July or August of 1970 I got a letter saying I successfully passed and had to come to fire headquarters and fill out a bunch of paperwork. You go there and you had to bring your birth certificate, your driver's license, social security which ever admin stuff an employer wants.

So, we did that. They gave you a form to fill out with your background information. What you've been doing, where you were born, are you a naturalized citizen, were you in the military, what kind of discharge did you have, the things you're doing now, who's your employer. All that stuff. They took a while to do the background check. Then they send you a letter saying okay you've been hired report to the academy to be sworn in.

Marcell (1970): When I first came on it was a multiple-choice test, general aptitude and then they had a physical. You had to do so many pushups, pull ups, sit-ups, and such. They would correct the test right then and there. You were told whether you passed or not and then you had to take a physical, you had to go see a doctor. They also would check to see if you were color blind, and they did that that day if you had passed. It was all done very quickly. When I took the test, I took it at Barringer, and they gave the test to the police at the same time. The police and fire took the test the same day at Barringer High School. You could have been a cop or a fireman.

Kelly (1971): It was a pretty simple test. They asked you pretty easy questions and easy arithmetic. I was still going to school at the same time, so I was familiar with just about any of that stuff. Then they showed you an aptitude test, like they'd show you a picture of a hammer and a monkey wrench and a screwdriver. Tell you describe one of them. So, the test was a joke.

The physical, I was in great shape because I was wrestling. You had to do something like fourteen pull-ups for a hundred. So that was no problem. And then pushups, you had to do forty for a hundred. Well, forty was a piece of cake, but he says if you stop, you're done. I was up to about sixty, but I wasn't stopping until my monitor said stop. And he goes, "How many is that?" I says, "Sixty." He goes, "Stop. You're wasting your energy." Then you leaped up against the wall to see your vertical jump. After that they had circles. You pick up a piece of wood and you drop it in a circle, and you'd bring it back to another circle. Then they had kazatskies. They were pretty tough. It was tough to get a hundred in them. You had to do ninety of them, so I didn't do too well at that, but I got ninety something. That was the test. It was hard to get a hundred.

Both Tommy Grehl and I aced the test. We came something like eleventh and twelfth. And up to number ten was veterans. They had veterans' status. We didn't have veterans' status. But there was like a couple thousand people took that test. And you could take the cop test at the same time. They said, "You want to be a cop or a fireman." because if you passed you could be either. You had to do the mental for the cop to see if you were not a nut. We both said no. We want to be firemen, no cop.

Romano (1972): At the time it was a general knowledge written test, math, English, reading comprehension, some mechanical ability. If this gear is going one way and this gear is going that way, which way will the third gear go? Things of that nature. The physical we took the same day. We took the test at Barringer High School, and it was a large group. Police and firemen took the test on the same day. Police went into several different classrooms and firemen candidates went into other classrooms. Then you took the written test and graded it on the same day. Those that passed the written took the physical the same day in the gym at Barringer High School. It was the old fashion type of physical, pushups, chin-ups, sit-ups, agility run, that sort of thing.

Rosamilia: (1973) You took a civil service test that ranked for the cadet program. They hired twenty guys. It was about thirty guys that passed the test, maybe a little more on the list. I took the next firefighter test too. I did okay on it, wouldn't have been made in the first group. Actually, it was very fortunate for me because otherwise I would have probably come on with that group of guys that wound up getting laid off in '76 and it would have really disrupted my career. I was able to avoid that. When they had those layoffs, it took two, almost three years for some guys to get back. They didn't come back fully until like '78. They had some CETA guys. Some guys didn't want to come on CETA, which was another Federal program, temporary hiring. Some guys didn't want to come back on that because it didn't go towards your pension. They remained out and they got rehired later.

Stoffers (1973): The cadet test was a physical and a written. The physical was push-ups, sit-ups, timed runs. Picking up blocks and bringing them from this circle to that circle. Squat jumps. I think pull ups also. Whatever a fireman's physical was that's what we got at the time. In '74 we were cadets, and we took the test for the fire department. The physical included climbing a ladder and there were other things involved. I think it was in East Orange. We just took it because if you got pulled in earlier, you would have been a firefighter earlier than the cadets were.

Burkhardt (1973): English, math, basic reading comprehension, stuff like that, multiple choice. Because it was the cadet program, we took it down at One Lincoln Avenue which is police headquarters now. Civil Service came in and gave a civil service exam. They graded the test right there and you took your physical. Your physical was the old sit-ups, broad jump, jumping jacks, all that stuff. Pull-ups and that must have been it, three hundred guys, four hundred guys. As it turned out, out of the twenty cadets that passed it, ten were fireman's relatives.

Morgan (1973): The cadet test was similar to the old firemen's test, physical, written. The physical part of it was pushups, sit-ups, running. Nothing like today.

Brownlee (1973): They had the written test and then we had the physical. And the physical was in East Orange, an East Orange firehouse. It was climbing a ladder, putting nuts and bolts together, sit-ups, pushups, tying knots, a couple of other things.

Coale (1973): The test was the old standard a, b, c, d, all of the above. Then they had a physical made up especially for firefighting. It wasn't the usual push-up and pull-ups. It was where you had to pull a hose and climb a ladder, and you're timed running up the stairways. So, it was on the way to a real fireman's test, not just physical ability, but job related.

Killeen (1974): A multiple-choice test, written test, plus the physical. That was a statewide test. You just opened up a booklet and checked off all the cities you thought you might want to apply for. When I took the test, I was living in Camp Lejeune. I came home on leave to take the test, a weekend leave. Came back to my legal residence. Actually, I was a legal resident of Belleville. Came home on leave, took the test, and went back home. It was like a weekend thing. I drove up, took the test, turned around, and drove back. If I had stayed being deployed, I don't think I'd be a fireman because I enjoyed going for helicopter rides and being on ships and shooting guns. That was great. But I was on leave, came home and took the test.

Camasta (1974): The weight on my test was either eighty written/twenty performance or fifty/fifty. But the physical examination or the performance part of the examination was a lot different. It was a lot more competitive. I'm pretty sure I took it up in Clifton. They had it at their training facility. And they were really close on eyeglasses because I remember the fellow either in front of me or back of me in line was Tex Bennett, who had very poor eyesight. He's now done quite well. You're aware of it if you came on the Newark Fire Department. So, he was sweating over the vision on whether or not he could pass with his eyeglasses. Because even though his eyeglasses functioned, I don't think they really brought him to twenty/twenty like you're supposed to have.

The thing that I always sweated out was the height. They had the height requirement. They had the height and also there was another fellow there who was sweating out the weight. He went on a banana diet because you had to be a hundred and thirty-five pounds. That he was sweating out the weight by a couple of pounds. I remember that being at the start of it. There was a doctor there and a nurse that did your height and your eyes and your weight. And a doctor, turn your head and cough type of deal before you even went on. The physical performance included sight perception. They had tubes all glued together in different formations and you had one model and four or five samples. And you had to pick the sample that was the model in a different position. Manual dexterity was another one. They had a mockup board with all screws and nuts on it and everything was timed. Aside from the efficiency of your sight perception and your manual dexterity, you had to do under the time too. How many nuts you got on the screws in so many seconds. And then I remember they had a hose drag which was the oldest two-and-a-half-inch hose in the world. It had a huge brass coupling on it and you had a hundred and fifty feet of that, you had to drag stretched out. Technique was very important. I always prided myself on doing quite well on that because Chief Tartus' brother, who was big and bulky, had a hard time with it. One of the tests I took at the time, it had rained the previous week that they had done it, so to make ours more competitive, they wet it down. You wet something down it always gets a lot heavier than when it gets rained on.

We had a hoist two-and-a-half-inch hose on a rope and pully. They had this flimsy steel five story structure that was their fire tower and you had to go up an aerial and onto that. You also had to run up that structure carrying hose. Everything was timed. It got to be very competitive. The people who came on the job, all worked hard to get where they were on the list. We probably were fortunate at the time. That was when Newark had EMS, so they had a call for a lot of guys. They went well past me on that list, but that got me on a little bit sooner. And Jersey City never did call me.

Straile (1974): The test was a multiple choice like state civil service exam. It wasn't as hard as I thought it was going to be. I graduated high school, so I guess I was able to pass the test. Other than that, I don't know how else to explain it. It was just your average multiple-choice exam.

We did have a physical that was grueling. That was really hard. At that time, you had to do chin ups, pull ups, sit-ups. It wasn't like the test where you run a track and go up and down a ladder and all. It was a grueling physical exam at the time. But I got through that too. I had just gotten out of the military a few years earlier, so I was still in decent shape, so it worked out very good.

Partridge (1974): Well, it was the first of a new type of exam that they had just devised that was meant to be more job related. The written was more fire oriented, less type of general math, English, science that they had previously had. They asked you questions that you had to know a little bit about the fire service to be able to answer. Now that type of test was later out as being too job related. Allegedly people couldn't get on the job unless they had some kind of an in, but at this time they were looking for job related. That was the test. And then the physical, instead of pushups and sit-ups and that sort of thing, calisthenics, had things like an aerial ladder, hose drag, dummy drag I think, things called spatial relations tests and manual dexterity tests. You had to align blocks into matching positions with sample blocks that were glued together. And you had to match up nuts and bolts and things like that. So that was the test at that time.

Banta (1974): It was a multiple-choice written test. I believe at that time they were using a physical that included what they called spatial relations which was putting the round peg in the round hole and putting the nuts on the right bolts.

J. Prachar (1978): A multiple choice test and you had to pass that. If you passed that, you went on and you took a physical performance test. If you passed the physical performance test, they did it that old fashioned way. They added up the two scores together, divided by two, and you got your score. Worked for me. The first part of the physical was you just had to climb a ladder and the thing was climb a ladder and hit a bell at the top. Just to make sure you can climb a ladder. Then there was a mocked-up hydrant and two short lengths of hose. You had to hook them up, make sure they weren't cross threaded. Then there was an obstacle course. You had to hop a wall, climb through a window, climb across a ladder on all fours, run back, pick up a first aid kit, run slalom through the cones, slalom back, and then drag a dummy twenty yards, twenty-five yards, something like that. It was a hundred- and twenty-five-pound dummy. When I walked into the gym at NJIT, I see these big monsters trying to drag these dummies and falling flat on their butts. I'm saying, "How's this skinny hundred- and sixty-five-pound kid going to be able to do that?" I realized they were trying to overpower the dummy. I just picked it up, put it at my hips, and away we went. I think the last part of the test was the stair climb. Throw a tank on your back, rolled up length of hose, and up three, four flights of stairs.

Daly (1978): We had a written and a physical. The physical was climbing a ladder, dragging a dummy, things like that. Not like the test now. Now they have to hop through a window, drag hose. It was a basic physical fitness test. Climb up stairs with a couple of lengths of hose under your arms, two flights of stairs run up, come right back down. Climb a ladder, had to ring a bell at the top. Basically, it was a test like any other. It was simple. Anybody could pass it.

Zeiser (1978): I do believe they made it a fifty-fifty weight on the physical part. At that time the written was basic knowledge, but it did have a math portion, an English portion. It was multiple choice questions. On the newer test, they talk about teamwork and stuff like that. This test wasn't like that. It was a multiple choice, general knowledge test. I remember studying for the test. We got that Arco book, at the time they had Arco. We'd go through questions and answers and asked friends that we knew that became firemen, if they had any material. Similar to if you studied for captain or chief or anything else. You talk to people. Oh, I got something, information that might help you. You would read it and hopefully some of it would sink in and be on the test.

The physical portion, I believe was a dummy drag, climbing a ladder. There was a window we jumped through. We had to jump over a wall. It was more like an agility test. Carrying a simulated first aid kit, like a toolbox, run it through cones. We ran up a set of stairs with a mask on our back as part of it. I took that test in I think it was '77.

Hopkins (1978): They had multiple choice and then you had a physical. I think it was fifty for the written and fifty for the physical. I know the physical part was in Central High School. The written part might have been in East Orange High or Clifford Scott. The written was all basic math questions I think and some mechanical things. I remember in the physical you had to climb a ladder or skate across a ladder. You had to drag a dummy, run in and out of obstacles, jump a little wall, run up a set of stairs.

Sandella (1978): It was a written exam and I think I took it in Barringer High School and then the physical exam followed. I don't recall if I prepared for it. I was much younger then and in shape, so I didn't prepare for the physical part. They didn't have those classes like they do now. And no I don't think there was much preparation for it. No.

Witte (1978): The test was nerve wracking because I didn't know what you did and how you did. You're trying to do the physical side and you're trying to do the best score possible because the physical was based on time. The faster you did, the better your shot. I remember going around obstacles with a first aid thing. I had to drag a dummy. Had to put hoses on a hydrant. Had to climb across a horizontal ladder, climb up a set of stairs with a hose line.

Kormash (1979): It was a physical performance test and multiple-choice questions. The physical was an obstacle course, dragging dummies, then connecting to a hydrant. I think there were stairs involved. Might have been a hose drag and running around cones, that was it.

Reiss (1979): There was a written component and there was the physical test. We were scored on both, later they changed it to just the physical. I took the physical part of the test at NJIT above High Street, up by Lock Street. I was number ninety-six on the original list. And I was offered CETA at the time that you were going on I guess, in June of '78, but I turned it down because the CETA program at the time was being investigated. And I thought, "Boy, I'll take this, and they'll investigate it and they'll throw us all out and that will be the end of the Newark Fire Department for me. So, I turned it down and waited and I came on in December of '79.

There was some physical training at the Newark Fire Department Training Academy on Jersey Street. I don't think I did too much for the written part of the test. I think that was just a general knowledge test. I don't think there was anything specific to the fire department on that.

Caufield (1980): It was a civil service exam, purely written. I being a disabled vet came out number one on the exam because of my veteran's status. I got the call from City Hall and my Uncle John swore me in. In retrospect I probably made more of a difference as an operator than I would have as a firefighter. Not that I would have been a bad firefighter, but I think I made more of a difference being an operator.

Almaguer (1980): Whatever the city of Newark offered us at that time, I don't know how I got the information or who gave it to me, but I did go to Expera of Focus. That was on Broad Street over there by Lackawanna Avenue. And through them, Focus, Expera, a Puerto Rican group, they arranged some kind of oral test to help us with the written test. And believe you me it became very, very handy when it came to taking tests. When they asked you about certain tools or certain construction that one might have not known at that time. Yeah, I went to Focus I think it was Expera and I remember a lot of people being there.

There was a written and then there was a physical and then there was a physical examination. The physical was taken at Newark College of Engineering. The gym was open for orientation. I think it was open for orientation. We knew about it anyway, but the actual test took place at Newark College of Engineering. It was a standard test that we used even up to the days when we were doing obstacle courses out there, more or less the same thing. Running back and forth with a hose. Remember now, this is 1977. Way back in the middle seventies. And I remember running back and forth, hooking up the hydrant, climbing a ladder, ringing the bell, going through a tunnel, dragging a dummy, obstacle course, and the best one was like going up stairs with a self-contained breathing apparatus on your back. They wanted to see how fast you could go up and down those stairs. We busted that record open. Me and my brother were the best in scoring that day.

I took a test for the Newark fire department. Filled out the same application that everyone else filled out. It wasn't for bi-lingual firefighter. What happened was on the application where it said Black, White, Latino, Other, Indian, all that stuff, there was a little section there that said bi-lingual. And that application that everyone filled out had that little box there where it said bi-lingual firefighter. During that time the Star Ledger was running articles saying they were looking for Latino firefighters. Obviously, I am Latino. I was born in this country. I was born in Manhattan, but my father's Cuban; my mother's Dominican; and I'm Puerto Rican.

Because back in the '60s there were no Cubans and there were no Dominicans. The only thing there were were Puerto Ricans. We were all Puerto Ricans. Anyway, it's a good thing. So, I see Latino, I'm not going to put anything else besides what I am and I am bi-lingual, so I hit that little box. Boom. Not knowing that that little box would be my curse. Because if I had not hit that little box, and I maybe put Latino or if I even put White, Caucasian, I would have come on the job in 1978. But they separated those individuals that marked that box, now we're separated from the list and then for the next three or four years we were in limbo.

I would like to give acknowledgement to Ray Aneses's father, who was Deputy Mayor at that time for Gibson. He was the big advocate of that list. If it wasn't for him, it would have died. If it wasn't for him and certain other Latino individuals in the city of Newark at that time, that list would have died and I would have been cheated because my written score was like eighty-five and my physical score was like ninety-eight. We found ourselves in limbo and then it was typical politics. Then all of the sudden I started to receiving notification that I had to take a Spanish test. I had to take a written Spanish test. I had to take an oral Spanish test. In the meantime, the list I should have been on, they were hiring guys. Anyway, I went through that process in Trenton, taking those bi-lingual tests, oral tests. And thank God I did good also, me and my brother. I don't know how many Latino people were involved at that time, but at the end of everything, the city of Newark picked out seven guys out of that list, out of political pressure or whatever it was. I have no idea. I was naïve. I was a young man. I was just happy to have a job.

There were lawyers involved. Ray Aneses was the one I got to meet. He was the one that called me up one time and asked me for money for a lawyer. And I was like, "Hey man, I'm married with two kids, working at Saint James Hospital. And I'm like, I can't afford lawyers or that kind of money." I think something went down. Ray Aneses used to call me up to keep me abreast about this list. And we were struggling to keep this list alive.

F. Bellina (1981): Down on Jersey Street, they set up a practice course. You jump through the window and all that stuff. They started it then. It was the first time. I think Stewart was the one that actually got it going down there, him, Ron Ballew, and a couple of other guys. They set it up outside. There was no interior. It was a very small academy. We would go down there every night and we would go run through the scenario. There was no tunnel, but it was like an obstacle course, and it was timed. The written was like nothing. It was just pass or fail.

West Kinney Junior High, that's where I took the actual written. And it was, maybe fifty questions, a hundred questions. There was really no study guide, maybe an Arco book. Because I remember at the time, I was trying to take the test for the Post Office too, coming out of Marines and it was like the same type of book that you would get. So, it's probably that same company. I passed that. I got the notification in the mail that I passed that. The next thing is the physical. We found out that they were doing the time test down there. One of the things was you jumped through the window, run through the cones, pick a ladder up. Run with the ladder. It was all running. It was up the staircase with a tank on your back and then down a flight of stairs. And also, the hydrant, you were timed to put the caps on. I actually built something at my mother-in-law's house where I had the caps. I would spin them off and spin them on. Somebody taught me how. First you put the cap on and reverse it. Hear the click and then go with it which was key. If I didn't do that, I probably wouldn't have passed the test.

Griffith (1983) I took both types of tests. I took the one before the consent decree which was in West Kinney Junior High. There was a written. Even the first one, the written was there, but it wasn't that intense. But not being a wise guy, I went to Seton Hall Prep, and you know I went to Sacred Heart Vailsburg, so I wasn't intimidated by that at all. I went in being used to taking tests. You took tests all the time. So, it doesn't really register with me as far as what it was. You know looking back maybe I should have been scared. It was general knowledge. I remember mechanical things, how a gear meshed. Then there were general questions. Some math, some English. It seemed to be the emphasis was on the physical part of the test and not so much on the written.

The physical, the first thing you had to do was climb a ladder, ring a bell. There was an obstacle course and then you had to carry a hose roll up the stairs. Somebody's standing up two flights and they said go, so totally unscientific compared to what we're used to today. I took it but I was thinking of going to college then so, I didn't really work out for it. Now the second test I took was then the consent decree test. It was a whole different lay out. Very scientific, everything was there. There were time clocks where once you broke the barrier it worked and it was more intense, but I worked out for it then. I had no disagreement with it, but my situation then was I was behind veterans. That was the only thing really that set me backwards, the veterans. They certainly deserved it. I had no issue with that. That's just the way it is. That's the rule and I certainly agree with it. And then you saw that morph over the years, but that was the test that I took.

Arce (1984): I did a physical test. I did a written test. The written was just a general written, high school. I think I did great. I was one out of the first ten. The physical test was more running. Now it's walking, walking fast. We ran. And it wasn't about how big you were, how strong you were. I remember that day, going to Trenton. I didn't have a ride. I had no car. I took the train and it's snowing, and I was late. In front of me were big guys. I mean body builders that worked out a lot. But they couldn't climb walls. It wasn't a big challenge for me because I was very agile, fast. It was an advantage to be small instead of being a big guy.

Weidele (1984): We had a civil service test with a written test and if you passed that you went to take a physical test in Trenton. Where you had to hook up to hydrants, run up and down ladders, jump through windows, and then just bring a hose line around the side of a counter and they timed you.

Nasta (1984): We had a written test which at that time was pass fail. That enabled you, if you passed it, to go on to the physical test. The physical test was timed. That's how you were scored. Your ranking came out according to your time on the test. So, I did a lot of working out at the Newark Fire Academy. They used to host the obstacle course every night. I did a lot of running on my own and I was down there just about every night practicing to learn how to do the obstacle course. In addition to running the obstacle course there was the rope evolution where you stood on a platform and there was a board with three holes in it. You threaded the rope through the three holes. That was a timed evolution also. From what I understand that event became pass fail too.

But the funny part of the story was, I was used to running the obstacle course at the Training Academy which was outside. My testing process was the first time that Civil Service brought all the candidates down to Trenton. And they hosted it in a gym. In the obstacle course, there was a part where you picked up a ladder and you had to carry the ladder upright and weave in and out of these cones. So, I picked up the ladder, I was used to picking it up from the bottom rungs because there were no height restrictions at the Academy. It was open sky. I was running through the gym, knocking the ceiling tiles out of the gym ceiling. The proctor was yelling at me and there was no way I was stopping. So, I was running and the ceiling tiles were falling behind me. I went through the evolution. I ran through the rest of the course. I got a perfect score. At the end the proctor comes up to me. He goes, "Listen, we're going to give you an opportunity to run it again because you were interfered with." I says, "If I run it again, I know what my time already was, do I get to pick the better time?" He says, "Oh, no if you run it again, that'll be your score." I says, "There's no need for me to run it again." So, I didn't. After that, they put a piece of tape on the second rung of the ladder when you run that evolution. So, nobody else could do that.

O. Johnson (1984): The test they used was the basic knowledge test. They gave you test booklets to prepare for it. They also had a preparation class for the physical part of the test. So, it was two stages. It was pretty good. We were lucky. They had something set up at the Shabazz High School which was Southside. The program was good. It gave you a little knowledge of it. If you applied yourself to it, then you did well. I would say seventy-five, eighty percent of the people who applied themselves did very well on the test.

DeCuester (1984): I guess it was the old test, not the biodata. The written was actually quite simple. It was like picture with the hammer and stuff like that. Then the physical test, dragging the hose. We went up and down, tying knots. I didn't go to any of the prep classes. I had the veterans' status, so that helped.

Giordano (1985): Well, that kind of evolved in my whole career. Entrance level testing back then was different. I'm going back to before I came on. I believe it was fifty percent on your cognitive ability, on the written exam, and then half the score was based on the obstacle course. And they have different components of the obstacle courses. It kept changing year to year, we were on the Federal Consent Decree order and the tests changed, hiring and promotional, every year after 1983. I don't think they duplicated one test, but the test I took was a physical and a cognitive skills test. At the time they even had things like follow the map, where are you? Are you at Joe's Shoe Store? Are you at Macy's Department Store? And it had a multiple choice, so you had to follow which streets were legal to go down. After the one time they did that, that part of the exam was eliminated. It was deemed to be discriminatory due to the statistical results against a protected group. It had an adverse impact on the results of the exam. That part with the map, I actually knew one or two college graduates. They couldn't do it either. I don't know what college they went to, but it was very interesting. That was the first part they eliminated.

So, when I came on, they had the basic cognitive skill test then the rest was on an obstacle course physical which changed and evolved into everything that now works. It was good for me. Then as we move forward, the next test exam, it was pass fail on the written. So, a person who got a seventy or a sixty or a seventy-three, whatever the determined pass point was. It was never set. Pass point on the cognitive was always set after the test was taken. They would lower the score to meet their goal of the consent decree to ascertain x number of black, Hispanics.

But in that core, they got many non-blacks and Hispanics that fell in the middle and got hired also.

I prepared for it. That's part of my story. I got involved with replicating the test, setting it up. We had it set up for anybody in the city that wanted to come. We had a lot of retired fire guys, too many to name, but they came before me. These guys would come and set the stuff up for guys to practice on. So, I was there every day and everybody that went did very well. People that didn't go, it was very hard, very few would make it. Probably through the regime of practicing. Who could run the fastest? Who could run this obstacle course?

It was under the Federal consent decree. The city would have one sponsored and myself and other guys we kind of built our own course. We would set it up. I would say it was not sponsored by anybody. It was just run through myself and members of the fire department. It was very well done. At that time, we set up a class, we saw the city was running one, the Vulcan Pioneers were running one. I had my bar on Bloomfield Avenue, the Three Twenty-two Club and I had many firemen in there. They were carpenters, welders, and they kind of built all this equipment. And it was great. We had Charlie Krutulis was a welder. He welded the mock hydrant. Brian Donnelly was a carpenter. He built the stairs. He built the window frame you had to jump through. I don't know who built the dummy, but we always had a dummy, and it was weighted a hundred and ten pounds. But we did all that and once again everybody who came into the practice classes did very well.

And somewhere in the middle, like every test, after the test was over the United States Justice Department would come in with Lawyers from Rutgers Civil Rights Division. I wound up going to Federal court, being deposed over running these classes. Where'd you get the money? Who built the mock hydrant? Who built the wooden staircase? And I named the firemen that produced all this stuff. It was so great. It was actually all part of the court hearing. But that was the beginning of a long saga with the Justice Department.

As my extensive experience went for minimal standards for hiring practice, I want to eliminate the whole physical and just you have to go up a fake aerial ladder and start the saw. If you could do that, you pass the physical because many people can't get that saw up an aerial ladder and start it. It's not happening, and it doesn't matter if it's a man or a woman. If you can go up three flights, carry that, and start it up, and maybe a claustrophobic test. I've seen it where some guys once the lights go out, they don't want to be a fireman. That's part of the old exam. They actually put you into a tunnel and you have to come out the other side. As soon as they put that door over the people, you heard in the microphone, "Let me out." They're done. The veterans who go to the front of the list, firemen's sons, it doesn't matter. I've seen it happen, supervising test exams for the union. We pushed our way right out onto the floor with the test takers in the department of Civil Service. It had never been done before. They actually tried to throw us out. I was the president then. I threatened them that we'll have two buses of people out here protesting. They were going to allow the Vulcan Pioneers in to watch and make sure everything was legit because nobody trusted anybody.

I must have seen thousands of people take tests. I've seen other people get second chances and some they didn't. It was a game. I was on the floor and that was one of the elements of the physical exam to be a fireman. They had the tunnel where they put you underground and you got to go to the center, crawl in, hit a light switch, back out, and go out the other way. You had to have the wherewithal to know where you were at, put your shoulder to the wall. If you come out the same door, you failed. I've seen both. I've seen people just panic. Let me out. They were claustrophobic and I've seen people, they just come out the wrong way. Because it was timed for speed so people are trying to do it in ten seconds instead of thirty. It moves you way up on the list. The Department of Justice changed it to you could take over a minute to do it. It was a disparate impact on a protected group. So that part was eliminated. They didn't want to discriminate against people who were claustrophobic.

We held on for several test cycles where at least the physical counted. And then we got to a major part where it was three different elements, and they were combined. And I think that was the last time it was competitive. It may have been competitive afterwards with the elevated climb and the tunnel just pass fail. Everything was just on the first part of the obstacle course which consisted of two mockup hydrants, two lengths of hose, you grab a ladder, and you weave it through cones. After that you went up and down ten steps, up ten, down ten, twice on some metal type industrial stairs that they use in like a warehouse. Then you jump through a window, you drag a dummy and that's what the test came down to. Who could do that the fastest? But I'm going to say maybe '90s, possibly in the 2000s, they did away with that too. Now the physical you take you pass with a minimal score. You're equal to somebody else who had some type of better score than you on the cognitive exam. Which takes us to a biodata.

I joined this group The International Association of Management personnel. It was a big think tank about testing and how to have diversity outcome-based testing. These professors and people that develop these exams, they could come into one percent of scoring any protected group by gerrymandering the scoring of the exam. And it turned out to be a biodata test for your life experiences. So, they would ask you, "Did you ever miss your turn going home? Do you miss it all the time? Once in a while? You never missed it or you always miss it?" So, at the end there's no right or wrong answers. They wait until everybody's answers are in and then they put it into a computer and spit it out so it's a negative one, a zero, or a plus one or a plus two. Depends on how it affects the different groups so they can get a diverse stratosphere of candidates. That's just one of the questions. Other ones were, "How many times were you picked for a sports team? Were you the first guy picked? You were never picked? Were you always picked?" It was just questions with no answers. It is hard for people to comprehend unless you went to all these focus groups and all these conferences. Later on, they went to video. They show you a small clip and then they would stop it and give you a choice in that video. Would you do a, b, c, or d? There was no right or wrong answer. The videos came from a small town like Olympia California. It had no bearing on what we were doing.

But the sad part is that to develop the test they gave out fifteen hundred question samplings. As I remember we were at Civil Service, and I was with the Firemen's Union and Captain Herb Volkert was with the Officers' Union. He spoke up and the people couldn't believe it. He said, "Hey, you're going to want us to verify these answers that are really not true and then blame us for them." Captain Volkert, who became Chief Volkert, was right on the money. They were asking for our fingerprint and validating that these were the right answers. How many times did you put a bicycle together? What you would say on a multiple choice on a video. Dealing with a superior officer, what would you do? These are all subjective things.

One of the videos was two new firemen in the firehouse. Ones lounging on the chair like he's been there twenty-five years and the other new fireman is emptying the garbage, mopping the floor, and the phone rings. The lazy new fireman's not answering the phone. So, which should the other new fireman do? Tell the supervisor, have a heart-to-heart talk with the guy, say nothing? At the end of the day, they want him to tell his supervisor. That may have been good in Olympia, California, but it's not good in Newark, New Jersey. That would not be the right answer. They had another scenario where a woman firefighter goes to put her gear on the truck. The first thing you do in the firehouse before that bell rings is put all your gear on the truck. You want all your equipment ready. The woman firefighter almost has her gear there and the guys are playing around with her being the new probationary firefighter. They say, "Helen you have to go make the coffee." She goes to make the coffee. She's almost ready to put her gear on the fire truck and the guys come out, "Helen, the probationary firefighter has to put the flag out." She goes and puts the flag out. Next, the supervisor comes out and looks on the floor. He's got a mean scowl on his face. He can't believe she didn't put her equipment on the truck. It's now fifteen minutes after the hour. She comes walking up and the video ends. What should she do? She should tell the officer, "I'll never do it again. The guys played a trick on me." And that's what they wanted. The company that ran that test was an example. They came in once and never came in again. No vendor ever came in and administered the same test twice.

N. Bellina (1986): Well, actually the father of a good friend of mine Al came on the front porch one day, I think it was in maybe '75 and he had these applications for the Newark Fire Department to take the test. And we didn't take it because we had long hair. "I ain't cutting my hair. What? Are you kidding me?" So, anyway, I think I took the test towards the end of '77. It was a written. I think the written was multiple choice. I took the test three times. That first test I came out like one forty-eight, but there were seventy-five vets on that test. Actually, I was in the high sixties. I don't know the vets scores, but they went to the front of the list. I had to wait. I waited until I think around the end of '78.

Now I took Jersey City's test also. So, I was on both lists at the time. I went down to Jersey City to get my physical to go on their job. My buddy Al called and said, "Listen, you've got to get home, see if you've got mail from Newark. So, I got home and yes, I did. I got the letter. It's got the mayor's signature on it. Report on Monday to the Training Academy. That's great. That was on a Tuesday. It was early in the week. Well, that Friday H. Lee. Serokin, the judge, threw out my list. That was the beginning of the consent decree, and I was done. I was heartbroken.

He should have let that run out then started new. They just killed it, killed me too. I was dead. So, it took me from '78 to '79 to '86 to get on the job.

I might have taken the test again in maybe '81, after my brother went on. I think it was eighty physical, twenty written. After that it was pass/fail written. It was still multiple choice.

On the written part, I think I pretty much had it. But I wanted to be in physical shape. That was my main concern, so I started running because my brother got on. But he just got out of the Marine Corps. Him and Scotty Gerow were running from Vailsburg to downtown with work boots on. I said that's nuts man. So, they had it down, but I didn't score that high on that test. Maybe the Academy was running something on the last test, but I don't think there was too much practice like they got now. I don't remember going anywhere to practice for that. I just did my own thing, going up and down the stairs in the house, you know, that type of stuff.

The last test was basically the same as the second test. There was an obstacle course. It was a little different than it is now. That first test we ran up the stairs with the tank on our backs. One of these tests had a tunnel. You had to crawl through with the tank on.

Sorace (1986): I took the written test which was pretty simple. They ask you like high school type stuff. After that we waited like a month and then we took the physical agility test. They had a course set up here in Newark and there was a group of us that would go down there almost every day and run it and practice. We all became friends. When we ended up taking the test, I came out number one in the state that year for the physical agility test. I was number sixteen on the entrance list because I had veterans ahead of me. I came out number one.

Masters (1986): When I first came on, we had the multiple choice, hundred questions, basics, some fire, some math, some written. Common sense questions, but most of your marks for that period, for the first few periods when this test came out was the physical performance. Newark offered classes down at the old training academy on Jersey Street three days a week and I was down there three days a week up to the test. I scored well on it. I got to be friendly with a few of the instructors that were there. You had to run for every portion of the test. It's a lot different than nowadays with pass/fail. Everything was your timing. It went through the couplings, the hose carry, the ladder raises, in a darkened tunnel shut the light switch, and the last was your dummy. Second part was climbing up an incline, doing some work with a harness on and your feet over the edge to see you're not scared of heights. But everything was timing and seeing how you went.

Ch. Centanni (1986): I believe our test was the first new testing process where they went into the obstacle course. We had a pass/fail written test which was the first part. If you passed that then you moved on to the obstacle course which was multiple graded portions. A very good test. Difficult, the physical was difficult. It was an obstacle course and it had several portions. There was an obstacle part that you ran through with a vest on; then there was a tunnel portion that you had to go through in the dark and do a search pattern; and finally, there was a scaffold climb which I guess simulated the ladder portion and the heights of the job.

The written portion I believe was basic math and some fire questions in it, but I think it was a basic test. There were some maps in there that you had to follow the street around to get from point A to point B, reading comprehension, things like that.

Lee (1986): It was a written and a physical test. Basically, the written was on basic general questions and the fire service. The physical consisted of activities I would do as a firefighter, carrying a dummy, going up stairs, going through windows, putting a hose onto a hydrant. I prepared. Unfortunately, I wasn't able to prepare fully because I was working a full-time job and I had two young children, so I wasn't able to devote all the time I needed to come out and practice. But I did have one or two practices.

Goetchius (1986): I took a written test of course. And I think they said passing was a seventy and they lowered the written part to get the numbers they were looking for. When it came to the physical it was an obstacle course and you took the incline doing the little job on top. That was being timed. I think now it's not being timed. Then the tunnel, that also was being timed and that came out on your final score. It was basically the same test they use today.

The written test count didn't count at all. It was a pass fail/written and the physical counted for everything.

Ziyad (1986): It was a written and a physical. They gave us a physical performance test at West Kinney Junior High School the first time I took it. The second time I took it they gave us a physical performance test and a written test. So, it was a written and physical performance.

The written test was basically a high school equivalency exam pretty much. They asked you basic reading, writing, and arithmetic. As long as you had a high school education level, pretty much, you should do well on it. The physical performance test was a speed test and a strength test. You ran an obstacle course, picking up hose and running up steps and running through an obstacle course. As well as, climbing a ladder and going through an underground tunnel.

I did prepare for the physical. I actually took the exam twice. Initially in 1980 I believe it was or '81. Me and my cousin Arnum Wapples, we both took the test. He prepared. He had gone to a couple of classes. I wasn't sure I wanted to be a firefighter. In fact, he had to call me up to remind me the test was that day. We took the physical performance test at West Kinney Junior High School on West Kinney Street. I know I passed, but I didn't do all that great because I didn't really prepare. He passed and he got on the job. The next time there were applications, my brother and my cousin applied. They took the test and they got on the job. Now I was encouraged. I took the test. What they did do was they had a preparation program. I believe it was part of the Newark consent decree, the State of New Jersey consent decree where they mandate some type of preparation for the actual test. So, I did go to the classes. Every day after work I would show up down at the Newark Training Academy and prepare for it. And I went to a couple of written classes. But the physical performance part was the biggest preparation they actually gave us. And I got a perfect score on the test. So, I guess the preparation did help me the second go round.

The way I see it, those individuals who showed up every day down at the Training Academy, those were the guys that ended up being in the top of our class. And I think throughout our careers, that kind of mirrored exactly what we saw. Those who prepared and put in the effort, literally got what they put in for. And one of the things I've always said throughout my life and especially I emphasized this once I got on the job is pretty much what you put in, that's what you get out. You put in half; you get half. You put in a whole; you get the whole goal and effort that you put in.

Alexander I (1987): The test that I took consisted of a written part which was just basic math, science and the second part was a physical part and which you had to complete a physical course in a certain time frame. The quicker you finished the higher your score was. So that determined where you were placed on the list.

In the physical part you had to take a hose line and run from one end of the gym floor to the other and connect to a hydrant. We had to also do what they call a ladder carry. That's carrying a ladder vertically and weaving through cones. We had to climb up a ramp, position ourselves with our feet hanging over the ramp and be able to pick up a wooden peg with three holes in it. And we had to pull a rope between each peg while standing on the edge. I guess they wanted to see what our balance was and if we were afraid of heights. The most important part was the tunnel where you had to enter one way and come out the opposite end. It was dark. You pretty much had to feel your way through. Some of the guys taught a technique that if put your shoulders on a certain part of the wall, the right or the left, that it would lead us out the way we needed to come. So that helped me and I was able to get through it. I scored pretty well. In addition to already being an athlete, like I said I played high school basketball and baseball, so my condition was pretty good.

I would still go down to Weequahic Park and do some running, do some calisthenics They also gave us practice courses down on Jersey Street, at the Academy. They had a mock test set up right out there and we were able to train right there. I went there twice a week because I was working most of the time.

Taylor (1987): Back then we had pre-training at the Academy. That's where I met you when I got into the Academy. I prepared and I was not the most athletic kid on my block, but I needed a job, and I was determined. That's when the stadium was still up in Weequahic Park, and I worked out and planned and worked. I went to probably every training session they had. That's when they were still down on Jersey Street.

Maresca (1987): We took a written and there was a physical. The written was pass/fail. it was all based on the physical which was kind of similar to the courses they run now. We had to drag a hose, hook it up to a hydrant. Then we took a ladder and ran between cones. We took a hose and ran up and down steps, twelve times, ten times, something like that. We carried a toolbox. Then we jumped through a window, crawled under some sawhorses and climbed out the window, and then you pulled a dummy twenty-five yards, whatever, a hundred- and fifty-pound dummy.

There were actually three parts. The second part was a tunnel you crawled in. It was like an M shape. You went in; you got to the middle; you had to go in to find a room; you hit the light switch; you had to go out the opposite end. And then the third part you had to climb up a ladder. When you got up to the top, you went to the edge of a platform, and you reached down and grabbed a rope. You had to thread it to either the right or the left side. That was the three parts.

Griggs (1988): The civil service exam at the time that I took it had a pass/fail written. The next phase was the physical performance. And basically, your whole grade hangs on how well you did on the physical performance. We had the hydrant mockup with the two and a half. The ladder-carry through an obstacle course. You had to go up and down stairs with at least a length of inch and three quarter. We had to go up, back down without falling on your back. We did that a few times. There was a dummy drag across the auditorium floor. They had a tunnel format where you had to go through the tunnel, switch a light on, and work your way back out of the tunnel. You had to hang on the edge of a platform. I guess they wanted to see if you could acclimate yourself to height and you had to do some kind of function with knots. We had a weighted vest I remember.

I didn't prepare as well as I should have. They had sessions held down off Raymond Boulevard at the Boy's Club. Chief Kormash at the time he was a fireman, and he was running it. I thought I knew everything. I thought if I went to the park and did my three to five miles running, I'd be good to go. But that wasn't the case. I went one time, and I should have gone numerous times. Only once I went and that was a big mistake. You have to prep for that. At the time that's what everyone was doing so I didn't pay attention on that part of the exam. But I did well enough.

DeLeon (1988): My test when I came on was the old before they erased everything and slowed it down. This was speed. Go through the tunnel, come out, lift a dummy, connect to a hydrant. Then you go from there, you lift the ladder, then you ring a bell. Then you come back down, then you go through the tunnel and if you come out the wrong way through the tunnel you failed because they were timing you. What helped me out a lot was at that time, I think Lonzie Ellison, who retired a long time ago, and a couple of other guys would coach me. And I would go down to practice. I had the motivation. I worked out really hard to do well. Gave it a shot, gave it a shot. None of it I regret at all. I like to kiss all of them if I see them around. I haven't seen them around at all since they left. They disappeared from my life.

When I took that test, I wanted to give it a go. Not knowing what I was getting into. Other than Gil Colon, I didn't have any other friends that were in the fire service. So, the insight for what I was getting into, it was like blind. Here you go kid. Go at it. The prep for the test, it was the same one they were doing since I'm pretty sure in the '70s and early '80s. All the way up until, I think mid to late '90s. They started changing that whole program.

Way before the biodata, I did the old school one which I like to say I'm glad I took it the old way because I worked for it and I earned it. No cheating, no short cuts, okay I'm gonna make it easy for you, go for it. I prepared a whole year. I used to work for a medical company, and we delivered oxygen. In the van had these tanks, seventy to a hundred-pound tanks. That's what I would do. Instead of taking the elevator, I would take that tank and run up say ten stories, I'd go ten stories with it. By the end of the day my legs were like Jell-O, but they told me that's what's going to happen when you take that test. The legs, the legs, work on the legs. I was really into it. I really wanted to do well on it.

Greene (1988): Well, initially we took a written test. It was not difficult at all. We took the physical test which was basically where at that time all the scoring came from. I believe the written was just a pass/fail and your rank on the civil service exam was determined by your performance on the physical agility test. I didn't prepare for the physical that much. No more than kind of like normal running that I had done. In fact, that was probably something that held me back. When I went to the test, I had no idea what I was doing. It was only because Alan Masters was there. He was ahead of me and I picked up some pointers from him like how I should carry the ladder and that's basically how I made it. Make sure that you secure the coupling to the hydrant tight. You don't cross thread it. You carry the ladder vertically not horizontally.

Sperli (1989): We had a basic written test. If you had a high school degree, then you could pass it. And we had a physical test. There were two classes that were hired from that test. I was in the first class and the second class had a retake of the test. It was the last test where all three components were actually timed. The first component was an obstacle course. You were timed on dragging hose, going up and down ladders, through windows, and dragging a dummy. The second was a tunnel that you had to go into. There was a light switch with a neon red light in the middle. You had to get to the switch, turn it off, and then go out the opposite direction. The third part your feet were dangling over an edge, and you had this block of wood with holes in it and a rope. You had to weave the rope through, and you had to go down touch the seat and then take the piece of wood back out of the rope. And then you were done. All three of these things were timed. But they hired my class and then they said that it was unfair. People fought it so the second and third components were just pass or fail after that, no longer timed.

The firemen's union used to have at the Boy's Club down the Ironbound, simulated testing. What the test was going to be with dragging the dummy and everything. They would time us and we would have weighted vests on. Me and my friend, who actually talked me into taking the test with him, Chuckie West, we were jogging just about every night preparing for it because we really wanted to be firefighters.

Alvarez (1989): At that time when I took the test, there were two portions to the test, the written portion and the physical portion. The written portion was pass or fail and if you passed it, you went on to the physical portion, the obstacle course. If you failed it, you didn't go on. I passed the written portion of it and then I was waiting for the physical portion, the obstacle course. And the city held the practices about a month and a half prior to the test. Where they had an obstacle course simulation set up at One Lincoln Avenue, the Police Academy. And so, I found out about it. They notified all of us and from day one, from the minute it opened I was there to the minute it closed every single day. I never missed a day, and I never missed a minute of it being opened. I ran that course every time I could run that course. Of course, the first time I did a horrible time. I threw up after it. I'm thinking I could smoke this thing, mister tough guy, and I threw up after. Then I took it slowly and I stepped it up and stepped it up because I had to get on this job, had to. So, there were other guys, "Oh, I did good enough. I'm not coming tomorrow." I don't remember exactly all the guys, but I think some of them never made it. But I ran that course. Every minute that it was available to me to run the course, I ran it. Because it all counted on that, on how well you did on the physical portion. So, I came out I think I had the second fastest time. And I came on with the first class.

Cordasco (1989): On the police test back then it was a written that was graded, and the physical was just pass/fail. It was timed pass/fail, three components. When we did the fire test it was pass/fail on the written and then everything was based on your physical. At that time there were the three components. There was the obstacle course, the incline, and then the underground tunnel where you had to hit the light switch. It was H shaped, but you had to do the U shape and you had to keep your right shoulder to the right side, left shoulder left side and come through. So that was the two different tests for the fire.

Because I was a cop, I had the keys to the Police Academy gym. They didn't have the armory at the time. My brother Chris and I would go there during the day. I would run during the day when there was nobody there. Then I would go at night and run it sometimes with instructors. And then Dave Giordano had the Boy's Club. So, we would go down for the Boy's Club. I'll tell you a funny story down there. It was a Saturday and Wayne Linfante and I were working the radio car. So, we called that we had a fight at the Boy's Club. We got changed. We had guys watching our guns. We ran the course two times and then went back to work. And that's a true story. Guys were hysterical. We had reliable guys watch the guns.

Daniels (1989): Oh, the test was pretty much a basic test, I think. There was reading. There was very, very little writing. There was multiple choice on the test, and they had a section in the test where you had to be able to look and see mechanical shapes and what goes with what. The math was basic math and fractions and times tables. That was the written portion of the test. It counted. The physical portion of the test was a little different.

The physical, the set up all hooked up at One Lincoln. It was in that gym. I walked in and I see all these people. There are a lot of people in there. So, I walk up in there and I see what they're doing. I thought this was going to be easy. I was a young guy. I was kind of cocky about it. I was like, "This is going to be a breeze." I saw people falling out at the end of the course and puking and all that. And I'm like, "God, this is going to be easy." So go through the course and there was the tunnel of course. You had to go through the tunnel and not come out the opposite way. Then you had a ladder where you had to do height coordination. You had to climb up the ladder. On the ladder, you had to weave the board then come back down. And they had the dummy drag. That was the last portion of it. All this was timed. So those were the things that you absolutely ran through each and every one of those obstacles. They had a window you had to jump through. They instructed you how to do it. So, a lot of people were taking their time, you know, jumping through the window or whatever trying to do it. I mean crazy.

You see guys going through the test, but I was kind of restless when I was young. I used to jump off stuff, climb buildings. As a matter of fact, people used to call me crazy, crazy Chris when I was growing up. I was naturally born for this stuff. I didn't know. Climbing up buildings from one story to the fourth floor. Anyway, when we were going through, I wasn't trying to take anything easy. I was trying to blow through everything my very first time going through this course. I jumped through this window. I didn't even touch the window. I jumped through the window, did a tuck, and rolled, kept going. I mean I was just excited. Then the last part of that test which is the drag, I started dragging that dummy. The dummy hit my feet and I fell back, boom. I got back up and I kept going. I did that and once I crossed the line, I remember what I thought when I came in. People doubling over. People vomiting. I felt like the room was spinning, but I was too fried. I went into the bathroom, splashed some water on my face. It wasn't as easy as I thought. I made it through, but it wasn't easy. So, after going through that course, after that day, then I actually started working out and preparing for it. I did because I realized that after seeing all those people going through what we did, I really wanted it. I wanted it. At that point I wanted it.

LaPenta (1989): We had to take a written exam. Oddly there were no firefighting questions on the written exam. It was just general knowledge questions, basic math, writing skills, memorization, had to read a map and answer questions to the map. And then there was a physical portion. There were three portions. There was an obstacle course you were timed on. And then you had to crawl under the gymnasium in a darkened maze. That was timed separately and then I think the last portion was we had to walk up an inclined plane and do like a block and tackle, do a task standing on the edge of the platform. They timed that and then they added the times together. That's how you came out. I think my entrance exam I was twentieth on the entrance list or something like that.

I prepared. I was a little overweight. I was smoking cigarettes, so I was living the dream. I was eighteen years old, living in mom's house. Not really having a care in the world. It's funny because I actually was getting in shape, wanting to be a fireman. I was also leaning toward going into the armed forces. I was leaning toward the Marine Corps. So, I kind of knew something was going to happen. Whether I got the fire department job or if I didn't, I'd be in the armed services, but I did prepare for it. I quit smoking and got in shape. I knew some guys who were on the job down here from growing up with them. And I used to go and hang out in some of the firehouses They'll tell you I was a portly young man so to speak. And then when they saw me, they patted me. They were like "Oh, my God. Who is this person?" So, I did get in shape for it.

David Giordano was running something down at the Boy's Club off of Ferry Street. My roommate in Newark was Chuck West. So, Chuckie and I would go down there. We it ran a few times. At the time you were able to apply for the job for the municipality that you resided in and also for the county that you resided in. So, I also took like the East Orange Fire Department test, the Montclair Fire Department test. I actually ran some exams prior to taking the Newark test.

I did that so I could be ready for the Newark exam. So, it kind of worked out to my advantage.

Tarantino (1989) I used to be in much better shape than I am in now. And I am pretty competitive, so I was like, "I'm going to beat everybody." So, I would train at night at NJIT parking lot. I ended up getting a length of hose from Dave Giordano. He owned a bar at 322. He set up that little training thing. I couldn't train when everybody else was training because I was working or going to school. So, I would run the NJIT parking lot every night before I went to work. We took the test. You know, you're nervous. You don't know how well you're going to do. I ended up coming out number one. So, I was one of nine that tied for number one in my class.

West (1989): What type of test did they use? It was a written test. I don't remember the type. The test has changed since then. Then they did a physical. The physical portion was really your test score, how you ranked. The written was just a pass/fail and then the entire rank was based off of the physical portion of the test.

Pierson (1991): They had a written which was pass fail. Then they had the physical which was a three-part physical. Two parts of that physical were deemed to be racially biased. So, I had to take it again. The obstacle course counted. The elevated climb which demonstrated you could work with heights and then the other was the tunnel crawl. And that was to demonstrate you weren't afraid of the dark. They were graded differently after that. They were made pass/fail I think. Basically, it came down to the obstacle course.

The obstacle course was tough. You were allowed to run, so it's pretty grueling. It was who was the fastest, so you had to get your time down real low if you wanted a shot. Even running those practice runs. You got the feeling that you were going to throw up. You really gave it your all every time, so it was tough. I went down to the armory to the practices.

Petrone (1991): You take a written exam which was pretty basic knowledge. I always felt that if you couldn't pass that you probably should be looking to dig ditches. Then when I came on it was a three-part physical exam. There was a tunnel that you had to crawl in. It was shaped like an E. You went in one end, it was underground, and you had to make your way to the other end and turn off the light. That was one aspect of it and then there was an obstacle course type aspect of it and the third aspect of it you had to climb up an incline, pick up a piece of rope that was threaded through a board with three holes in it. You had to unthread it, rethread it and put it back down. And that was the three parts of the exam. It was an aggregate of the three scores and that's how you got placed on the list. They timed you on everything.

Castellucio (1993): Well, you had the written exam which was pass/fail. And probably a third grader could have passed. Then the way they scored us was on the physical exam that they timed you. It was the type of exam where you had to actually run through. That was how they scored us.

You had a ten-pound vest on you. You had to run I think fifty feet to a hydrant hook up dragging a line. Hook it up. Unhook the other line on the hydrant, run fifty feet or so to the other hydrant, hook that one up. You had to run and grab a ladder. Run through some cones carrying a sixteen-foot ladder. You had to go up and down stairs about ten times. You had to jump through a window, run through a tunnel, jump through another window and then you drag a dummy across the floor. It was pretty tough.

I went to the armory every night that they had it. I ended up there four times, but before the armory even opened, after work I would go over to a high school track field and I would run every night preparing for it.

Snyder (1993): The written was pass/fail. Then they had the physical part of it and that's where you're graded based on your time. And that's how you were ranked. It was an obstacle course. You would take the hose, hook it up two times. Then go through cones with a donut roll. Then the same thing with a ladder and then you had to do steps. You had to touch every step with the donut roll on. And then jump through a window and carry a dummy like two hundred feet. Another part of it was it was a pass/fail where you had to hook up a peg. You had to stand over a ledge and go through the peg system. The other one was a little tunnel you enter. You're almost like a rat. You had to go through the tunnel, turn a light on, turn it off, and then come out. Pretty simple. Some people failed although I don't know how. I prepared for it. I mean I ran the practice course. I probably ran it twice a week to prepare for it. I went to the Boy's Club. Giordano ran that with a couple of other firemen like Angelo Centanni. And then they had one at the Roseville armory. We did that. I only did that maybe once a week. But I was practicing already. And then I went down to Trenton, took the test. I was as sick as a dog when I took it. I still did pretty well. I think I had pneumonia. I still came out fifteenth though. I really had to stop before I did the peg system and ask for a drink of water because I was so dehydrated.

When they appointed me, I came on a week after my class started because they kind of messed around with the residence saying I didn't live in the city which I did. It took a week to get that squared away. I was going through the process the whole time. I was on the job. I was off the job. I was on the job. Meanwhile, there are a lot of emotions you go through. Of course, my dad did everything he could to try to stop the train from derailing. So, me and like nine other guys came on a week after the class started. We all graduated together.

Bartelloni (1993): We had taken a written test first which was a pass/fail test, not a difficult test. And then once you passed, everything was based on the physical. We had trained at the armory on Roseville Avenue for maybe a month. I still remember looking at the faces of some of the guys that were there. It was 1991 or 1992 when we were taking the practice. And then the exam followed, but it was all based on the physical. Whatever you scored on the physical time wise put you on the list. I did fairly well and was in the first class when they hired.

Gail (1993) I did full training, got in shape, lost a lot of weight and practice, practice, practice at the Armory, made a lot of friends. I went to the union and the Community Relations practices. Went to everything they offered.

The written was pass/fail. It was basically math and science questions, some grammar questions. All of the weight was on the physical portion. Which was why it was so important they you practiced because there was a lot of technique involved. It wasn't just the fastest or strongest. There was a lot of technique involved. So, you really had to practice it or else you wouldn't do well.

Ostertag (1994): The test was a basic written test. It was basic knowledge, but you had to think a little bit. It could have one of two answers like any test. So, you had to put some thought into it. The physical performance was strictly based on how fast you can run and go through the course. The fastest guy was ranked number one. Now it's a little different. Now I think you can kind of walk through the course. Now they keep downgrading it. But they put a weighted vest on you and you had to run a course, connect the hydrants, run up ladders, carry dummies, drag hose. You had to practice for it, pretty strenuous. The city put on a mock test that was open to everybody taking the exam. Everyone was able to go down to the armory to practice. I was down there every single night. I was one of the best guys down there because I did it every night. When I got to Trenton I fell with the dummy and lost a lot of points. I still ranked like fifty-six. But you had to practice. You had to go through it. The more you did it, the faster you got. They also had a pass/fail section. You had to climb a ladder to a certain height, walk to the edge of a mock roof, put your feet over the edge, and perform a task up high. It was pass/fail. It was timed though. After that they had a tunnel, you had to go through. I guess they tested to see if you were claustrophobic or not. So, some guys failed that. Some guys failed the height thing.

Ramos (1994): There was a written portion of course and no oral. Afterwards they had the physical test you would take after you found out whether you passed it. The written was pass or fail. The physical test was based on time. The better time you got the higher you were on the list.

The physical components were stations you had to pass. The first situation was hydrants that were set up approximately fifty feet away from each other. You had to disconnect one feed line from one hydrant. Run to the other one. Take the hose off that hydrant. Run back to the other one and connect it. Then from there you were to go to a ladder carry. You had to carry a ladder straight up in the air through a maze of cones that were there. There was a tunnel crawl that was about half the distance of the gym. You had to jump through a window, a mock window system they had there. And you also had to drag a hundred and twenty-five pound dummy the whole distance of the course which was about fifty feet at the time. But that was the killer. Today they have a different test. Our test was based on time. We had to run through the course. Today they want you to walk through it. It's fast paced, but it's not the same thing that we took. It's a different test today than the test we took.

What I did to prepare for the test was basically train on my own. I had work at the time as security. I had three jobs actually when the test came up. I worked at Anheuser-Busch, as security and on weekends I would deliver beer for them. And I worked at night as a driver for a valent parking spot on One and Nine in Elizabeth. So, I used to drive from the valet parking at night, which was from eleven to seven, I would rush over the Anheuser-Busch and start that shift which was from eight until four. Go home and sleep and do it all over again. So, I did that for about two years. At the same time, I was getting ready to take the test. I would train with a vest and run up and down some stairs at Anheuser-Bush sometimes after work. I would stay for an hour, put the vest on and run up and down some stairs they had back then. They had the old metal steps that are outside. I would do five floors of it. Also, the firemen's union had a mock set up for us as a practice. I did that also with them, but I was only able to get to that particular spot one time a week. You know I wouldn't be there all the time, but some guys were there all day long. They spent the whole day there. I would go there, one time through the course and leave because I'd be too tired, too hot to do anything more. My mission was to get accustomed to the apparatus we had to use, get accustomed to the course. Get a feel for it basically. If it weren't for that it would have been difficult to go to the actual test and pass. I recall when I did go to the test in Trenton, there were guys there that had never gone through any practice test. They were big guys that lifted weights. They're thinking the fire department was all about weights. They didn't understand it's more a stamina thing than anything else. They're going to go there. They'll get to the first little test area, and they would just drop out. You would see them come out one by one. And I'd get happy. That's one more for me, one more spot for me, one more spot for me.

Richardson (1994): It was the basic written test. Kind of like you're located here. What's the best way to get to this incident over here all streets named with trees, go one way north and that kind of thing, a logical type test. I believe there was some math. I remember the physical part more. We did practice at the Armory. We did do a lot of practicing at the Armory. Drag the hose, connect the hose to the hydrant, disconnect the hose from the hydrant. Bring it back to the other side. Reconnect it. Carry a ladder. Place the ladder back into a stand. A hose roll, go through a window. I think we climbed the warehouse stairs, you had to climb up and down those a few times. Came off that and then grabbed the dummy and did the dummy drag and you were done. For our test we could run. I know the new test they have to walk, and it was a weighed vest, but we were able to run. And then we did the maze. It was a timed maze and you had to go through it, find your way to the light switch, turn it off and get out the other side. And then you had to stand on a platform with your toes over the edge and reach out and untie a rope. It was out in front of you. I think that was pass/fail, but the obstacle course was timed. And then you came out on the list. I think I was number fifty.

Jackson (1995): I recall going to Barringer High School one early morning to take the written part. When I passed that section, I got a letter in the mail to go to Trenton to take the physical portion. It was an obstacle course and it was a matter of getting through the obstacle course the fastest. The faster you got through the obstacle course the higher you were on the list. There were three or four classes from my list. I believe I was the third class, but I should have been in the first class. I did well in the practice sessions, but when we went to the site there was the vertical ladder that we had to climb. In the practice session it was in the open air, it went up to the top where you had to ring the bell. In the test facility, it went in between towers. So, it became dark. You really couldn't see. It was different so I wound up slipping down the ladder and I missed two rungs. When you slip down the ladder you had to make up your rungs. So, the second separated me from being in the top ten to being in the top hundred.

I was fresh out of high school, and I played basketball recreational and also in high school. I was in pretty good shape and once a week I would go to the practice session that they had at the armory on Roseville Avenue. When I would go there, I would go through the course maybe one or two times a day. And then I would go home and just relax. For the written part, being fresh out of high school it was kind of basic for me.

Y. Pierre: (1995) What type of test? Different types. Physical, mental, stress, I mean they tested us to the max to make sure we are capable of doing the job. That's for sure. I trained practically every day. We'd go running, exercising every day. They used to have a training camp at the armory. I went there two, three times just to make sure I got a great idea of what the test was going to be about at the time. We trained very hard.

Farrell (1996): The entrance test I took I think was probably the best test they could put out there. And it's evolved now to a completely different test which I don't agree with. For years they took the written and the physical, they combined your score and they ranked you. Well, the consent decree takes its place and says okay the written now is going to be pass/fail everything will be graded on your physical. That was still okay because you know as well as I do, you don't have to be a rocket scientist to be a fireman. But you do have to have cognitive skills. You have to be able to learn. Because you come on this job, you have to learn. Just because we don't sit here and try to break down the Pythagorean Theorem, you still have to be able to learn. You still have to be able to progress, especially if you want to become an officer. You're hitting the books. You know how challenging that can be. But you still have to be able to learn the pumps. You still have to be able to be certified on the ladder and engine. And you still have to learn things so to have that ability to learn, the written test is absolutely necessary. But pass/fail, I'm okay with that. Here's the grade you have to make. You got a seventy-one. You got a ninety-nine. And you're still dead even going into the physical. I'm still okay with that because at least you have kind of cognitive skill that you passed and said, okay, you're smart enough. You got the brain skills. Okay, you can learn on this job.

The physical, tremendous physical, it encapsulates this entire job. By the time you pull that dummy across the line, it's a very similar feeling to how you come out of that fire building. You're drained. It's tough. The fire building is still tougher because you've got the heat and everything else on top of that. But it's still a very great, job related physical. And it's the same physical they have today, but it's only pass/fail now. The one I took was also geared towards the smaller quicker guy. Well, my test you're climbing in and out of windows. You're climbing underneath things. It was a little bit tougher. It was a little bit tougher to a big guy than it was to the guy who was five foot nine a hundred and fifty pounds. But to me, do you want that five foot nine, hundred-and-fifty-pound guy come and carry you out of a building? Or do you want a six foot two, two-hundred-and-forty-pound guy come to carry you out of the building. But be that as it may, it was a great test. They evolved it a little bit better. I actually like the test now better than I did when we took it. But it was still a very challenging test because you're running against the clock. At thirty-one years old I was running against nineteen- and twenty-year-olds. It was a fair test. I think that's the way they should have it because it's very black and white. Pass/fail written, and the physical, Neal Stoffers ran a minute twenty-nine and Danny Farrell ran a minute thirty, you're just ahead of me on that list. Cut and dry, there's no "V" formulas, there's no middle ground, there's no way to skew this. That's the way it was, and it was ranked. And that's how we got hired off that list. And I think it was a perfect test.

It's evolved now with the biodata, with the teamwork assessment video where there's no true right or wrong answer. I don't agree with that. I think that's just a way to manipulate the list. You've got two different types of people on this job. You can either do this job or you can't do this job. Sex, skin color, it's all irrelevant. There are some women, I'm sure, that can do this job. We have a hard time in Newark finding that woman who can do it, so they've manipulated this test in my opinion to really get more women on the job. And truth be told, we've never had a woman in the top three hundred on the list. This current list now, you have ten women in the top three hundred. That's a big difference.

Roberson (1996): There was a written and a physical part. The written was pass/fail and the physical part was, at that time, you actually had to run the course. And it was based on your time. You got your ranking according to veteran's and non-veteran's status.

The physical test was an obstacle course, the hose drag for the hydrant. You had to carry another hose through a window. Climb through a window, grab a ladder, go up a set of stairs, down a set of stairs, drag the dummy. And then you had to climb up a ladder, on the ladder was a rope, and you had to take one piece from one end and put it through the other end without falling off. The trick to that was to know when you go down to pick it up, you don't bend over because all the blood rushes to your head. You had to squat down, pick up one, then squat down, pick up the other one. The last part was the tunnel where you're actually in the dark. You had to find your way in through a tunnel which is shaped like the letter E and turn a light switch on. Then get out as fast as you can. I did that in like eleven seconds.

I prepared for it, absolutely. Found out they had a practice test course to run. So, when I first ran the course, it took me five minutes and thirty seconds. I found out it wasn't the physical aspect, but it was more your physical stamina and endurance. This job is based on not how strong you are, but how much endurance and stamina you have. So, I was going through the course twice a week. I went from five thirty and I got my time down to a minute and twenty seconds. And I actually ran the course in a minute and eighteen. Yeah, that was my giddy up.

Meier (1996): The written was pass/fail. Everything was based on the obstacle course and then there were two other components with the tunnel and working with height and they were just pass/fail.

The obstacle course started with a hose. You had to bring a hose down to a hydrant, connect the hydrant, disconnect the hydrant, then bring it to another hydrant which was fifty feet away and then reconnect it. Then it went to a series of obstacles. I remember there was a ladder, you grabbed a ladder, you went through the cones. You had to grab hose, go up a flight of stairs. Go back down to the bottom. Go back up again and come back down. And it was all within maybe a minute and a half. So as fast as you could do it. You were graded on just the obstacle course.

I went down to the armory and what's cool about the armory was there were all other candidates that were interested in getting on the fire department. There was a little excitement there. You got to meet guys you actually got on the fire department with, and everybody became friends. We were in close contact with each other and kind of embraced the entire hiring process. Then I got to see them in the Academy and I'm still friends with them today.

Rodrigues (1996): The test was back in '94 and it was multiple choice, the written test. And then there was a course you had to run; the whole course was in Trenton. The first part was you actually had to run between hydrants, hook up onto one of the hydrants. Unhook the other one. Run to the other side of the hydrant, hook and unhook. After that you grab a ground ladder, run between the cones without touching the cones because then you would be penalized for it. After that you would place the ladder on a stand. You had to place it there. Right after that you had to grab a roll of hose, run up the stairs. On the top of the stairs, you had to put both feet on the landing in order to qualify, then come back down. I believe you had to do that three times. Once you come down, you head over to the other side. Then you had to jump out the window. At the end was to drag the dummy backwards. That was the first part of it. The second part of the physical was to go in a tunnel where you cannot see anything at all. Go along through the tunnel. Obviously, you have to put your shoulder against the wall and then you have to hit the switch in order to turn the light on. Once you turn the light on, you got to go out from one end to the other. They were timing you. Back then I believe I did it in eleven seconds only. I still remember that. And the third part was you were hooked to a rope. You had to climb up set of stairs. And then once you got on top of the platform, you had to have your feet out maybe a couple of inches. Then you had to actually pass a rope through some sort of plate with holes and make sure that it doesn't come loose. After that you have raise your arms up in the air. And that would be it.

Montalvo (1996): It was the old test. We were allowed to run. I remember we started off connecting the hose to the hydrant then we would carry a ladder through an obstacle course. We would jump through a window, run underneath another obstacle, and finish off carrying the dummy.

I did prepare for it. Back then I was working as a truck driver. I was working the midnight shift. I would get up in the morning, go run two miles, go to the prep course, run the prep course. Go run a little bit more then go home and get some sleep, go to work and start all over the next day. I did that for about six months.

Willis (1996): The physical part was tough. The cognitive was okay. That biodata, they were instituting that at the time. They were just starting to institute it and I didn't like it, but I did alright on it. I scored fairly well, made it on. I would say mid-level status. You know, out of the top hundred I was in the middle. There were a lot of good guys up in the front that really did well.

Freese (1998): This is in 1990s, early 90s, they had a written which was a pass or fail and then they had an obstacle course which you ran full speed and that's what you got ranked on. Your time and speed on the physical exam.

The obstacle course was a setup of hydrant, ladder, stairs, and dummies. But the way it started was you had to uncouple a hose from a hydrant, throw it over your shoulder, run across I believe it was about seventy-five feet. Couple it back to the other hydrant. From there you would go grab a bag, go up and down stairs. I don't remember how many times, but quite a bit all this while you're wearing a fifty-pound vest. After that you had to go up to a straight ladder and you had to climb up and down. I remember also climbing through a window, running across carrying a dummy. It was something to that effect.

After that I was involved with testing two other physical exams. That was the third since I came on the job. So, I'm getting a little mixed with both, but pretty much that's what it was. Uncoupling hoses, running back and forth, climbing up the stairs, going up the stairs carrying a hose bag, climbing.

After that test they changed it. You couldn't run anymore. It wasn't about the speed. The written test started counting. They did a biodata. Since Newark was a consent decree city, our civilians that are interested in practicing in taking the test would have an obstacle course on Roseville Avenue, the old armory. And I was detailed there a few times to help coach and help teach the kids how to run the obstacle course.

Highsmith: (2000) I had a written test. It was pretty easy, adding, subtracting, following the map, pretty much. And a physical test and the first time I ran the practice test, I pretty much passed that. I started working out. I quit my job and worked out on a daily basis so I can make the job. I only went to one practice session, then I worked out on my own after that.

Carr (2000): My written test was the one where we had to follow directions A to B. It was that and a couple of math questions and stuff like that. And then the physical portion of the test was the individual run. It was highly competitive. We had to practice. We went to the Armory on Roseville Avenue and then we had the test down in Trenton. Our class and I think the next two classes after us were allowed to run. Then after that they came up with the biodata. The biodata and everything else came shortly after that.

We had the ladder carry, jump through the window, and the one where we had to go in the dark tunnel. And we had the dummy carry at the end. It only took you about one minute and maybe eighteen seconds. That's all you had. We all sat and puked. Some guys had on tights and knee pads. It was crazy. It was highly competitive. I don't even remember exactly where I placed. I know that I was like number like forty or fifty something.

When I prepared for the test, basically my father was like eat this, eat that, run some stairs in Weequahic Park. Get yourself in shape. The written test to be honest with you, it wasn't really that difficult. It was basically critical reading. Just like anything else, critical reading, following directions and that was it, so. I left out of there feeling good about the written. You went to the practice site to put your hands on all the equipment you had to use and for the most part if you did well at the practice site you were going to do extremely well at the actual site in Trenton because the parquet floor was less friction, so you could move faster. The threading to the hydrant was a lot easier. Those things right there were a lot easier when you actually took the actual test as opposed to taking the test at the practice site on Roseville Avenue. It was a lot easier down in Trenton.

Rosario (2002): It was the first one to do the biodata, but it was all written at the time. After our class they started doing the video. So, we did the biodata and then you did the physical where you did what we called the three minutes of hell. You started off pulling a hose line down seventy-five feet, then you made a turn and you went to a hydrant. You took the hydrant cap off, put it back on. Then you went to a rubbish box, carried that for fifty feet out, fifty feet in. And then came the hard part and that's while wearing a forty-pound vest, you grabbed the forty-pound high rise pack and you had to go up stairs, which was six steps up, six steps down. I believe it was six times. Then right from there you would pull a dummy for seventy-five feet. You'd pull a fifty-pound box up, like you were pulling the flies on a ladder. So that simulated that. You'd bring that up and bring it down controlled. And then grab the fire extinguisher, seventy-five feet out, seventy-five feet in. And then pull a two-hundred-pound dummy backwards for seventy-five feet and that stopped the time. Once you finished that, then you went into a makeshift tunnel and that was timed. You had to get through it. You get through that and all you had to do after that was go up two stories of ladder, ring a bell, come back down, and that concluded your test for your physical.

I prepared a lot. At the time I was working as a mailman, so I was doing a lot of walking anyway. And then they set up the practice course in the Armory on Orange Street and Roseville. So, you could go there anytime during the day and Newark had it set up so you could practice. So, every day after work I would stop there, practice it until I got my time down to about two minutes and thirty seconds. When it was time to take my test, I scored two thirty-five. So that put me in the top tier. I was number two on my list.

Kupko (2002): We were the first on the Newark fire department that took the biodata. So, it was a traditional written exam which was basic reading comprehension, simple math. You had that biodata which was a character profile test. So, you're asking the same questions, you know just changing the name from Bobby to Larry to Susie and seeing if you're consistent with your answers across the board. And the physical, that was the obstacle course.

The physical was very straight forward. At the time I was in college. I was playing two sports. I was an athlete, so taking that was fairly easy. It was just a matter of going to the course over at the Armory and practicing over and over and over again. Shaving seconds, shaving seconds, doing everything you can to insure you had a pretty good spot because at the time the physical portion was weighted very high in terms of how you scored on the test. Now it seems to be just a pass/fail. That's what they've dumbed it down to.

Mickels (2002): I took a multiple-choice written test and then afterwards I took a physical performance test. There was also a biodata portion of the written exam. The biodata portion entailed personal questions, questions about my childhood. It asked me some scenarios. What would I do if this happened or that happened? And it asked me some questions about scenarios. Did this ever happen? How did you react to it? What did you do? Questions that appeared to want to know more about my personality, my character in my younger years and presently.

The physical test was very challenging. The physical was a course in which I had to perform physical activities that simulated what the fire department work that I would probably be faced with in a real, live scenario within the fire department. Dragging a manikin, a dummy, putting up a box, and the most challenging for me was the stairs. I believe a thirty-pound vest, going up and down the stairs; I'm not sure, twelve times, something like that. Back and forth carrying a box and I had to do it at a rate of speed. I had to do it in a fast pace.

I prepared quite a bit for it with other individuals like myself who were interested in getting the job. There was a course that was set up at the Roseville Armory. We practiced quite a bit there with a vest that I purchased on my own, back and forth. Did that every day along with others that were interested. In fact, it was interesting. There were other towns too that were studying and having their test around the same time. East Orange, I believe we trained with East Orange quite a bit. So, I prepared quite a bit on the course itself and also on a personal level. I was at the park every day, running, training, pushups, at my local gym preparing myself that way as well. Along with preparing on the actual course that was going to be used on the day of the test.

Gaddy (2006): Pretty much, a, b, c questioning for the written and then we had to do the physical. The physical was the part you were graded on. That was the part you had to kick in. I just had a kid and I was just focused on getting the job. I never had a police record or anything like that, but I was in the streets hustling. So, my mind set was, what can I do other than make this fast money that's going to catch up with me one day. So, I took everything, and I passed it. But when it came to the physical, I didn't go over for the physical for months. I went there the last day as they were closing, and I saw what I had to do. For those three days, because my test was on a Tuesday, I capitalized on everything they wanted me to do. The only thing I was nervous about was the fire hydrant. I wasn't nervous about the stairs because I was imitating the stairs in my house. I have a three-story home. I would run up and down stairs with weights on my back. I had it in my backpack, and I'd just run up and down stairs all day long, every day for those three days. I would run around Newark to get my stamina up. It's more about stamina. I wasn't worried about that. I was playing basketball. When I went and took the physical, I should have aced it, but I was so overzealous where I was going up the stairs, I had to restart the stairs like maybe four, five times because I skipped it. So that kind of wore me out. When I got to the dummy my knees buckled; I fell; and I got immediately up and yanked it. My time was three eleven. You needed to pass with an eight three oh seven or three oh five at that time. So, I looked at it as, "Damn, I kind of failed myself." But to be one eleven out of five hundred, maybe a thousand candidates at that time, that was pretty decent.

Jenkins (2006): The entrance test, well a regular written directional test where you can follow directions, there's basic math, that's about it. There was a whole lot to the test back when we were taking it. Then they had the biodata part. I had to do the physical also. I really didn't know what to prepare for the physical. I just went in, took the obstacle course and passed it. I heard about the union course. During the times they were doing the course I was working at the Post Office, so I didn't have enough time to get from my job to the training course.

Figuereq (2006): We had biodata, the written, and then we had the physical, the three parts. Back in '99 I think that test started. I took the one with the hundred questions for the biodata. You had to write down the answers and then basic written and math. Once you passed that they gave you the physical, but you didn't know the results of that until after you took the physical. There was a whole controversy. People were complaining. All three parts counted equally.

The physical is the same one they've had for the last ten years. For us it was try to make it under three minutes and ten seconds to get a hundred percent. I did two forty-six. You had to stretch a line across about fifty yards. Drop it, disconnect a two and half hydrant cap, put it on the other side. Walk over, pick up a K-12 saw, go around a cone, put it back in a box. Do a pulley, hand over hand. Bring it back down. Grab a forty-pound bag, the whole time you have a forty-pound vest on doing this. Then you do the steps, eight back and forth. Drop the bags again. Pick up another line with a tip, go around a pole, bring it to the end. Drop it. Pick up a fire extinguisher. Go around another cone. Everything's about fifty yards. And pick up a dummy, drag it for maybe twenty-five yards. Drop the dummy, pick up a box. Go around another cone, put it down and pass the finish line. That's the one they're still doing today.

Then the maze, you have to do the tunnel and they give you forty seconds to finish the maze. And once you're done with that there's a pass or fail. You have to go up a ladder. I think it was probably thirty feet up. You go up rung by rung and ring a bell and walk back down. Pass or fail also, I think it's thirty-three seconds' time.

Medina (2006): I took a multiple choice and there was a biodata. No romances, are you a team player, that type of question. We also took a physical. But if you didn't pass either of the first two parts, you couldn't move onto the physical. You had to get under a three oh five, three minutes five seconds, fast walking. That's what it was, forty-pound vest and pretty much it was an obstacle course. That was graded, but I think the written part didn't count as the same. It wasn't thirty-three, thirty-three, thirty-three. It was not even. I think the physical proportion counted a little more. I did pretty well.

I boxed for twelve years. So, I was always active. I was running around. I ran track in high school, and they had an obstacle course on Roseville Avenue, the Armory. They had an obstacle there and I finished at two forty-four when I took the test. Two minutes forty-four seconds. That was down from three oh five. So, I scored pretty well.

Dugan (2006): First it was written and biodata. The written test was pretty easy in my opinion. The biodata was maybe the second time they started doing the biodata. And it was the written biodata, before the video biodata. Then we also did the physical test. It was not like it is now where all you have to do is a minimum time and pass. It was you want to try the hardest you possibly could to get the best time you could. I came out number twenty-nine on the list. And that was also before all the veterans. We had only maybe eleven or thirteen veterans on our list. After the war, it's a lot more now.

K. Alfano (2006): Yeah, the written was multiple choice; the biodata was multiple choice; and then the physical test. I went down as much as I could to the Armory, and I trained for it. Because I wasn't going to college, so I got in there as hard as I could. I did pretty well. I came out number seventy something after the whole test was graded. The physical part I think I was one of maybe twenty guys that did the best. The physical was one third; the biodata was one third; and the written was one third.

M. Bellina (2008): The written exam and my class was the first class that had the video biodata. If you passed that you did the physical exam. At that time, we had to do it under a certain time. You were competing with your time. Now I think it's pass or fail. If you do it under five minutes or something like that you pass.

Our physical was, you wore a weighted vest, and you ran an obstacle course which was dragging a length of inch and three quarter a certain distance. Taking a hydrant cap off, putting it back on. Taking a K-12 and going around a cone, putting it in a box. Simulating hoisting a ladder. Then you had to put a high-rise pack on your shoulder and go up twelve steps. Then you took an extinguisher and went around a cone. And then you dragged I think it was a two and a half around a big pipe that they had out there that they got hooked up on something and there's this box you put it on. And then I think you had a certain amount of time to ascend a ladder. After that course you had to go through a maze. I went to the Armory to prepare. They had the course set up so you could practice on it. That was something I really had to push myself to do.

G. Centanni (2013): When I took the written it was a very low-level test, just very remedial math, reading comprehension. And then a biodata, there are three right answers and one wrong answer and they weigh whoever answers the question the most and a physical. The physical was a pretty good, strenuous test. We had to wear a weighted vest and go through a whole obstacle course, hydrant, stairs, dummy drag. Under three minutes is a perfect score.

G. Pierre (2013): Oh, our entrance test, my test one of the last things got changed out. It dealt with a psych test, an educational part, simple math, a little reading, and then the physical. The physical was very grueling. I put a lot of time into the practice for the physical test. You had to do the carrying of dead weight, running up and down the stairs. You had to run with a weighted vest. You had to carry the toolbox and you couldn't run. I ran a two forty-seven which was pretty impressive from what I could tell.

To prepare for it I did a lot of cardio. I did a lot of running with the weight vest on the trend mill prior to it. They changed the practice to odd times, so you had to take off work or slide out of the schedule. I was working for a donation center, and I would leave the donation center for an hour, another hour and a half on my lunch break. It was a lot of training. I did one of the diets. I just wanted to cut fifteen, twenty pounds at the time. But the physical part was very demanding, very demanding. At that time, you didn't know who was actually going to be in your academy class. I remember walking out with one of the guys. We walked out and I looked at him. He looked at me. I don't know. I don't know either.

The one thing good for me was I'm almost fresh out of college. So, you could say the initial part wasn't that hard on me because I still had that fresh book knowledge there. I was a good student in college. I got two degrees from Delaware State University. I got a degree in business administration, and I got another degree in Hospitality and Tourism Management, and I graduated from college cum laude. So, I didn't have too much of an issue with the math, the reading and arithmetic.

They did a social testing on it with a lot of teamwork. You had to make sure everything was teamwork, teamwork, teamwork. I did some studying for that part of it. I had to make sure I was in bounds with that. That was the last part you went through. I remember coming into the room. You're sitting in the room with a psychologist. He's sitting like three feet from you, the room's dark, you sit at his desk. He's got reading glasses and he asks you like probing questions. "You said on this question you went to high school and got out in June, but on the next one you said you went to high school, and you said you got out in July. From June to July, why'd you say June?" I didn't say that. If you didn't say it, tell him you didn't say it. You had to answer two hundred questions on my test. You had to stick with the answers and be honest. They're messing with you. There was no real way to prepare for that. You had to concentrate. The test is set up to ask you the same questions three or four different ways. That's how they find out if you're consistent in your answers. This was two thousand eleven. I didn't have a video camera to record.

But honestly it took me nine years to get on. Even with all that it took me nine years to get on. The first time they called my name, I had a job in Hospitality and Management. I was a food and beverage director. And I relocated for the job and didn't come back. I got the letter to actually come back for the testing. It was a letter where you had to respond back in a certain amount of time. I had the opportunity of flying back. I declined at that point. I was going to go with my career. I wish I had started then, but at the same time you never know. It was probably better for everybody.

Ended up getting laid off a couple of years, but it's good that I got the job when I did. This is a young man's job, but you have to have a little maturity to really respect it and protect it. The first time I took the test I kind of like played around with it. I didn't really want it. But then you come home. You see the application for the job. You see your family's going on. You try to go for the job, and you come back two years later. Your pop and your uncle are still doing the same thing that you left behind. You got more family on the job. You come around like I did. You give it a hundred and ten percent. I put it off. I put it off, to get the job. The first time I tested beside thirty-five hundred other people. And the second time around the numbers went up to like six thousand people. So, you really got to be in the top ten, top twenty-five percent to get the job. To be even considered for the background check that comes after that. This is all the second time.

Rawa (2013): Actually, I hate to say this but the written was really easy. It was just a basic standardized test. I think the part that people complained about the most was the biodata, the little video portions of the test. With the biodata, they'll show you a scenario of firefighter that does his laundry and they'll show a little clip of the guy walking away from the washing machine. Then another firefighter walking up with his dirty clothes, looking to see if he can put his dirty stuff in there. He sees that there's somebody else's stuff in there and then they stop the video right there. It will give you four different responses as to how to react if you were in that situation. I'd say about two of them are decent answers, but I guess they look to see which one is the most voted for. Basically, to confuse you kind of, there's no really right or wrong answer.

Then the physical part, which I never trained for, I showed up the day of the test and that was the first time I took it. Your rank was from a combination of written, physical, and biodata tests, one third, one third, one third. Now I know it's pass fail for the physical. My nephew's taking it. He's going through the process now and it's a little different for him than it was for me a few years ago. I found out afterward that they would run training courses over at the Armory. I honestly didn't know anything about it. Didn't know until the day I came on the job. The day I went to go take the test; it was my first time doing it. I do wish I had taken advantage of that now, when I look back. I could have been on a class sooner.

J. Centanni (2014): The civil service test for Newark, we had to take a written and then a physical, a practical obstacle course that was timed. The written was basic math and reading comprehension and then you had to watch some videos to see how you worked with other people. And they grade you on that. The obstacle course had different fireman activities you have to do. Like carrying a saw, hooking up to a hydrant, raising a ladder, climbing stairs with like a weighted vest on. It was timed.

Garay (2014): We took the written exam. And then after taking the written portion and biodata, we were called to do the third part which is the physical. We trained on the obstacle course, and I loved the fact that this job keeps you motivated to work out and to maintain some kind of work out regime. It's very demanding on the body so I liked that because I've always liked working out and challenging my body. I really got involved in the obstacle course. After I took it and passed, I was just waiting for the time to come in. I completed the physical part in three minutes eleven seconds. My rank after the veterans was one eighty-three. They combined the physical the biodata, and the written test.

Fortunato (2014): The test was written, physical, and biodata. The written test was multiple choice. They chose the scenarios with the biodata, and then the physical. During the obstacle course of the physical you had to wear a weighted vest, I think it was twenty pounds. Had to do hose drags, had to simulate going up I think it was twelve stories with a high-rise pack and going down. How to do flies like you're raising a ladder. Carry a fire extinguisher. You had to carry a box too.

I think that was about it. Then you had to climb a ladder, like an eighteen-foot ladder and go in a maze, come out.

Earp (2016): The test was a written part and then they had a video with different scenarios on situations that would take place in a firehouse. Washing clothes, would you take another firefighter's clothes out of the washing machine. What would you do in that situation? Would you tell the other firefighter, or would you take it out yourself? Situations like that, just to see the type of person you are. What type of character you have because this is an environment where you have to be friendly and respective to other people's belongings and space. When you're around a person for twenty-four hours, they want you to be able to cooperate with each other.

There's a physical part where you have to climb the stairs. So, there's a lot of physical endurance. You climb the stairs. You do the hydrant test where you put the cap on. You pull the dummy. You drag the hose. You have to drag it around the pole. In the last part you carry a box. That's the last stretch. At that point you're exhausted. Then after that you crawl through the dark tunnels to find your way out. And you climb the ladder, the ladder test. You get scored on all three parts. You get three different scores. So, on the written part you would get a score and on the video scenarios you get a score and on the physical you get a score as well. And they add up the three scores and they average it out and they give you your total score for the exam.

Corales (2016): The test was simple reading, multiple choice questions about how you would act in case of a situation that arises. A few math questions, simple math that I can remember, it was nothing difficult. But it was basic. And the video question that they ask you is the one that actually would describe what you would do in a situation which was pretty cool. They gave you a physical. I trained hard for it. I took a couple of friends of mine because I felt like I wasn't able to do it on my own. It was just for motivational purposes. We went to Ironbound Stadium where they taught it, on Saint Charles Street. We ran up the steps. It was a total of fifty-nine steps that we ran up. Me and my son, to this day we go out and run those steps as well to imitate what I was doing. And we set up our own course there to get ready. We had weights and crates and we dragged hoses back there. It was pretty neat. It was a childhood friend of mine that I did it with, so we kind of shared some laughs in doing that as well, so we had fun.

Then we went to the armory. I remember waking up early in the morning, four-thirty in the morning about twice a week. I did it for about two months to get a practice run in which helped out tremendously. I remember the first time, toward the end of the course, I fell on my back. I had spaghetti legs. I couldn't get up. And I'm like, "Whoa, I got to get some work in." The day of the test I remember toward the end of the run I was making great time on my test. I picked up a box which was the last part of the obstacle course that I had to complete. The Jersey City firefighter was telling me you're doing great time, you're great, you're great and I stumbled over my own feet out of nowhere. I took two steps and hit the floor with the box. I wasn't able to get back up. The firefighter had told me just think about that box. That's your son's toolbox. You got to get it out. You got to get it out. So, I was able to finish the course which was an accomplishment for myself from all the hard work that I had put in prior to that and leading up to that day. And it gave me a whole different respect for what I was doing. It was an opportunity that I thought I let slip away because I didn't think I made the time necessary. But here I am.

Alexander II (2016): The Civil Service test they gave us was three portions. The first portion was a written. I guess it was math and like critical reading. The second portion was a team assessment and the third portion was a physical test.

The physical was tough. It was tough. I think you had to pass it in five minutes. You weren't allowed to run. You had to walk it. It was pretty strenuous. It was pretty taxing. At the end, a lot of people hit the ground and tried to recover. The first stage was a hose drag, like you drag a hose down a certain distance. At the end of that, there was a fire hydrant. You had to put the cap on the fire hydrant, make sure it was all the way on, on tight. After that you had to do stairs. You had to do twelve flights up and down. So, you go up and down, that's one flight. You had to do that twelve times. You had to do a dummy drag. You had to carry a K-12 saw around a cone a certain distance away. Drag a hose line around a pole. You would run down, have the hose line, turn around a pole and bring it back. So, the hose line would kind of get snagged on the pole. Then you had to kind of fight through that, fight your way through that. Then there was a teamwork assessment. That's the portion when they gage how well you interact with other people and how well you can work together in a group. They added that. Pretty interesting questions. One of the questions that sticks out is, say you're washing clothes or somebody else in your house is washing clothes, and you need to wash clothes also. What would you do? They give you four choices. One is like obviously wrong and then one is somewhat wrong and the last two, they could go either way. So, I guess they kind of gage your score off of what everybody else does. What everybody else says on the test. That was a pretty interesting portion of the test too. All of the portions were weighted. You still had to get a certain score. I believe it was above seventy to even pass it and then based on where you got above that, they ranked you on your score. You still had to get a passing grade.

Cruz (2016): We got the letter that there was going to be the test. We had to report to Rutgers. There were a lot of candidates, and the test was very long. We had to take the written exam then we had to go to the video portion the same day.

We had to watch the video and then answer questions about the video. We were scheduled later after that to go take the physical, the obstacle course kind of test.

Academy

Conville: The Academy when I went on, I would say we only had firehouses. But whatever training you got was what you got in the job. We were appointed as the openings came. It might be five or ten, because a lot of the veterans from the First World War were retiring. They were staying until they were sixty-five. When they had a couple of openings, you would get the job.

Conover: On Eighteenth Avenue right there in Vailsburg. I think it was just a couple of weeks. We were taught the basic things that you had to know. Newark built a nice training academy Down Neck after I was in for quite a few years. Down there you really got training that we didn't get when we came in. For example, the new fellows coming in, in case they weren't used to a gas mask, what we called a smoke mask on the fire department, but actually they're just like a gas mask. They get training with the darn things so they don't panic. They'll understand it's a little bit harder to breath. They'll understand what they can do about it and what exactly is happening. It's a lot like the training you got when you were in the service.

Ryan: Yeah, we were in the Academy I think a total of three weeks. We stayed in the Academy for three weeks and then were assigned to the firehouse. Deputy Chief McCormack was the head of the Academy. Chief Drew, he was a captain then, he used to teach truck work because he was in a truck company. I think he was in Seven Truck at the time. Then there were a couple of other instructors up there, firemen instructors. We were there a total of three weeks and then we were assigned to the companies. They taught us basic firefighting. I don't think we even went on a pumper. Taught us basic ladder work, basic hose work; didn't have a drill tower or anything, really. They had an accident previous to that where the rope broke when they were on a life belt and two of the fellows came down. My brother was at the academy when the accident happened. They were coming down a rope from the third story and the rope broke and the two of them fell to the ground. One fellow, he was hurt really bad, and the other fellow was hurt. He couldn't perform regular firehouse duties either because he had a fracture foot that never healed right. He always had a limp after. The other fellow was in bad shape for years and then he died. He was hurt internally.

J. Doherty: What they did, they latched onto the G.I. Bill, so that we would go to the Academy on one of our days off or whatever it was. Since we were enrolled in it and they counted it as a school, we got seventy-five dollars a month from the G.I. Bill. I think I did that for about two months. They taught us fire prevention. But aside from the G.I. Bill no Academy at all. We went straight into the firehouse.

Gibson: I think there were eight or nine of us got made that same day. The Director said something, and he rued the day he said it. He said, "When you come in the fire department here, we take care of you. If your wife is sick, stay home and take care of her." I did and they were pissed off.

I didn't go through the Academy when I was appointed. I went straight into the firehouse, to Thirty-two Engine. There was no Academy then. It was right after that that they started getting active with the Academy.

G. Alfano: I never went to the Academy and I never went to school. Maybe three days in all the time I was on. You went right to the firehouse and that was the school.

D.C. Griggs: I was with a group. There were approximately thirty of us. I was very disappointed when the Star Ledger came out prior to me getting appointed saying that they needed fifteen members. And not knowing how Civil Service worked. Sometimes you ask guys after a period of time, they're not interested. I happened to come out nineteenth. I was a veteran, but there were twelve disabled vets ahead of me and according to my markings I would have been in the fifteen, but I actually came out nineteen. But it didn't matter because they still swept right up to thirty guys.

The Academy itself was very boring because we practically sat for two weeks. The chief up there was an old timer, a real old timer. He was not about to do too much moving about. He read to us and questioned us and one day we were taken out to hook up to a hydrant. One of the companies came up and we stretched some hose, didn't charge it. We made connections to the hydrant and the pumper was explained to us. That was it.

Duerr: There were six of us that went up to the old Academy on Eighteenth Avenue. We didn't get too much hands-on training because of the facility. Most of it was in the classroom and classroom activity. If they had a ladder drill or an aerial drill, they would call up Nine Truck. They would raise the aerial to the front of the roof to the Academy and we'd climb up the aerial. We had Burrell masks at that time and we'd get to use the Burrells off the rigs that they called in. I think the training was about five weeks.

Schoemer: I went right to the firehouse. After a while they set up the different tours to go to the Academy. So, actually you worked five days a week and weren't compensated for it. Because you worked in the firehouse days, they would set it up so you would work Saturday and Sunday days and the rest of the week you went to the Academy. Five days you studied in the Academy and you still went to work nights.

A. Prachar: I was appointed with a group. I can't give you the exact figure. I believe it was a 183 of us that came on at the same time, divided up among the four tours. I had two uncles that were on the job and through their influence I was able to get the position I wanted at Engine Ten. It was the only opening at Engine Ten and I got it. Reason being that I walked past the firehouse every day to go to school when I was in grammar school. And it was the only firehouse I knew in the city and as far as I was concerned it was the only fire department in the city. And I asked for it. I got it and I spent many years there.

I went right to work. We didn't have schooling until months after we went on the job. I was assigned to Engine Ten, tour four with Captain Hanburner. We were on I guess, three months, four months. The first thing that Chief Schoettly taught us in the fire academy was that everything we learned to do in the firehouse he was going to try and break us of now and tell us the right way to do it. But he said, it's too late now. You're already ruined. I'm going to say we went for two weeks and then we went back to the firehouse for a period of time. I don't recall. Then we went back for another two weeks and then we were given certificates telling us we were firemen. This is maybe eight months after we had started the job.

They didn't teach us much, really not too much. Everything that we learned basically we got in the firehouse. I mean, book watch right on to being on the nozzle to driving. We had all this experience, but evidently it was a requirement that we get schooling whether we were learning anything or not. They teach us first aid. Some of us had basic first aid, but working at Ten Engine, we had more than enough first aid cases come right to the door that what they taught us in the Academy was an afterthought. All my training was in the firehouse. Anything that I got out of the Academy was book assignments which I honestly truthfully feel never helped me and that sending us to school was just a requirement that they had to fulfill. And anybody that I went to the Academy with would tell you the same thing. It was a total waste of time. The only thing that we had different in the Academy that I can remember was a film of the birth of a baby. Because I never experienced that in the firehouse. Other than that, it was on the job training.

We went to the firehouse at night and to the Academy during the day. I slept a lot in the Academy. Engine Ten at that time was probably the fifth or the sixth busiest company in the city. I remember the first year I was on it was the first year that they broke a thousand runs which was quite healthy then.

Bitter: When I went on you worked. The Academy was up on Eighteenth Avenue. We went to classes from eight in the morning until four in the afternoon, class day, that night we went to the firehouse on nights. But we went to classes every day for four weeks. We worked nights like Monday and Tuesday, off Wednesday, Thursday, and Friday. Then you worked days in the firehouse and then the next week you started classes again. They did that for all four tours. They did that for two weeks and then two weeks later you went again.

We were getting off from working nights and then going straight to class. Classes all day, you go back to the firehouse that night. And then came the weekends, Saturday and Sunday you were on days. So, you did that for two weeks. Then you had six weeks later while the other tours went to class. It worked out where there were five days in that week in the Academy plus the two nights working. Work the two days on the weekend and the next week the same thing. Classes all week, you worked your two nights. No such thing as overtime or penalty time, comp time or anything. Those days you did it.

Cardillo: Well, they taught us couplings, male, female, and hoses. No pumping, we didn't have a regular pumper there. They showed us the masks. That was the Burrell.

Elward: I reported to Eighteenth Avenue. I think there was only eight of us. Unfortunately, a guy that got killed on the job, Hugh Gambacorta, got killed at a fire, was one of my classmates in the Academy. And I think they beefed the class up. They had guys like Joe Critchley. One of the guys in my class at the Academy, Jimmy Murry, his father was one of our instructors. He was a very good speaker.

I mean it, he was dynamite. Old guy, Joe O'Conner, I think he did most of the physical training. The Academy was good. We got a whole month in.

Schofield: I came on in March and back then you didn't go right to the Academy. We went to the Academy in May. You were on the job a certain amount of time until they got a group together. Then you went to the Academy. That was on Eighteenth Avenue. That was the Academy at the time. Came in March and graduated or completed the general course of instruction on June 14, 1963. Joe Redden and John P. Caufield signed it.

Cosby: I was appointed as an individual at that time and I spent three months in the field before going to the Academy. I had already trained on the job when the Academy came. I went with Ronnie Heath and Jerry Hatfield. I don't know when they came for sure because I came on by myself. That was all that was left on that list, Ronnie Heath, Hatfield, and myself. We were in the Academy a month. We had classes like first aid and they showed us how to jump off of a building into a net. How to hold a net and we practiced raising a ladder. And then they were trying to also show us how to scale a wall with Pompier ladder. How to rescue, how to use a mask and all that, they had us doing that. By me coming on alone, I guess, they needed me at the time. They waited for more to come on then they'd run a class. That's why, I figured, they waited like that.

Dalton: We didn't have the Academy like the Academy is today. The building on Eighteenth Avenue was the Academy for us. We went up there every day and they would take us down by the fireboat and train. But they didn't take us into active firehouses hardly. We were there about two weeks. They taught us the basic rules and regulations of the fire department and everything else. Then they would take us out, make us learn how to hook a soft suction on a hydrant and all that stuff. I guess it was just lucky that we got busy so we got the right training to be good firemen for the rest of our career. It wasn't much of a training school compared to what they get now.

Gaynor: What we did was work in the firehouse nights and go five days a week to the Training Academy. There was no contract at the time see. So, the city had the liberty of doing that. But for the most part it wasn't bad. A couple of nights we got caught where you went directly from some type of fire and then started in the Training Academy at the regular starting time. Maybe fell asleep in class and didn't smell good either. But it only was a four-week course. And Stanley Kossup was one of the new captains who was the instructor along with Carl Stoffers at that time. David Kinnear was the Battalion Chief and Joe Drew was the deputy in charge of the training academy. The Academy was on Eighteenth Avenue, the site of the current fire headquarters. Eddie Lee was one of the firemen there. I'm not sure I can recall any of the other names.

They taught us safety. I can remember the drill with ladders and the apparatus, getting to know the apparatus. Some people did okay. Danny Tauriello was the chief of apparatus who certified us at the time. You could jump off the front of the building into a net if you wanted. Rich Nolan and Bob Peppi I think did jump off the front and into a net held by eight or ten men. But there was another place on the side of the building where you could jump off. And everyone was required to jump off from that position once.

Perez: I went straight to the firehouse and I tell you about nine months later they sent us to Eighteenth Avenue, the Academy, which was a joke. It was like a two-week course at the Academy and that's it, went back to the firehouse.

Calvetti: When I was on the job maybe two and a half years I went to the Academy. I knew most of the stuff already. In fact, I was studying then too. Because the guys I was with, Ricca, Bitter, Chrystal, they were always studying.

So, I was up on a lot of this stuff. When I went to the Academy I was like a pain in the ass. The captain down there, he did know his job, but certain things he didn't know. Like one day he's telling us about working off a ladder. He's working to the same side as he's got the leg lock in. I said, "That's the wrong way to do it. I should work on the opposite side. You leg lock to the opposite side you're working on." "Don't tell me. I'm a captain at One Truck." "I don't give a shit what you are. I'm telling you; you made a mistake." So, he looks in the book. "Oh yeah, you're right," he says. He was a captain and he didn't do that kind of work. He had his firemen doing it. I knew he was wrong when he said it. And then after that we got to be pretty good friends, him and I. And he used to bust my chops here and there and I'd bust him right back.

I'll tell you another funny story. We were going to graduate from the Academy. Now everybody's got to jump into the net from the first landing, maybe ten feet. So, the whole class does the ten-foot jump. Now he wants volunteers to go up to the next level. Nobody volunteers. He picks me. I said "You got to be crazy. I ain't going up there to jump." He says, "Why not." I said, "Cause there's no fire on my ass. If there's a fire on my ass, I'll go up there to jump, but just to jump to please you, I'm not going up there." He said, "I'll show you how to do it." I said, "Go ahead." Well, he went and jumped, and don't you think they missed him, the guys on the net. He fell; he hit the edge of the net; and hit the ground. He was out of work for about four or five months. The guys didn't catch him in the middle of the net. You got to have at least eight men on the net. That's what the minimum was. The more the better, but at least eight were supposed to be on the net and it was like a big bull's eye in the center of this net. It was in a quarter fold. You had to open it up. I guess it was like a ten-foot diameter net by the time you got it opened up. He jumped and he didn't jump out far enough. He hit the edge of the net and he hit the ground. He ripped the net right out of the guys' hands. So, the net broke his fall. It could have been worse if he missed the net completely.

Lawless: I came on in '66. After I went through two sets of riots, I finally went to the Academy in '68.

Benderoth: I went to the Academy two years after I was appointed. Two years later. Me, Jimmy Donlon, Kevin Rafferty, all the guys that were in busy companies, we go up there and Chief Drew says to us, "Well look guys, you've probably seen more fires in the last two years than I've seen in my whole career on the fire department. So, we have to put two weeks in." What they do now, we did it in two weeks. We did first aid which we always did in house. Overhaul, everything that we were doing in the field. But we had to put the time in. We graduated in June of '69. One of the guys was disappointed. He was Down Neck. He was the newest guy on the job when we went to the Academy. Everybody else had been through this stuff.

Miller: No, you didn't go to the Academy until six months later. We went during the late summer, early fall. At that time, you just walked in; they'd tell you what your assignment was; and you walked into the firehouse without any equipment, without a helmet. The guys there fitted you up with a helmet and a turnout coat and boots that were on the rack. And you could use them until you went and got your helmet made for you at Cairns.

It was a week or two weeks, but we were at the Academy up on Eighteenth Avenue. They were showing me things like how to use the mask and I had already used it at quite a few fires. So, they were teaching me something that I had learned out in the field and learned out of necessity or I would have been hurt.

Dainty: The Academy at that time was a little Eighteenth Avenue firehouse. The Academy was on the first floor and upstairs were offices just basically the admin staff. The police department had a crime lab in there which consisted of one little room and the third floor was a gym. There were probably about forty of us in the class. And basically, book learning. There was some hands-on, but they didn't have any facilities to do any live burns. They didn't have any stairs to climb. We did do ladders. We did mock hose stretches. Towards the end we did go into some buildings that had burned and pulled some ceilings and stuff like that, but we had little of it. And one strange thing was they still had the life nets on the trucks. So, there was a fire escape on the side of the building, it would have been the number four side, when you looked at it, it was small platform, so they put a ladder up to the platform instead of using the drop ladder and you would go up on that and you would jump into the life net.

I think there were like seven or eight people on the net. It was spring loaded. You opened it up and it was kind of there and the big thing was don't walk over there with the net flat. Walk with it on end so the people didn't jump ahead of time. So, we all did that. There were a couple of guys who weren't really enthusiastic about jumping into the net. They had this big red dot in the middle of the net that you were supposed to hit. It was a pretty big shock when a guy dropped into it with seven people holding it. Even though there were huge springs that were probably about eight or ten inches and maybe two inches around to help absorb it. You held it up and then you were supposed to naturally come down with the weight and the shock. But very shortly after that they removed them from the trucks. I don't know what the reason was, but they did, so that alternative was gone.

I knew two guys in the class. John Salvato, who I had gone to grammar school with and I never saw him again because we went to different high schools and Anthony Vintola. Anthony and I went to the same high school. So, there was somebody there that I knew. There was nobody from my neighborhood. But then it's like everything else. You make friends. You go on to crews you know for the rest of your life. They did well.

Ray Fredette was there as a firefighter and Ray had eye issues. They were very good about not dismissing guys for physical issues because of the fact they were already on the job. They would take care of them as much as they could.

Chief Kossup was there as a Battalion Chief, as a newly made Battalion Chief. Ed Wall was there as a Battalion Chief. I'm trying to remember who the deputy chief was. He was a slender guy, but we never saw him. His office was upstairs. We'd be sitting in the classroom and all of the sudden you'd see a body come like a shadow in the back. It was him poking his nose in to see what was going on. They had a couple of displays that were there at the academy. They had a hydrant. They had a board with different tools on it. The one thing that they had that is no longer in use was the ticker-tape type system. That was in the back. They would sit there and you had to learn that to some degree so when you got to the firehouse you had an idea of what was going on. That was unique, so we might have spent four weeks, six weeks, maybe eight weeks there. I have no idea.

Almost everybody in the class, I think except for one or two guys were veterans from Viet Nam. So, it was easy as far as structure, taking orders, following orders, discipline. Everybody was in the military, so we knew how it was supposed to work and the fire department back them was a semi-military organization. We've gotten away from that. But back then, 1970, it was. The higher you went, just like the military, the higher you went on the pedestal, the more Godlikeness. That was pretty good.

We did very little hands-on. They would bring companies in just like they did later on, but it was hard because you had no facility. It was basically an old firehouse that was converted into classroom space. So, whenever they needed equipment or hands-on they would pull a company, they would usually go to the Central Ward where most of the burned out buildings were and do something there. And we did that for several days.

Weber: I don't think I saw the inside of the Academy for instructional purposes for two years. So, by that time I was a seasoned pro. They taught us a little bit of rope work, tying knots things like that. And the basic underlying philosophy was if you tie a rope to a tool and it doesn't fall off, you've done a good job.

Saccone: I went to the Academy a year after I was appointed with another class from 1970. That's how it was in those days. You didn't go right to the Academy. At that time the only training we ever had was at Eighteenth Avenue. And a matter of fact, the Director of the fire department right now was the one that trained us. All I can remember is we had to throw a thirty-five-foot ladder and raise it against the building on Eighteenth Avenue. We were trying to raise that ladder and it was going back and forth. We didn't know if it was going to go into to the street or not. And we were told that we had to jump into a net. That was an issue. If I remember correctly, we didn't have to do it. It was up to your own initiative. That was basically it. There wasn't really that much training at that time. Most of the training that was done was done in the firehouse because you were working with people that were very knowledgeable. It was really up to the individual to learn. If you walked into a firehouse and just stood there and didn't want to learn anything or do anything, that's what happened. Your mind just blocked it out.

Daudelin: I went straight to the Fire Academy. I think it was two weeks, up on Eighteenth Avenue. They taught us basic firematics, some first aid. Kossup was a battalion chief then, a new battalion chief. We did a lot of courses on firematics. We didn't do any smokehouse or anything. We had the old Burrells. And what they did for a smokehouse, I remember like it was yesterday, they brought us down to a vacant building that they had tarpapered over the windows. They put off a couple of smoke bombs in there and that was our one and only smokehouse training. But basically, in those days it was more on the job. Because at that time there were still people who went straight to the firehouse. Eli Savarese was in my Academy class. He was appointed that summer and they put him in the firehouse and then pulled him out of the firehouse.

P. Doherty: We went right to the Academy. We were the first class in a couple years. There were twenty-six of us and we went right to the Academy instead of going to the companies right off the bat like they were doing. We were in the Academy four weeks.

We raised the wooden Bangor ladder every day. They taught us the Burrell, how to use the Chemox and how to dispose of it. We jumped into the net and we went to abandoned buildings and stretched lines and opened roofs, used hooks and axes. We were given all around training. We learned about the alarm system, how to book alarms and what the return calls were, how to take companies off when they came back, first aid, and pump school. We went to pump school down below Special Service with Danny Tauriello. He took us through the whole evolution on the pump, how to work everything on it. We went down into the basement of Special Service. They had the engines up on blocks and they had pumps and everything down there. At that time, they used to do the repairs down there. And so, we went through the whole scenario of how to pump. You could just look right at it and see it without the apparatus panel. It was the whole breakdown of the whole thing. It was very good.

The evolutions that we were taught in the Academy were exactly what happened in the field because we had some pretty decent people up there that were teaching us. Not the upper echelon, the people that were actually teaching us to stretch the hose lines. What they would do was they would call up an engine company that had a lot of experience and when we would go down to check lines and everything, we would be with that engine company and truck company. Truck Five was up there teaching us with the saw and all of that. Twelve Engine and Twenty, they had some quality people teaching you the evolutions when you went to the Academy. Basically, what you learned from stretching in the Academy up the stairs, you had to do the whole thing and they monitored you all the way up and around. It really was done that way, a little minor tweak here and there, but you really didn't have to concern yourself because you really knew how to do it. That was the way they did it in the field.

Marcell: I got put on on Friday and I reported to work the following Monday. Didn't go to the Training Academy, just went to a firehouse. About two or three years later, I went to the Academy. By that time, I had a lot of experience. We had a lot of fires. They taught us fundamentals. In those days hydraulics was kind of big. They'd do different theorems about that. Kind of like the things you would learn when you were trying to study for a promotion, different theories. Most of the fundamentals we learned on the job from the guys who would break you in. This is how we do this. When we get to a fire, we put the ladder up. When we get to a fire, we put it into pump. We take the hydrant and stretch in and feed the engine and then take a couple of lengths of hose off the back and so on and so forth. It was just more elaborate training than that, but the actual Training Academy was only a week and a half, two weeks. Not much.

Kelly: We went to the Academy for a week and that was it. The Academy was on Eighteenth Avenue. You had to jump off the building into the net. And they taught us how to do the mask with the air cylinder, but masks were just coming into play at that time. And a lot of the older guys, we found out, didn't use masks. They couldn't get used to the feeling of the mask. So, they could eat a lot of smoke, the older guys. They really developed that ability to do that. But I would say we were the first ones that really got used to that mask, that MSA mask. We didn't use the Burrell. The Burrell was right before us. They had just done away with the Burrell and they came in with MSA mask when we came on the job.

Romano: We went to the Academy. There were four of us that were hired on the same day. And we went to the Academy which was located on Eighteenth Avenue at the time. I have to be honest with you, the training we got at the

Academy was piss poor, next to non-existent. We raised a few ladders. They taught us how to put on the MSA, how to use the mask. How to carry a hose roll and that was about it. And after two weeks of that, they sent us into the firehouse.

Brownlee: We were a class of twelve, went to the Academy one month, and learned the fire tetrahedron. We did ladders. We did a lot of ladder work. We did the church raise. I almost fell into the Passaic River. A little bit with the masks, we did the Chemox; we did the Burrells, but we weren't supposed to use them. Then they showed us how to use the MSA SCBA and that was about it.

Rosamilia: At the time the IAFF lobbied and wound up with this program, federal grants for recruiting. It was a recruitment program for mainly the larger cities. What they did was they provided them with funding to hire cadets, send them to college. So, you went to Essex County College and half of your time was spent there and the other half was spent working either classes at the Academy or sometimes in the firehouse. That was a nice opportunity.

They had twenty spots open. The city applied for a grant. Chief Wall at the time was president of the Officers' Union and so he had a little in, I guess. The Training Academy applied for the grant and they got a grant for twenty members. You had to be between the age of eighteen and twenty-one. If you had service time it would be minus-ed to make you qualified to be twenty-one. Two guys came on with that program. You took a civil service test that ranked. They hired twenty guys.

It was about thirty guys that passed the test, maybe a little more on the list. They made twenty guys and then the whole thing was you had to go two years to college. Basically, it was a two-year program with a little bit of on the job. They would send you out to the firehouses in pairs on a schedule during off school times when you weren't in class. That would be part of your requirement and a lot of Academy time and classes.

At the Academy they taught us how to drive the apparatus. They taught us basically all the stuff that you would be getting in the Academy. A lot of that was just administrative. Just to get us together and see what we were doing and doing inspection. But it was the general kind of class that you would be in at the Academy.

They did that for a year and a half, but more and more it became send you to the firehouse. Early on they gave you a lot of stuff because they had their own responsibilities, too. If they had a class, they didn't have as much time for us. So, if they had a big training thing going on for the department then they would schedule you more to go to the firehouse. If they were free, then you would do more stuff in the Training Academy.

I took the next firefighter test too. I did okay on it, wouldn't have been made in the first group. Actually, it was very fortunate for me because otherwise I would have probably come on with that group of guys that wound up getting laid off in '76 and it would have really disrupted my career. I was able to avoid that. When they had those layoffs, it took two, almost three years for some guys to get back. They didn't come back fully until like '78. They had some CETA guys. Some guys didn't want to come on CETA, which was another Federal program, temporary hiring. Some guys didn't want to come back on that because it didn't go towards your pension. They remained out and they got rehired later.

Bruce Morgan and I were teamed up together. So, he was pretty ambitious. He dragged me through a few extra courses that I really didn't want to go through, but I was his partner, so I did it with him. Actually, we wound up finishing a semester early. We had doubled up on some courses, so we finished in a year and nine months. We approached them and said we're done with our school. It's summertime, why don't you advance us now? So, Kossup said, "Let me run it by them." They said, "Okay, we'll advance you now if you have no school to do in the fall semester." So, they did. That's how you ended this thing. Once you met your requirements, you got basically a promotion through qualification to the rank of firefighter.

Burkhardt: The provision for cadets was two years college. You went year-round to college and in the summer when you weren't carrying the full number of credits, they would put you in the firehouse two, three days a week for anywhere from four to six hours. They would take you out probably by midnight. That's how the city gets their money's worth out of you. But the cadets weren't in the firehouse the first eight months probably because we carried so many credits. I carried the max and when we weren't going to college, you had to go to the old Training Academy on Eighteenth Avenue and take fire science courses. A couple of courses Kossup taught down in Essex County College and we'd have to go there. They tried to keep the twenty guys in the same classes throughout the whole curriculum. They didn't want us to bond with other people because there were a bunch of firemen coming in there. The young guys have long hair. The firemen used to frown up on Eighteenth Avenue when they'd see us come walking in there with some wild outfits. I was one of the short hair guys.

But what they would do was if the Training Academy was closed, we had to go down and cut the weeds and prep the Jersey Street joint to get the boat out. So, we were like the janitors for a couple of weeks in hooking that thing up. Once we got the knowledge of the fire department, we went through almost like a Training Academy like the new recruits do now. In fact, Joe Lange and a couple of other guys, John Kunze, a lot of guys, Billy Tansy, Craig Elton they all came on at the same time. We had already finished the class, so we had to almost teach them. That was back in '72. We kind of mixed with them and then the Training Academy chief, who was Wall at the time, thought we were ready to be sent to the field. They tried to keep us all in houses with chiefs. The firefighting force wasn't ready for the young long-haired guys coming into the field. Guys wore wigs in the firehouse, short hair wigs. The firemen weren't happy with us because they thought we were on the fast track to become captains and taking jobs away from everybody else. They were misinformed too that we were socially promoted, that we never took a test when in fact we did take the test.

Then the fire department offered an exam in the middle of our training for the college and a lot of guys took the fire entrance exam. Me and about five other guys were the only ones that passed. When the firemen heard that they went ballistic. It was a couple of other things, but the firemen weren't too happy with the twenty hippies coming into the job.

Stoffers: We were in the Academy. We were in class in Essex County College. After I think it was six months or a year, they'd bring us out to fires. Okay, there's a fire. Let's go and you pull, and you help them out and you learn that way. They had us down at the Academy whenever we weren't in school, teaching different things, learning the ropes. You're not there every day because you're in school also. So, if there is one week where everybody had classes all week long, you missed that week in the Academy. And then if you had only three classes on Monday, Wednesday, and Friday. Tuesday and Thursday you were in the Academy. If you were in school Tuesday and Thursday then you were in the Academy Monday, Wednesday, and Friday. I forget how the schedules went now, but we had Captain Steinbach down there. He was one of them. Chief Kossup at the time Battalion Chief. Chief Wall was the Deputy. Ray Fredette and Bobby Melillo. That was the main body, and they would teach us like you would do with the recruits. Start with that and work this way. Then at college you would get the physics, chemistry, your typical college graduation plan if you want a degree. We didn't go into the firehouse until a year and a half later. We were working from six until ten, something like that, just to see how it goes. I think we did days too, but I'm not sure. We worked straight through the summer. It was a job. You just treat it like a job. Maybe we did have off during the summer and that's when we spent most of our time in the Academy.

Morgan: Depending on the sessions at Essex County College, but we were doing probably about twenty, twenty-four hours a week in school and about the same in the firehouse. The hours we worked in the firehouse varied, depending on school. We were all pretty much in the same classes, either morning classes, afternoon classes, or evening classes. When we weren't in school, we were in the firehouses or up at the Academy or down at old Two Engine where we took classroom instruction down there. We learned the ropes of the fire department before they actually put us out in the field. They probably had us down at Two Engine for I'd say maybe six months. We learned the old bell system, the tapes, the joker, the different signals, different requirements. The things that you would learn, regular firemen would learn actually when they came on the job. We were learning this pre-firefighting, before we became firemen. We had quite an extensive knowledge going into the firehouse, more so than a lot of the older guys used to have when they used to come on the job. If they were lucky, they got a week or two in the Academy and then shoot out to the firehouse. A lot of times the guys would stay out in the firehouse and then three or four years later they'd come back and start learning things that we were learning. By then they were already pretty experienced and it's basically a waste of time for them. Going into the firehouse we knew quite a bit with regards to the way the fire department operated.

Going through the cadet program, I think I had a unique opportunity and advantage over most of the guys who came on the job back in that era because we were slowly phased into it. We used to go to the fires. We used to help stretch lines. We used to overhaul after the fire was knocked down. We saw quite a bit of what was happening out there prior to ever being exposed to actual firefighting. The guys back then used to come into the firehouse, not even out of the Academy because they didn't even go to the Academy then. You got made on the list; you got put into a firehouse; and fifteen minutes later you could be going to a fire. Now that's an experience where you're going to be in awe. Maybe you never saw a fire before in your life and now all of the sudden you see this burning building and you're going to be going into it. We had a really, really great opportunity with the cadet program because we were allowed to see all of that prior to it. So, we were really set up for it. We had, I believe, a tremendous amount of experience prior to going into the actual firehouses as firemen with the cadet program, that really prepared us.

Coale: I think the Academy was only eight weeks. I can't remember to tell you the truth. It seemed like forever though. It seemed like forever. It might have been less than eight weeks because they wanted to get us out in the field. They were short at the time. It was the new Training Academy which was right there on the river. They just opened that, but the tower wasn't finished yet. It was basically class work, that's all we did. And we'd go out to different sites in the city to do actual hands-on training. We learned basic firefighting, the ABCs and the triangle, the whole thing. But it never taught us what a real fire is like of course.

Killeen: I think we were the first class in the Academy to have it paved. I believe the first class; the driveway was still stones and we had it paved. I forget the actual length of time there, but it was for real. In my mind it was all for real, everything was for real. They gave us homework. I remember one time I went down to Thirteen Engine, and I asked them if I could look at one of the masks because we had to do a diagram of the breathing apparatus. So, I'm doing homework, like grade school stuff. I'm taking a compass and making perfect circles. I don't know what the hell they thought of me doing that. They might have thought I was out of my mind.

We had a small class, maybe fourteen guys, real good people, real sharp people. Going to the Academy was good. The instructors were good. After you get out of the Academy you hear different things, but we had good people. Eddy Wall was in charge of the Academy. Chief Tartus just got promoted to Battalion Chief. A couple of guys, they were beat up. Like Harvey Wiseman, somebody I remember. He was in the Salvage. He was Eli Savarese's Captain for a while. He's down there. In the Academy he was a very good. Teaching us ropes, we learned a lot of things from these guys. These guys were older, and we learned a lot of things from them.

They took us out for driver's training on regular pumpers. We had the B model Macks, the gas models. We had a truck down there. They took us out to Weequahic Park to learn how to tiller, which to this day I cannot tiller. I couldn't tiller then, and I couldn't tiller now. I remember trying to back in. I sat forward, backward, sideways. I couldn't do anything. I couldn't get that thing in. We had fifty-five-gallon drums. I'm knocking them over.

One time, we're doing battering ram stuff. There's a freestanding wall maybe about two courses of red brick thick. We're by Twelve Engine with the battering ram. I remember specifically them telling me, there's two handles on the front. One is like a hand guard for when the battering ram goes through the wall to prevent you from breaking your hand. The second one is where you keep your hand and then you have the one in the back. So, you go boom, boom, boom. I put my hands in the front where I can get some good leverage, right. And we swing it. Right through the wall, those guys ran my hand right into the brick. I thought it was broken. There was a guy there, Lou Bellini, he was holding me up and I was in such pain, I must have been white. They sent me to Doc Devlin over on Roseville Avenue. Doc Devlin looked at the hand and it was okay. I did a lot of stuff with an ace bandage wrapped around my hand.

But I tell you what; we had a real lucky class. Grumman Engineering, Grumman Aerospace modified a fire engine for New York City. It had a remote control on the nozzle. It directly operated the pump and they brought it to us to try out. This is why I am so upset with this department. We're down at the Academy. We got all these recruits and as you maneuvered the nozzle it would increase the flow forty-five gallons a minute at a time. The man on the nozzle increased how much flow he wanted, not the guy on the pump. So, if you had kinks or no kinks, you controlled the amount of water and the nozzle reaction and everything. This is amazing. It had a little spring antenna that wouldn't get damaged. It was a concept thing. We got to use that to play around with for a little bit. Then somebody else brought a big air bag that the stunt men use. It ended up at the end of the day, I think myself, Kevin Drennan, a couple of other guys were standing on the top of the metal ladder on the side of the Fire Academy, going off doing flips into the bag. It was powered by air fans. It had big holes in it with canvas over the side. As you jumped in it would blow the air out, but you wouldn't hit the ground. First you would do the first floor, then second floor. Then we were doing swans. See if we could do swans. We were doing flips, landing on our backs. Doing everything. We had a lot of fun.

For my class it was advantageous. We had good instructors. We had a lot of things to play with. It was great. The Academy was a good time. They took us to fires. You get to work at fires. We thought we were hot. We had no idea what the real world was like, but at the Academy life was good. We were there maybe two months, April, May, might have been for April, May and we came out sometime in June.

Banta: We were on Jersey Street at the Training Academy. There was a group appointed in '73 and I assume they went to Jersey Street also. So, if that's the case, maybe we were the second class. I don't know if anybody prior to '73 group went to Jersey Street. It was paved. I don't remember if it was two weeks or four. I'm leaning to believe it was only two weeks at that time. They taught us basic firefighting; we had the smoke house. We had the tower where we operated; how to stretch lines, air packs, first-aid, just basically everything they still do today. Our live burns consisted of palettes and hay in both the smoke house and the top of the tower. We did the church raise in the Academy parking lot. As a matter of fact, we had a guy who was in our class that ended up being assigned to a truck company, who wouldn't do it. And every time they kept asking for somebody to come and do the church climb, he always managed to get himself to the back. He never did it. And then they came out and they assigned him to a truck company.

Camasta: The Academy was on Jersey Street. I think we were the third class through the Academy. Chief Wall was the training commandant, and we had some real older characters. They had Harvey Wiseman, the legendary Salvage captain and you had Steinbach. Huge German guy with a flattop haircut. Carl Duerr wasn't there at the time. So, it was before him. Ray Fredette was. He was a fixture. They were quite proud of their Academy and the stuff that we're familiar with that are gone now, all worked at the time. The whole east end property. That was all functional, so that was a lot of fun.

It was a pretty regimented ordeal. I can't remember if it was six or eight weeks. It was at least six. It might have been eight. We did everything and you were busy the whole time. I was previously attending fire college before I came on the job. I was going to Union County College taking fire science courses. And while I was there, I met different fellows from other fire departments. This is how I networked myself to find out who was having tests and stuff like that. Relating back to the Training Academy, one of the things that I found helpful is Chief Buccine. I went to school with him. He was a newly promoted captain in Twenty-seven. And I did a little bit of buffing while I was in the Academy at Engine Twenty-seven. Theoretically I should have just seen firehouse life, but the two times I went there, Engine Twenty-seven had their only two fires for 1974. That's why they only let me go there twice because it was bad nights both times. They had a monstrous tire fire the one time. It seemed like we rode forever on the back of that FWD to get somewhere down the port to get to all these tires. Then the other one was a structural fire they had somewhere. Then they wouldn't let me ride there anymore. I was able to do that while I was in the Academy.

Straile: I went to the Academy on Jersey Street in Newark. The Academy was good. We had some really good instructors. That we learned a lot from them. They said our class was like one of the best classes they ever had down there. Maybe because it was such a small class. They were able to dedicate more time and stuff to us. So, we learned a lot. They were good instructors. Liked every one of them.

You had classroom work that you had to learn different formulas, ratios, how to pump, gallons per minute the whole thing. And then you had the physical work where you went out. We had to climb ladders. We had to learn how to use the tools. You had to go up in the smoke tower. You had to learn how to use the SCBA which was an important part of the job. All in all, it was a well-rounded academy. They taught us a lot. We learned a lot.

Partridge: We had, I don't know if I remember the exact number, I believe we were like twelve. There were two different cadet programs in the history of the Newark Fire Department. The first one involved guys who were supposed to be pursuing a college degree at the same time they were coming on the fire department. This was a different type of program. This was more sort of an outreach to the community to get people into the job. The requirements were different. I'm not sure exactly what they were, but we had something like eight firefighters and four cadets if I remember correctly.

The Academy was interesting because it was kind of like my first clue that the Newark Fire Department often operated on a shoestring. I frankly excepted more from the largest city in the state. The instructors that were working there at the time, they were pretty good. We went into some stuff that I never really thought we would get into as recruits. I mean by the time we left the Academy we were trained to drive apparatus. We had a really good portion of the class dedicated to hydraulics. We had a Battalion Chief there, Chief Tartus, who had been a teacher and was very up on the subject. He taught us hydraulics. And I remember being very surprised that this was in the curriculum for a recruit class. And they went into a lot of what was known at the time about fire behavior. We did the usual drill field evolutions and stretching lines, climbing ladders, going through the smokehouse and so forth. To me the best part was they took us out to vacant buildings a lot. That was different than using the Academy facilities because you could actually learn how to cut roofs, pull ceilings, stretch hose lines in differently configured buildings. I thought that was pretty good, but honestly, I excepted more from the city of Newark. I expected a much bigger, better facility. I expected more organization. I expected a kind of stricter discipline during the course of the Academy. I think we were there like six or eight weeks. It served its purpose. I mean we went out into the field and by all account from the guys that were already working in the companies, we were well trained.

J. Prachar: We did five full days and like three and a half days. We graduated on a Friday. We didn't do a full ten days in the academy, because our graduation was Friday in the morning. And I think we only did a half a day on Thursday. We learned basic stuff, how to raise a ladder, how to wear a self-contained breathing apparatus on your back with the face piece and not panic. How to crawl through a smoke-filled building and not get lost and not panic. Learned how to take some heat, unfortunately, in my case I learned how to take a little bit more than I was prepared for. We had a fire burning in some pallets and hay on the third floor of the drill tower and the drill was a couple of guys go to the roof, pop the hatch when they're told. Three guys without tanks run a line in. Three guys with tanks head up the stairs, relieve them. I don't remember who the three guys were that brought the line up, but I remember the three guys that went up. We were the first group. We were myself, Mike Mitchell, and Jimmy Murray. And we went up.

I decided I was going to grab the tip. We went up. We relieved the guys. The instructor is half a flight below us. Tells me to open the line up and hit the fire door. Hit the fire door, then he said open the door up. I guess Mike Mitchell must have opened the door. We crawl in, hit the fire. The instructor tells me to put it on fog. I put it on fog, hit the fire and the next thing all hell broke loose. It got hot and I'm screaming. I'm screaming and this guy is saying, "It's okay. It's going to be a little hot. Just keep working the line. Work the line." I'm screaming. I scream to Mike open the windows up. He opens the windows up. We finally get it down. Now the thing is this stuff was burning for about twenty minutes before we get up there. I was in pain. I walked downstairs and you were the first guy I saw, and you asked, "What happened to your neck?" I reached across the right side of my neck with my left hand and pulled off all my skin and said, "Shit, this ain't good. This ain't good."

That was my second week on the job. That was Tuesday. I think that was Tuesday which would be the twenty-seventh of June. The twenty-seventh of June I went to the emergency room. I came back, finished out the week. I wasn't doing any drills. Graduated with a big old nasty bandage on my ear. Spent three weeks on light duty in Special Service.

Mitchell: What'd I learn in the Academy? I guess the book knowledge of firefighting, practical stuff. Not really stuff you learn in the field.

Daly: I think the Academy for two weeks and then they shipped us in the field for the summer. And then in October they shipped us back to the Academy to learn more. I thought that was a waste of time because during the summer I learned a lot more than I could ever learn in the Academy. That was a very busy year. We came on in a very busy time and I think we learned more outside the Academy than you did inside.

We learned how to stretch hose, masks, the smoke tower, going into a burning situation in a close spot to see if you were willing to do it. Some people couldn't do it. They had to bail out, me I enjoyed it. I'm a masochist or a sadist or something, but I actually enjoyed being in that type of situation. My one real memory of the Training Academy was when we did the church raise in the parking lot. Everyone had to go up and over it in their turnout gear and if you didn't you had to go in to see the chief. But my biggest memory was doing the church raise and climbing up and over that in the parking lot with guys you don't know holding onto the ropes and holding on to the bangors and just climbing up and over it. Anything I did in there was just for fun except for the book. Marty Cawley came out one in the class. I came out two in the class.

Zieser: We went on in June and did like eight days in the Academy. And then because you only got eight days in the Academy they brought us back again for additional training, another month of training. Basically, that first week we learned our SCBA, donning our equipment, using the SCBA. Then we learned ground ladders and just some basic hose line stretches. When my father came on you didn't get any formal training. They put you right in the firehouse and it was the captain's job to train you. So, at that time I don't think it was unheard of that the guys didn't really think that eight days was a good number or bad number. What they experienced was going right to the firehouse. I can tell you this though, by the time we went to the next set of days training in October, and they put us there for a month, they were going to teach us how to stretch lines. I think most of us were pretty well seasoned by then. Not that they couldn't teach us anything new. But they were just reinforcing a lot of the stuff that we already learned, especially if you were fortunate to work with good companies, busy companies. I remember my captain always taking me out and doing some sort of training. In my eyes it worked out great because it was on the job training. It was a busy summer, and we learned a lot.

Hopkins: We went through the Academy. The first time for about a week or ten days and you learned the basics. The bell system, you learned the signals and when they would send you out on a run you had a certain type of signal. And then when you returned or when you were on a fire scene you made a signal and that was it. Yeah, you learned basic firehouse life. What a hose was; what a hook was. Basic stuff and then they sent us into the field all summer. And then we returned I think it was in late September or October.

Sandella: As I recall we went to the Academy and we got some paperwork and stuff done in a short period, maybe a matter of days. Then we went right into the field. So, we didn't do much in the way of training when we were hired. We had a live burn. I remember Ray Fredette burning some pallets up in the tower. The one memory that I have about the training was the church raise.

Chief Wall was the Commandant, the deputy chief and we were setting up the church raise with the tormentor poles and the ropes. The ladder was a fifty-foot ladder, and it was fully extended standing up straight into the air. The tormentor poles would be out there and the guys level the ladder, holding it in place while guys would climb up to the top, go over the top, and come back down the other side. And it was pretty scary if you weren't familiar with ladders. You had that long climb, you had to actually lift your weight over the top, and the top of the ladder was only maybe about a foot wide if that much. It got narrower as you got to the top. I recall Carl Duerr explaining it all to us. Chief Wall said, "Alright, now Carl will demonstrate." Captain Duerr turns green, but I got to give him credit. He went up and he came back down. He went up; he went over the top; he came back down; but he didn't say much. He just walked into the Training Academy. He wasn't too happy. But the church raise was interesting. That's one thing that we did. I don't think we did that on our initial stay at the Academy when we only did a couple of days. We had gone back after a few months in the field, and we may have done it then.

Witte: I was there. We were part of that rapid, rapid class. The first class was forty-nine guys in June which I missed. That was eight days and out. We did the same in July. We were eight days and out and then come back in the fall for four more weeks. The first time we just learned how to put a mask on. That was it, basically. Then they said, go out there, you just hang with the captain. I think we dragged hose and threw ladders. I can't remember now. I just remember eight days out. Hey, you learned how to do a mask.

Kormash: We didn't go to the Academy for long. We went in on December nineteenth. We had the Christmas holiday, New Year holiday, I think right after the New Year we were out. They couldn't do live burns. I remember that because I believe Prachar got burnt in the class before. So, they didn't want to do that. They did a little smokehouse stuff. Then Public Service stuff, MVA stuff, repelling, ladder raises, hose stretches, sprinklers and standpipes, all of the basic firefighting strategies and a little building construction. That was pretty much it.

Reiss: We were sworn in on December nineteenth in a blizzard. Everybody made it there and then we started the Monday. So, we were actually only in the Academy for three weeks and that included Christmas and New Year's which we didn't work. We had very few days in the Academy. We didn't touch a hose until the last day. It was too cold first of all and we didn't have the time. They were trying to get us to learn how to use the SCBA and things like that. They really didn't have time to do hose work, just too cold. We spent the whole Academy with Carl Duerr telling us that we're all going to get burned because somebody in a previous class got burned. It's so hot in there you're going to get burned. We went out there on that day, it was like five degrees out and the water was freezing when it hit those stairs in the Academy it was so cold. So that didn't quite happen.

They covered first aid, the SCBA, kind of the rules of the department, how the department operated. We had a lot of classroom work on firefighting, but not the physical part of it. We did go to a couple of fires and pulled ceiling and hose. But it was a very quick Academy. We were in and out. There was a live burn on that one last day in the burn room on the top floor. Everyone took turns and by the time the third or fourth group went, the water was frozen on the stairway all the way up. That was a little interesting.

Almaguer: Seven guys went to the Academy for I think about a month. I think we were there close to a month. They introduced us to the Newark Fire Department. They introduced me to firematics, introduced me to the fire engine, to the fire truck, hoses, wrenches, the compartments, tools that we need to get familiar with, standard operating procedures, etcetera.

We had a live burn. The drill tower was in use. They used to love lighting that drill tower up. I'll never forget. We had the tower and then we had a building on the far end. It was a one-story building. They smoked it up and they wanted you to go in there with the mask, walk around it, and come out. Whereas the tower was stretching a line with a mask and putting out a fire.

I'll never forget the first time putting on that SCBA mask. The guy told me to go in to the smokehouse. He was standing outside and all this smoke was coming out the door. He says, "Okay, you're next. I want you to go to the left and walk around and I'll meet you here." I said, "Fuck this. I'm going back to Saint James hospital." But then they pushed me along. That was just an exercise. Imagine being in the real thing.

F. Bellina: Went through the full Academy, I want to say it was six weeks maybe. It was good because I learned from Carl Duerr. He knew pumping. He knew hydraulics. He knew water. He actually did a good job with that. Boehringer was involved, Chief Boehringer. Fredette was there and I learned ladder work too. We learned what they knew, the '70s. That's what we learned from them. It wasn't the new stuff. It was about what they did. They went out of the book, but it still related to what they did. It wasn't that big of a change. I actually learned a lot. I learned the job from them, as far as the mechanics of the job.

Wapples: Appointment date is November 2, 1982. And I felt as though I wasn't going to be appointed because it was almost a three-year period. I was going into the third year and our list was a two-year list which they got an extension on. When that list first came out, they made guys in May of 1980. We came on in a class of eleven. They brought us in because it was a political matter. It just so happened that Gibson wanted to show he was bringing in people for the fire department. Where I had scored on the test, I would have been number sixteen without vets coming on. It was getting very disappointing to me to know that I was up so high, between thirty-three and forty-six on the list. Back then, I was twenty-four and I had a child. This was something I was really looking forward to because now I had an opportunity to better my living standard. And to get caught up in the politics that went along with it was kind of tough to bear with. The list was in the process of expiring and it was just a whole bit feeling towards local politics within this town during that period of time. But I hung in there, stood in there and waited around and it came through finally.

We spent six weeks in the Academy, a total of four weeks initially. What happened when we first came on the job, after being in the Academy for two weeks, we realized we were going to get laid off. They brought us on the job; we were in the Academy studying diligently and putting our whole hearts at it. Next thing we know, after the second week, we get our slips. We're getting laid off in another two weeks. So, we did the four-week period. What happened then was we didn't get laid off because it was a forty-five day notice they have to give. So, they opt to put us in the field. We all went to various locations. After being in the Academy for four weeks, they felt as if we were qualified enough to go out in the field and to learn from the captains out in the field. We all went to different firehouses. Then after being laid off for a six-week period, we came back to the Fire Academy and did another two weeks. And then the graduation ceremonies came. Nobody wanted to come back in the Academy after being out in the field for months. It was just something where we just passed the time when we came back because everybody knew everything basically then. It didn't make any sense bringing them back in from the field at that time. But if you put your mind to it, I'm sure that there were things that we did learn by coming back, so it paid off.

Griffith: My firefighter class in '86 was sixty-five guys, a very big class. In fact, it was so big what they did was split us up. They put us all through mask training for a week. We were all together for a week and they did mask training and general knowledge of the fire department and all that. I was in the group that they kicked out into the field. So, we went right to the field. I ended up on the third tour in the third battalion. They didn't really teach us how to use a hose. They taught you how to use a mask. That whole getting thrown out was insane. However, when we went back to the Academy, now we were in the field for six weeks, Captain Duerr gave us a test. We went over some things for a couple of days. He gave us a test and then he got up and he yelled at us and screamed at us. He said, "These are the worst grades on this test that I have ever seen." And the deal was when guys came back, we got this. Because you're in the firehouse and the guys are telling you, "Listen, they're going to tell you to do it this way, but this is the way we really do it. And don't do this and don't do that." Each house has its own way of doing things. You got back there. You thought that you knew it all. So, when he graded it, he really wigged out. They never brought up a class like that big again. It was crazy because guys would think, "We know this. We don't have to go through that." Every now and then different things and guys would snicker. So, it wasn't the best. Today that wouldn't fly.

When we went back in, it was the same course. I think they modified it a little bit. They had a pump simulator there and you got into friction loss, I remember that. We started with what fire is and the fire tetrahedron. Then we went into friction loss and pumping and ladders. There was a progression there that we went through. They did live burns and you put it together. It was nice to see it evolve. They wanted you to run the line a certain way and flake it and all that. And now guys knew little tricks and little things. Where'd you get that from? I thought it was good because I picked up what I saw in the field going to fires. But this was like an explanation to that. This is why we do it. This is how we do it. It answered a lot of questions. So, the Academy was good. This was Puffy Freda. It was a really good program. Of course, when you got out of the Academy and into companies you thought you knew it all and you never do. You never do. Even the day you're leaving you're learning something new.

Arce: I was there for about two weeks. The reason we were there for two weeks is because they were short in manpower and there was a lot of work, a lot of fires. So, we actually got trained out in the field by going to fires, fighting fires and going to a lot of incidents. We were doing four to five thousand runs per year depending on the company you were in. We're doing thirty runs, ten hours, twenty-five, ten hours. Of course, we had a lot of boxes, which were pulled boxes or whatever, but during that time we also had about a thousand fires, dumpster fires, car fires were enormous, and a lot of house fires. In the Academy? I don't really know what they were teaching back then. I know I had Captain Duerr and Fred Shackleford. We did a lot of hands-on. We had the drill tower where we used to burn.

Nasta: If I remember correctly, they hired sixty. But we had a weird Academy class. Our class went to the Academy for two weeks. Then we were sent out in the field for basically the holidays. They brought us back in and they split us in half, somewhere around February. They split us in half to finish two more weeks in the Academy. But of course, we'd been in the field for a couple of months and back then we were catching work. We were catching a pretty good amount of work. So, we went back to the Academy. We knew everything. You know how that goes. The first two weeks everyone was kind of shy. The second two weeks, nobody really listened because, like I said, we were experienced. We were out there for a couple of months. We didn't do any marching or any drill type things like that. I'm guessing because they knew it was going to be a short period of time. As recruits we didn't know it, but I'm sure the staff knew the deal. Chief Freda was in charge of the Academy back then and Captain Duerr was one of my instructors and Ray Fredette, Gene Anderson, Bobby Melillo. We went through the normal stuff. They taught us fire science and we did live burns and we did some rope work. I thought it was a fairly solid education, but I had nothing to compare it to. But we learned what we needed to get by. First day in the firehouse, you're glued to the captain. You just follow the captain.

Weidele: Yes, we went through the Academy. I think five or six weeks, that's what it was and we came out early because they needed people in the field. They said they were going to bring us back and give us other training. Once we got in the field, they knew they were never going to bring us back. So, then we remained in the field. They taught us fire suppression, teamwork, camaraderie, how to deal with the public too. And make sure that safety is the overriding concern at fire grounds. If something doesn't feel right, let your captain know. Certain guys were skilled in certain things like electricians, building construction guys, and you learned a lot from them there too. It helped you in the field when you were overhauling or fighting fires, guys brought things to your attention about how to pull ceilings, how to pull moldings, how to force doors. So, it was really interesting when I went through. They had real good instructors. You had guys with many years of experience and you were just really excited, I know I was, to be there. When I left, every day I went home. I told my friends and parents all the things I learned. I was so excited.

O. Johnson: Our class was approximately sixty guys, split in two. And it was kind of strange because the first half of the class went to the Academy. The other class was out in the field. So, when the other class came from the field, they were like we know all this. They were a little cocky. They had the quick orientation. I guess roll calls were bad, so half the class went to the Academy. The other half of the class went into the field. You had the basics, but it was on the job training for those guys. So, when they came back, it was like, "Oh, we did this already." After that we all came together as one group, and we basically finished the course. It was a little different then.

I think the Academy was like six weeks. It was a very fast class. It was good. They stressed the importance of it, but they stressed look we're not going to babysit you. You know what you need to do. You got to continue your reading. You're reading this. Your confidence you build from your experiences. You always ask questions, and you keep learning. And that's what they did.

DeCeuster: We were in the Academy eight weeks. I got to clean the bathroom a lot because we'd go out to lunch and have a few drinks every day. It was hard to stay awake after a while because some of the instruction was a little bit boring. Basic firefighting, you had the tower, smoke tower, went up there. Now of course they've changed, setting up all the operations, chain of command. I remember when I did the swearing-in we were at Eighteenth Avenue in what used to be a handball court and Carl Duerr is going, "For the next eight weeks, I'll be your mother, your father." It was like watching a movie about Marine boot camp. Sargent Ernies. I'll be your mother, your father, I was like I heard this shit before. So now we're in the Academy. He introduces Deputy Chief Freda, Puffy Freda. Puffy comes out, "What a great job, come into work, wash your car, go to sleep." I go, that's my dad. That's my hero there. Puffy was a good man, too, a real good man.

Giordano: They had knocked me off the list for whatever reason and I was put into the next class. I wound up being sworn in by myself and with Battalion Chief Gaynor. We were sworn in in the director's office, John Caufield. That was pretty memorable and then I went on. I wound up in the same office at the end of my career. The wallpaper was still the same. I had my family and Chief Gaynor had his. They turned to Chief Gaynor and said, "It's about time you broke down and spent some money and got a limo." They thought he got the limo because he was the battalion chief and when he said no, they turned and looked at me. They told me, "Don't worry, you won't be using it." They made me go to the Training Academy and go to work for that half a day. My family went out to eat to celebrate. I don't know for what reason, but I was going to be a one-man class.

I went to the Academy. Deputy Chief Alfred Freda was the commander and my training, I was mostly with Captain Carl Duerr. He was a tough son of a bitch, especially for new people who really didn't know him. But he was a great guy. He really taught you a lot of the basic things you used to learn in the Training Academy. He went through all the rigors of Firefighter One, really took me through the whole basic course. Everything he could. But a lot of evolutions you have to do with other people. I had to take tests, exams, everything I could do as an individual. But things like raising a three-man ladder and other things you do in tandem as a group, I couldn't really perform those. I think I was there at least a month, maybe even six weeks.

I will say some captains befriended me and would come down and spring me out after lunch for the rest of the day. Take me to the firehouse and take me on some runs and so forth. So, I started to make a lot of friends and people I met through the Academy. They already knew I was running training things for a lot of their sons, family members, or people they knew from the neighborhood.

So, I guess the city felt I had to go back and complete the class with some group evolutions. They actually hired sixty firefighters at once. Everybody went to the Academy for a week or two. Kind of like the course that you and many others went through where they just threw you into the fire and brought you back later. That's what they did. The first thirty guys in alphabetical order had minimal training. They went into the field. I was the second group. We finished the whole academy. And they came back and finished. We all graduated together.

The first day I kind of lined up with guys who had shiny new turnout gear and mine already had been out in the field to working fires. It was filthy dirty. I remember we were all standing for line up and Director Kossup came down the line. He asked me, "How do you like the job?" "I love it." It was a great group of guys. We broke into three divisions. Eddy Griffith was from the line division, so naturally they put him in charge of our group. And two others were in charge of other groups.

That was my training experience. I was assigned to the field for ten months and then a whole class coming in so I went back and did the traditional course to graduation. We had the party at my bar. It was a great graduation with a great group of guys. Chief Centanni made chief of the department. Other guys were deputy chiefs, battalion chiefs, all guys from that class did great things. It saddens me to say there's a good bunch out of the sixty that are not with us any longer. So, life's been kind to many and not so much to others.

Lee: We went to the Academy, but because the class was so large and the Academy could not accommodate all of us, all sixty-five went for the first week. We did all the orientation and filled out all the necessary paperwork. Then thirty some odd, were put out in the field while the remaining members completed the Academy. At that time, I think it was an eight-week course. For seven weeks we were out in the field and at the end of the seven weeks we came back, and we completed the seven-week course. The first week we did basically just paperwork and how to put on our turnout gear, but no major training. The training was taken up when we got in the field. They did teach you how to put on an SCBA.

When we went back to the Academy, we learned all the fire scenarios, how to properly carry ladders. How to properly stretch hose lines. We had controlled burning. We had search and rescue. We had rappelling from what we used to call the Borden building. We did all the evolutions which made you a Firefighter One at that time.

Sorace: We had sixty in my class. I believe it was sixty guys from Newark. And we had two guys from Millburn that were in our class. We were in Newark's training academy on Jersey Street right down by the river. The first week was sixty guys in it and then the second week thirty of them went out to the field. The top thirty stayed in class. I stayed in the Academy because I was in the top thirty. We were in the Academy a couple of weeks then we went out to the field and the first group came back to the Academy. We were done.

They taught us basically the IFSTA firefighter manual, the basic manual. We covered everything. How the fire department used to be, alarm systems, hose, engine company stuff, truck company stuff, first aid, CPR, basically everything that's firefighter entry level that they learn today. There wasn't too much Haz-mat back then. Now I understand there's a lot more Haz-mat in the Firefighter One program. We did live burns, some live burns in the training tower.

Masters: My class was sixty-two guys and two members of the Milburn Fire Department, Bernie Cunningham and another gentleman. I'm still in touch with him. He's a senior captain up in Millburn. We did four weeks in the Academy. We were so big the Academy couldn't hold all of us so what they did was, the first thirty-one stayed in the Academy and the second class went out into the field for four weeks. I was in class A, the first thirty-one. And then once we graduated, they came back which had its pluses and minuses. When they came back, they thought they were seasoned veterans. It was kind of hard for the instructors. Chief Freda, Captain Duerr, a couple of other gentlemen, Ray Fredette, Bobby Melillo. So, there were little discipline problems with the second class.

They taught us everything you want to know about firefighting as far as what goes on with the engine, the equipment, friction loss, pump pressures, how to calculate if you're going to take three lengths, four lengths, five lengths. How to improvise if something goes wrong on the fire ground. They teach you as a driver, how to get water, always give your company water first. With the truck, they taught you everything with the aerial placement. Two guys always going in with the engine. Two guys do the roof duties as partners. Back then we were the last class to get tiller training. That's what we broke in with. I broke in on Seven Truck with a Seagrave. The majority of guys knew how to tiller. And then once in a while our spare engines were the old Macks where you had to double clutch and all that. I was on the tail end of that.

Goetchius: Well, it was a little strange. We put a week in. They split our class up. There were sixty of us. We put a week in and then they threw us out into the field for I believe it was five weeks. Then brought us back and retrained us for another five weeks. So, we already knew what was going on in the firehouses and how lackadaisical it was. When they brought us back, they tried to make it a paramilitary operation; having us march out in the field, climb the tower every day. So, they tried to put discipline back into us. That was interesting. They kind of gave you the feeling that, don't believe everything that goes on in the field and you have to really keep on your toes at times.

N. Bellina: Well, we had sixty-four guys, so they broke us up into two classes. We all went in for a week and then my classes went out first. The other class stayed in for three weeks I think it was, at the time. We went out to the firehouse, and they just sent you basically anywhere. You weren't doing anything. You were just following, staying with the captain. That was basically it. Depending on the captain that you had, he would bring you inside or would he not bring you inside because they didn't like that idea of you just having a week. But then again, these guys had nothing anyway when they came on.

The week of training was just a bunch of different stuff. It was a whole big pie of the job at the time. I'd say a little bit more of it was towards fires. Because they knew one class was going out. And about the firehouse, the other members you're going to meet on the job and how to act. What to do. If the senior guy tells you to something you do something. You do it. Your thing was to say yes. That was it.

At the end of the week, the class that was going out was shown the mask. They did bring down a pumper or they had one there. We worked with the hose. The ladder, we did put a couple of ladders up to the fire escape on the drill tower. Not too much though because they had sixty-four guys in that one room. So, it was a lot to go through and when we went out to do something all sixty-four went. It wasn't like they broke off the class that was going out first and left the other class in there. I don't think they had the people at the time in the Training Academy to deal with the sixty-four, so they had to take everybody out at one time.

Ch. Centanni: We had a pretty big class, '86 I think we had sixty-four members in our class. It was an election class. So, they were supposed to do nothing. It was a time Sharpe James was taking over for Gibson. So, there was a big political ta-do and right before the election Gibson winds up expanding and hiring a bunch of firefighters and a bunch of police officers. As a matter of fact, I was just with Sammy DeMayo and Anthony Ambrose, the police directors in Newark and we all came on the same time, during that same experience. We all came on that same month of April.

I'm going to recollect the best I can, I think we were a really unique class with that too. I think I was in the Academy for two weeks. They taught us how to use the SCBA, how to put on our turnout gear, what the bells meant and sent us to the field to fill in overtime and vacancies for the summer. Then we came back and completed the Academy. I think it was a total six weeks. But ours was staggered. We did a couple of weeks then we were in the field for a portion of time. Then we came back. They split us in half. Half stayed in the Academy and the other half went to the field. Then they came out to the field, and we went back to the Academy, and we had a graduation at the end.

A lot of the stuff I learned stuck with me my whole career. You learned the basic fundamentals of fighting fire. You learned how the department worked, how to pump a little bit, the operation of hoses, ventilation, and rescue. I think they built our confidence up with a slide to life off the roof of the tower. It was a five-story building. Smokehouse, live burns which were real live burns, class A burns at the time. But some of the things stuck with me forever. Carl Duerr was the captain. He used to say, "Understand the evolution you're involved in. Use common sense with it." I use that with basic size up and a size up to everything I did my whole career. Whether it was on the fire ground or administratively, it really was a good little thing and it stands true today.

Ziyad: Went to the Training Academy, when we did have a real Training Academy down on the water front, the old Training Academy. We actually had one of the largest classes in the history of the fire department. We had sixty-four firefighters in our class, including two from Belleville, that made it sixty-six.

We had two guys from Belleville, first time they had brought in two guys from another city to train with us. So, we had sixty-four people in our class which at that time was the largest class and still might be the largest class in the history of the fire department. They actually put us into the Academy for one week to learn the fundamentals, to learn how to use the SCBA and then they split the class up. I was in the top of the sixty-four. They left thirty-two guys in the Academy and they sent another thirty-two out into the field after they learned to don their gear. They put them in the field. So, for eight weeks we were in the Fire Academy learning, as Captain Duerr said, learning the fundamentals of the job.

We were in the Academy for two months and then they sent us out into the field. We never went back after that. The other half of our class was in the

Academy for one week. We did two months straight. Then I went out into the field on a temporary assignment. The other class came back into the Academy and they had to finish their eight weeks. I can't imagine what that felt like.

It's funny; some people think that it's a job that you have to a vocation for, where you have to be involved, you have to have some experience. Because firefighting is a no experience job. Literally you learn everything. You learn the fundamentals, you learn the science of fire, you learn rescue techniques. You learn what water does, you learn to put the wet stuff on the hot stuff and it goes out. You learn building construction; you learn team work. And you learn things that you didn't think you learned. You learned about the fire engine. You learned how to don or put on the mask and wear the equipment and how to use the equipment. How to do it efficiently.

You learn so many different concepts that involve just leaning on each other and life skills. But the main thing you learn is you learn service to the community. A lot of us with our lack of experience didn't understand actually what firefighters actually are. We think they're these big guys who were just heroes and they just do crazy things. They run into burning buildings. But the reality is, the key of it is you're serving your community. You're serving the citizens of Newark and you're serving people who you don't even know. You're literally putting your life on the line for individuals who are not relatives to you and properties that are not your own property. You learned how to serve, to truly serve a people in a city and your job becomes one of service. Giving up time and giving up your life in some cases. Giving up your health in some cases for people that can't do it themselves. So, you really truly learn what service mean.

Alexander I: I went through the Jersey Street Academy for a total of six weeks. In six weeks, I learned fire science. It was just amazing how much I was taught and how much I was able to retain of what they were teaching. Just learning the fire science, learning first aid, understanding building construction, that was so important. Learning the different tools that firefighters used. The breathing apparatuses, I mean it was intense.

We stretched hose, learned how to operate the engine pumper, learned how to operate the aerial ladders, learned how to climb ladders. Actually, that was my first-time climbing ladders. So, I had a fear that first week. But I had some great instructors and they got me through it. And I never looked back.

Maresca: We had eleven in our class, and it went down to seven very quickly. Three of them were thrown out within four years. And then one was with Webb when Webb died and it kind of shot him and he never came back. They were very good friends and he never recovered after that traumatic incident. I think he went out on stress leave or something.

We were in the Academy October twelfth, and we were out the first week of December. They taught us basically the job. Back then it was a lot of hands-on. As much as I heard growing up, still I didn't know anything about this job. So, they did teach me a lot. We did live burns. Back then it was on Jersey Street, and we had the tower. We used to do live burns with the pallets and the hay and things that you can't do now. The burns were probably a little bit more intense, but it was a good learning experience. It prepared me well for the job.

DeLeon: I went to the Academy on Jersey Street. I had Chief Alfred Freda, Captain Carl Duerr, I believe Damian Emerick had just started the Academy at that time after his accident. Ray Fredette and Bobby Melillo, those were my instructors from seven in the morning. We left about five o'clock. We did everything. At that time, I didn't know exactly what we were doing it for, but we did the housework. They explained what we would do, why we were doing it. And the outcome is when we went to the firehouse that's exactly what we did. So, we were being molded from day one. I was trying to get acclimated. I thought it was just learn, learn, learn and you go to work. You start your job.

It's funny, I still have that notebook somewhere. We learned everything from the Essentials for Firefighter One and Two with the chapters. Every week you do something different. Then we'd go out, we'd do the hands-on. Once we started getting into that, I liked it. I started loving it. I loved the hands-on. All firefighter stuff, turnout coat, you got to put it on quick. This is what it's used for. We had the three-quarter length boots. We didn't have leather helmets, but I didn't even know they had leather helmets. Just had this big black thing which I still have to this day somewhere. The hands-on was fabulous. From there what didn't they show us? They did what they could with what they were allowed to do. We did the slide for life which they stopped doing. Which was going on top of the drill tower, which is not there anymore, hooking up your harness, clipping onto the rope and sliding down to the apparatus. Which was another moment where like alright, this is it. I'm done.

We had the old drill tower in which we did live burns. That was interesting because there were a couple of times where I was pretty far into the second floor when we were doing the live burns and one of the guys would grab my collar and start dragging me out. I'm pushing back in. I'm saying, "What are you doing? What are you doing? Let me go." We had no water. The fire was getting out of control. I didn't understand at that time. So, he did the right thing. I didn't know better. Then he came out, he goes, "You crazy kid?" No. I'm into to this. I like this. We're supposed to do a search. We're supposed to work ladder drills and hose stretching drills. But as far as hooking up to the hydrant and stretch that line, I had full faith that I got water. What's the problem? So, they took it from there and they go, "No kid, get out."

But it was a learning experience. I remember one time they told me, "Okay, don't wake up the captain unless there's a second alarm." That didn't make any sense to me. A second alarm, if I don't leave from the get-go, the captain's going to rip my head off on the house watch. What later I found out was that if they have another fire going on, look at the card, see where you're due, so if you do get the second alarm or they already make it an eleven, doesn't sound good, you have to go wake up the captain. Give him a heads up, what's going on. Later on, I look at my notes, I started laughing. Look at this, I wrote down wake up the captain on the second alarm, but I didn't have any reason as to why or how I should do it. Those things you learned.

Fast forwarding to before I retired. I end up doing an Academy class myself. I was the lead at our instructor level two. I did everything that I was taught plus more because we had a lot more resources. We did the live burns out in Morris County and Union County in a concrete building. So, I used to say, "Eh, that's not fire." Training went all the way down to propane which they use to heat up and a fog machine, they used a fog machine and that was it. And they put palettes, a little bit of hay. I guess the old school got ingrained in me, so when they went to that I was calling people wimps. This is not learning. You need to light stuff up. You need to get a feel for what's going on.

They had a control room and they shut everything down. I guess they looked at the casualties around the country. And they say, "Okay, no more of that. Okay, we're taking that away." They started resisting it and they didn't make it the way it should be. The only thing that was really close to it was the simulator that they had at the Academy where they go in a container. They start a fire. They start a flashover. A couple of guys freaked out and ran away. I tried to grab them, pull them back in. I said, "Where you going? You're running, nothing happened to you." "Look at my helmet. Look at my shield." I think we ended up putting aluminum foil to cover it so they don't have to worry about their shields. Yeah, what a difference.

Taylor: I went to the Academy for six weeks. That's where I met you. They taught us safety, self-safety firefighting. Carl Duerr was there. You were down there. Freddy Shackleford, Chief Freda. Really a great help getting me acclimated to the fire service.

Griggs: My class was I'd say twenty-five to thirty guys. We did six or eight weeks in the Academy and learned basic principles of firefighting and just getting used to being in the firehouse also. We did a lot of marching, ladder raises. They would have companies come down which was nice. They'd have an engine company come down. We'd stretch hose up the tower, a concrete block building, four stories. They were constantly stretching hose, putting up ground ladders which was good. They'd have a ladder company come down. We'd get to meet the companies and they would talk about what to expect in the field. What was going on in the firehouse. We would talk about firehouse life which none of us really were familiar with. They did live burns at the end which was great.

Greene: We did six weeks in the Academy. They taught us very elementary firefighting, how to use an SCBA, how to don and doff the firefighting equipment, through first aid, CPR, ropes, knots, climbing ladders, a little bit about hose, nozzles, nozzle reaction, positioning, saws. Some of it would be chemistry of fire, the effects of fire, smoke, etcetera.

Sperli: I believe when we started the Academy there were around forty guys. And then we had a couple that jumped over to the police department, a couple of other ones that falsified documents about not having a record and they ended up getting caught and taken off the job and residency problems too. At the Academy we got general book work mostly, the basics of firefighting by the books. And they tried to prepare you for the way it's done in the firehouses which is a lot different than the book work.

Alvarez: The Academy was six weeks, exactly six weeks. We had a total of thirty-two in our class. One of the guys was from Maplewood. We were training him in the Academy because Maplewood was a smaller town. They don't hire as many, so he was in the Academy with us. So, it was a total of thirty-two, but thirty-one Newark guys and I believe unfortunately three of them didn't make it to the end. They were taken out. They didn't fail the class, but apparently, they found something in their history, something that didn't coincide with the information they put down on their application.

They taught us the very basics, hose, ladders we had a few engine companies come in. We had ladder companies come in. I think there was one live burn. From what I hear, today they do a lot more. Half the day was classroom work and half was outside. I felt at the time for the number of instructors that it was too many guys for not enough time to be hands-on. They were only using a few guys to do certain evolutions and that's all you could use. You didn't really get the hang of it.

They didn't break them up in teams. They didn't have teams like the Academy now. Now there are a blue team, red team, green team and they break them up because for a while there they were going out of town. They were actually splitting them up into academies in two different counties. Their academy class is longer. It seems like they're a little bit more prepared as far as academy wise than when I was there. There were just too many guys for too few instructors to handle the hands-on evolutions. In the classroom everything was fine, but the actual hands-on itself it lacked.

Cordasco: We went to the Academy for six weeks. It was actually pretty funny because Wayne Linfante and I went through the Police Academy. We were on the police for four and a half years when we switched over. So, for Wayne and I it was actually pretty fun. Learning the stuff was good, but we were like two of the guys everybody looked up. A couple of funny stories, it was Carl Duerr's last Academy class. He was very knowledgeable, but he was very strict. He would bust everybody's chops for their pants, their shirts and stuff. So, one day he calls me out and he goes, "Cordasco." You had to stand up and say, "Recruit Cordasco". So, I stood up. I go, "Yes, sir." He goes, "Are they your police shoes?" Because you had to have the oxfords and I had diehard Sears highlights. I said, "Yes sir."

"Alright, sit down." Usually, he made us go to Katzin's or Lee's right there to get the right uniform. And they go, "How come he didn't make you go?" "Eh, privileges." We had a lot of fun.

That December it was freezing. A lot of our outside activities were canceled. We actually had zero-degree weather the one week. We watched officers training films because it was actually too cold to go outside, and they had nothing else for us to do. Actually, there were a couple of nice days, so we were doing water and Joe D'Alise, who was a fireman still at the time, was down there. We did the water, and we were breaking down the hoses. Back then we had the three-quarter boots and Wayne, not on purpose, he got water in Joe D'Alise's boots. Joe was pissed because they take forever to dry. So he goes, "That's it. You and Linfante. You're not getting paid this week." Since we had flipped over from the police, our checks were the only ones that were never right in the Academy. I remember we got a check for a dollar ten. So, he had seen our checks that day and he had said, "That's it. You're getting nothing." The checks came and it was like a dollar ten, a dollar fifteen each. We had to wait for Kenny Blaha to bring manual checks our whole Academy time.

Another funny Academy thing is because it was so cold, we weren't really doing anything. It was one Friday afternoon; we're sitting in the classroom for like an hour. It was two thirty to three fifteen, three thirty. So, I went to the bathroom and all the instructors are just hanging out in the one room. So, I come back in. I fix my books. I push the chair in. I look at the guys. I give them the thumbs up. Said, "We're up." I put my jacket on and I walk out the door. So, they're all looking. Now we had to park over by the smoke house. They're all watching me walking. I know they're all looking at me, but I'm not looking back. I walk to my car. I get in my car. I see them because now I'm facing them. He's really leaving? I pull around to the front door; I flip them all the bird; and I take off up Jersey Street. I sit at the top of Jersey Street. I see them all running to their cars. So, they're all getting into their cars and they're all taking off. Monday morning, we come in and one of the guys is looking for me. He got in trouble. He got caught leaving. So, he comes up to me. "Matty, I got caught leaving on Friday." I said, "Alright." He said, "They want me to do a report." I said, "Alright, do your report." He says, "Well, I have to put that you told us we were up." And I turned to him, and I said, "You put me in that report I'm throwing you in the river." So, what he did was he put in the report he had to drive one of the guys home. That's why he left early.

We had a good time in the Academy and guys liked it. We were in for Christmas and New Year, so we actually had a little lunch time party. It was with the instructors. We set it up. We did some basketball because they had the two squads, A and B squad. I set up basketball games down at River Bank Park. So, we had a good time in the Academy.

Daniels: It was twenty-six of us. We were all gung-ho, fantasizing about working together. We got that far, still had no clue. Even though we were in the Academy we still had no clue.

I want to say we were there three weeks. No longer than four, but I'm pretty sure it was three weeks. They made a big deal out of it too. There's never been another class that stayed in the Academy and did three hard weeks. They were out marching us all the time. We were a bunch of guys that don't know anything, we were all standing at attention, uniforms worn and making sure we were right because the Academy had those kinds of requirements. But I'll tell you what; I enjoyed my time through the Academy. Some of those people that brought me through, like Chief Freda, Puffy Freda, I admired Puffy very much. He didn't know me that well, but I just thought that he's so cool and calm about everything. Fred Shackleford was hard, but he really wanted the best for you. Chief Jones at the time was chief of the department. So, there were just a lot of people who really poured into us and it made an impact for me.

We learned fire dynamics. They gave us tests all the time. They used to have the old smokehouse and at the time that was what we were using. We got the basics of how to do the job, just giving us some ideas. There are things that they taught me that saved my life in a lot of situations. So, I learned how to take care of myself. I really learned how. They made sure. Those basic skills of teamwork, that was good. Relying on everybody and pulling your weight. The instructors used to say that our job is to make sure that everyone goes home at the end of the day. And then they said, not only do you have to trust the captain to look out for you, but you have to look out for yourself. You need to make sure you understand how to do a size up and understand what you're looking at, reading smoke. I used that stuff and I taught that stuff when I was a captain to my crew. It has saved my life and it was based upon stuff that I learned in the Academy. You can't learn this stuff any place else. I had no previous experience with any of this. I really learned how to learn, observe, and do the job. The skills, the basic skills that they gave me to start off with are just as important from the beginning of my career to even now in the middle of my career.

LaPenta: My class was like twenty-five-ish, around there. I think we had like seven vets. I had a guy from Maplewood taking our class. Then a couple of guys towards the end got booted out for whatever reason. I think someone lied on their application and someone had a criminal record that they didn't mention. So, I think we were close to like twenty-three when we graduated finally.

My Academy was like six weeks at best. They taught us basic firefighting knowledge. I was into the fire department, and I had friends on the fire department in Newark and in New York City. I was reading trade magazines and I had the old timers here in Newark giving me their old books. Read McAniff's book on this and read Clarke's book on that. So, I was home, not even on the job yet reading about this stuff. When we got into the Academy there was this tall guy, he had curly hair, used to be a fireman at Six Engine, great guy. No names but I think his name is Neal, but they taught us basic stuff. I mean they were just really introducing us to the world of firefighting.

I think that most people that come into this profession, they're car salesmen or they worked in a retail store and sometimes it's culture shock. "Oh my God, I can't believe I'm doing this." They showed us a video of guys getting injured on the job. It was a safety video. You've got guys getting electrocuted and guys blowing themselves up. You see people in the classroom, "Oh my God I'm signing up for this? You're only paying how much to kill myself?" So, the first couple of days they come in. They yell at you. They're trying to teach you respect and how to work together as a team. Firefighting is a team job. You have to have respect for the officers, respect for each other. But basically, it was just drilling in how to do the job safely. Stretch lines safely, learn how to raise ladders safely, going over the general orders, teaching us about friction loss and nozzle pressure and how to use hand tools properly. It's probably more involved today than it was when I came on the job because of certain standards, the State gets involved in there which is good. It's a good thing. But back then it was basic. It was just; here it is; here's the job. Do it and when you get in the field then you're going to get why. Even when I came on, we got a lot of experience.

Tarantino: To be honest with you, I can't remember learning anything. There are certain things on the fire department I really just don't remember. I remember there was a lot of classwork. I remember that Puffy Freda was our commandant and Carl Duerr was the guy who was doing everything. But our class was that class that if you remember with the judge's decree, they were going to throw the list out. There wasn't the right racial mix, so Judge Politan declared the city a state of emergency and they put together two lists. So, it was my class in August and the December class. And then they got rid of the list. It was fast. From when I took the physical to where I came on the job was ten months. I mean it was very fast. Guys wait years. It was immediate for me. I think Duerr took his vacation. He really wasn't even there. Eli Savarese ran the whole thing and Eli's no stickler for stuff so we kind of really didn't do much. We learned how to use a mask and I remember rappelling. I remember raising the ladder with the Bangor poles. I remember raising that. I don't remember doing any first aid at all, not one thing of first aid. We did a lot of marching. I remember doing a lot of marching.

West: My class I believe was twenty-three people. I went to the Academy on Jersey Street. Coming from a volunteer department, I knew sort of the basics, but certainly nothing coming to a big city department. Almost hard to describe the wide range of different topics that you learn in a big city academy. Dragging hose, throwing ladders, truck work, engine work some small EMS stuff, CPR, but certainly your days were filled with different things down there. There were not many quiet days during the Academy.

Pierson: We did three weeks in the Academy on Jersey Street. They taught us how to stretch lines. Don and doff your mask and put your turnout gear on. A little bit about ventilation. And we had to rappel down the old fire tower. Did a couple of live burns. Out of the Academy I was assigned to Five Truck. It was only temporary. I did the summer at Five Truck. It was two to three months. Then we had to go back in for one week and then they put us back out to a full-time assignment.

Petrone: I came on with a class of twenty-nine, maybe thirty. Something like that, it was somewhere in that neighborhood, and went to the Academy on Jersey Street. For the most part they taught us to put on our masks. Harry Carter, I think was the commandant. And Captain Wargo was one of the training officers and Captain Jack Camasta was one of the training officers. Basically, from their experiences, if you can put on your mask, everything else you'll learn in the field. You're going to go to fires. Everything taught down there was part of the curriculum. But they were big on explaining to you that all this stuff in the books is great if the fire read the book. Since fire didn't read the book, it did whatever it wanted, you're going to have to learn it in the field. You learn it from guys who have lots of experience and basically that's what we did. So, they more or less taught us to put on our masks. We had to get through a confined space by taking off the mask, pushing the mask ahead of you while you're still wearing the mask. For the most part they taught you the ABCs of fire. Like I said, they were big on trial by fire. Get out there; guys out there will teach you.

Castellucio: Went to the Academy on Jersey Street. They taught us how to don our masks. We did a lot of that. Ladder raises, we actually did a live burn, we did search and rescue in the smokehouse. It was pretty good. It should have probably been a lot longer. But they taught us the basics and said when you get out into the field, your captain's going to teach you and you'll learn.

Of course, they had a captain's exam, and they didn't want to pay the overtime, so they put us out on a Saturday. The city skated because I think the only thing that came in was a car fire and a small brush fire in Branch Brook Park. And here you had forty red-ass firemen who had absolutely no clue what we were doing.

Snyder: We had forty-nine guys. We had Captain Pignato as a training captain. You came in a couple of times and Chief Nasta broke his leg, so he gave a lot of classes. We were in the Academy on Jersey Street for eight days. They did do one day where they came into the field and then they came back to the Academy. There was a big fire on Route 21. There was a big factory. So, they brought everybody out and we did probie stuff. What stuck with me was a lot of dangerous stuff, whether it's chemicals or using foam. But I can honestly say I never even turned on a hydrant in the Academy. I never did it. When I got to my first job, I was hoping I'm doing this right. I didn't want to sound stupid and ask. So, I kind of figured it out. It's common-sense stuff. You have common sense on this job, you'll do fine. When they sent us out it was about getting guys into the field. They needed guys. The State law said you're Firefighter One, you're a fireman. It didn't take that long. Now it takes like six weeks.

Bartelloni: I'm not sure of the exact number of guys in my class, but we were definitely anywhere from forty to forty-five people, somewhere in that neighborhood. We went to the Academy for two weeks and to tell you the truth, I think they did a great job for two weeks. They did go through everything that you'd be pretty much doing in the field. But there's nothing like the field, the real world. You know when I think back on it, what they taught really did pertain to the nuts and bolts, with the engines, pumping, climbing aerials, saws. We put fires out, car fires, which at that time there were tons of. But they prepared you as best they could in that two-week period and then we went to the field.

Gail: I went to the Academy for three weeks. In the Academy we learned a lot of book stuff. They taught us raising ladders, dragging hose, pulling hose off trucks. They taught more how Newark did things versus how the industry standard was. I think that's changed a lot. Now it's a lot more the industry standards. Then they tried to combine a little bit of both. Now they try to give you the industry standard and say Newark does it a little different because we have this type of building and because we have this type of truck. They try to adapt it to the equipment and the infrastructure we have here. They taught us a lot of the physical stuff, a lot of pulling hose and packing hose, climbing stairs, and climbing ladders with all your gear and equipment. It wasn't difficult. I don't remember it being difficult at all. I was only twenty-two years old, so I was in pretty good shape. But it was minimal. They didn't teach you a lot. No hazardous materials, no weapons of mass destruction no blood borne pathogens, none of that stuff. It was really pull hose lines. When it starts getting hot open up the hose line. That's what it was. And they taught you how to put on your SCBA. They spent a lot of time on that. That was important. Other than that, there wasn't a lot of standard stuff to teach. It wasn't the curriculum from the state like there is now. But they got you to the point where you could operate in the fire department in Newark. There was a lot of on-the-job stuff. As soon as we came out of the Academy, I went to Vailsburg for one day and then the captain there said keep trying on your SCBA. Keep doing it. He went over a lot of stuff. I think at that time in the fire department a lot of the stuff was learned on the job, more than the Academy. The Academy gave you the very basic and when you went out in the field you stuck with the officer and the apparatus. You learned on the job. It was a great way to learn.

Ostertag: We only had twelve guys. Twelve and one guy left. He was a cop, he came as a fireman, and he went back to the cops after his first fire. Third Battalion, caught a good job with a truss roof, went back to the police after that. But we were in the Academy two weeks.

They taught us basic firefighting, no Haz-mat, no special hazard stuff, nothing specialized, like ropes and rigging or the airport. None of that stuff.

Ramos: When I went to the Academy there were twelve of us. My illustrious Academy lasted only three weeks. It was classroom work, books, the regulations, the proper way to use the equipment, hose, ladders, power tools. That was probably for the first week, then the second week we went outside and worked with different apparatus, different hose, different lengths, different dimensions, raising ladders, rescue situations, scenarios, things like that, the smokehouse. That was about it, your basic Academy stuff. It wasn't as strict as today. Today it's more set in military style where they march you. Ours was more relaxed, maybe because it was just twelve. That was a different situation. It was more relaxed.

Richardson: Yes, twelve of us and one guy went back to the police after getting burned at his first fire he went in. He was on Rescue. He burned his ears, and he was like, forget this. He was a cop. He had come over from the police department. He took a leave of absence from the police department, burned his ears. He went back to the police department. He's like a deputy chief over there now, so that was probably better for him. But there's only eleven of us left on the job.

They gave you all your safety. You knew exactly how to stretch the line, how to put on your gear, how to put on you SCBA, tactics of how to get out of situations, tactics of how not to get into situations, most of all keep your mouth shut, listen to the guys that are ahead of you and have the knowledge. I had the benefit of coming on the '90s and still having the guys that were from the '70s and the '80s. I had that knowledge with me that these new guys don't have, but all the books and everything and the fire tactics and the fire tetrahedron and all that kind of stuff. That all is great to know, but it's not the knowledge that you get when you're on the fire ground and you're stretching that line in and you're taking that roof and you're cutting it and what's really happening in real life. It's very hard to teach in the Academy. They give you the outline and the basics of it. But it's true. Learning is really on the outside. They went through all the books, and they gave you all that base knowledge that you needed. So, it was tough. We had live burns, but you didn't have all technology you have today for the teaching. The tradition and everything were bestowed upon you in the Academy and they explained that to you. What that tradition was and what the fire department meant. Besides learning how to be safe and how to use the equipment they were giving you, but you got a lot of good tradition stuff.

Jackson: I want to say we were in the Academy for twelve weeks. They taught us what I think at the time was Firefighter One. There was also the hands-on aspect of it. It was a pleasure for the department to have their own academy on Jersey Street. So, we were able to do a lot of practicals. We had live burns. We had the smoke house, and we had the open space so we could do more things. I learned a lot there. That was the turning point for me because coming on, me doing a career where people are leaving the building and you're going in. It doesn't sit well with a person who's sitting on the outside who hasn't been to the Academy. Who doesn't have family members on the job. Who hasn't experienced it. But your first time going through in a live burn situation or your first time crawling around in a dark building where you can't see anything, your first time having to trust another person or multiple people and one another. You're either going to love it or hate it.

Y. Pierre: I believe we were in the Academy eight weeks. They covered everything. Things that I never would have dreamed of. The ladders, hose lines, pressure, hydraulic pressure, raising a ladder, how to get smoke out of a building. We were so low it didn't make any sense. We didn't learn anything because there was so much happening. We were thinking to ourselves, "Oh my God, that's what this job is all about? I don't think this is a good job for me." We went through the first live burn, I was like, "Oh my God, oh no we don't need this." I was a Marine, but Marines don't play like that. We shoot at each other. We shoot at other people. But getting burnt alive is just a different scenario. It's just a whole different scenario. I'm sorry to say. No, no comparison. As a Marine, you know, you got one shot, one kill okay. Get the enemy before he gets you okay. But running into a burning building and you're just getting cooked alive just did not make any sense. That did not make any sense at all.

Farrell: There were eighteen in my class. We were mostly appeals. They went roughshod through our list and just booted guys just by what their name might be. To tell you the truth, they never even had an appeal on me. I never even went to the first level of appeals. I had to go and hire a lawyer, but they put me back on that next list that we got on a year later. I thought all eighteen were appeals, but there were a couple of guys that actually weren't appeals. I think probably sixteen out of the eighteen guys were just appeals from the class the one year previous. They just ran roughshod through and said let them fight their way back on. They had nothing on me. I was born and raised, grammar school, high school, college, my jobs from the Foodtown on Mount Prospect Avenue to Kaslander Lumber, everything was in Newark. My father was on the job thirty years. They were searching for a certain something back then. That was the big transition period where they were really making a push and they just didn't like the make-up of our list. They just ran roughshod though it to get the numbers they wanted and unfortunately, I was one of those casualties. But I fought and I stuck to it.

I know a lot of guys who didn't have the resources to fight through it. And probably never took this job because they didn't know somebody on the job who could help them through that process. That's where United Civil Servants came in for me. I joined them as an associate member of the United Civil Servants to help me through that process. If I didn't know them or if I didn't get contacted by them, I would have probably just kind of shrugged my shoulders. If I didn't have a background in the fire service, I would have probably shrugged my shoulders and said, "Okay, I didn't get called." I never got called. Why? I wouldn't have known until I got that letter from Trenton which came months later, too late to fight. But I knew what was going on, so we started the fight early and that's how I got back on. So, I fought for this job. Nothing handed to you. It makes me appreciate it more sometimes. I came out number forty-eight on a list of so many thousands and got bypassed. I was going against twenty, twenty-one-year-old guys at thirty-one years old, I think I earned it.

I think we did eight weeks in the Academy. Now they do a little bit longer. They go twelve weeks now because they do Haz-mat and stuff. We only went eight weeks, and we were longer than a lot of the classes before us. Years ago, they used to go in for a couple of weeks and then they threw you in the field. You did a lot of on-the-job training. We went for eight weeks in the Academy. It was a great Academy. It was a great class. We did really well. Honestly, to this day I think we had the highest test score, average test score of any class. To this day, I don't think anybody's surpassed us yet and that's twenty years ago.

You learned out of a book. You learned out of the IFSTA book. This is how you carry a hose-line. This is how you raise a ladder. They teach you firefighting out of a book, like they're supposed to. I guess that's the legal way of doing it. When you get to the field you realize it's done a little bit differently. I mean they taught us everything we really needed to know. We did a lot of live burns. We still had the old Academy down on Jersey Street. We had the old smokehouse and then the old tower. We were doing rappelling. They had us really active. That was the best part of it. The hands-on training because this job is mostly hand-on.

Roberson: We had thirty-five guys in my class. My class was named after Marcus Reddick who died in a fire rescuing a woman out of a window. She fell on top of him. She survived and he passed. We actually hung a helmet up in his honor. We learned the mechanics and the basics of fighting a fire. How a fire starts, how it reacts to different things. How it spreads. The literary part of the class was great. We actually benefitted from great instructors, Chief Nasta, Chief Donnelly, Chief DeCeuster, who was a captain at the time. The practical was even better. I wound up finishing second in my class academically, behind James Costa who is a chief now. And the physical part was great. I mean they had us in the smokehouse. We were fighting fires. It taught you the basic principles of fighting a fire and also surviving in a fire. Because the principles are life first, then building. Then everybody goes home safe.

Meier: There was a June and July class, back-to-back classes in the summer of '96. And I was in the second class. I remember it was thirty-five guys. We went through the Academy in six weeks.

We learned a lot. It was good. We learned overall firefighting skills and the ins and outs of being a Newark fireman. My father being a fireman, it was very easy for me. The guys from Irvington always looked up to Newark and I always looked up to Newark. It was a big city, so I got a lot out of it.

Rodrigues: My class was thirty-three guys, and we went to the Academy on Jersey Street for twenty-eight days. They taught us fire behavior, engine company operations, ladder company operations, obviously sexual harassment, blood borne pathogens. I remember we did a lot of hands-on outside and live burns. We also did rappelling back then.

Montalvo: In our class there were twenty-one men. All of us finished the Academy, all of us together. We did the Academy in twelve weeks. They taught us all the basics of firefighting. We started off with written questions for the Firefighter One exam. We started studying for that. And then we did a series of live burns, went through the smokehouse, basic EMS, basic Haz-mat. We did that for twelve weeks.

Willis: My class was thirty-five. There was supposed to be thirty-seven. Two people I think had problems. They were removed, so there were thirty-five of us. We went through. Everybody went together. We worked with each other. It was really fun. Got to make a lot of friends. The chief, all the instructors, everybody. I miss them. I miss Ray Frost. Ray Frost was a good guy. Died young. And a few other guys that are gone that were there. Chief Snyder, he's a good guy. Tough on me, but he meant well, and you learn from that. All of those guys, they were good.

My wife always makes fun of me. She says, "I don't know how you guys learn your job." Total when we went through, counted it on the calendar, it was seventeen days. When she totaled everything, counting ceremonial, it was about twenty days. More or less here's your equipment, you're going to learn your job real quick out there. It was an interesting first month.

We learned the basics, the fire department, a few of the rules. Some were on the books. Some were off the books. How to enter the firehouse was a big thing and that was off the books. The guys would talk to us. You knew it was something not to talk about. Other than that, Chief McGovern did a good job with Haz-mat coming in from Rescue One. He wound up being my chief when I came into the field. Chief Connell was really good. He was a good instructor, and he was fair. We had Sadrud-din, spoke softly, but he meant well. Chief Snyder, strict on knots. We had to pass with knots, or we weren't getting out of there. You had to learn all this stuff quick.

We stretched hose. We did live burns. We had our own Academy at that time, so it was easy for them to do everything right there. We had to march. Marching was a big part of it, structure, jogging. Other than that, it was pretty much learn as you go. They gave us the instruments and tools. We went out there and played the chords.

Highsmith: I went through the Newark Academy on Jersey Street. We were there possibly six weeks. Somebody made a comment about, do we have to go in the fire. If we feel it's unsafe, do we have to go in? And that got passed around the fire department. And they gave us an extra week of the Academy because of that comment. The first thing was I learned it's not as paramilitary as I thought it would be. Me being a military guy, I was looking forward to it, a paramilitary situation. I found that it wasn't. So, I couldn't show off my skills. The class itself as far as basic firefighting with Chief Sereico, Captain Stoffers, Chief Connell, I thought the class went very well. I tried to come out on top, but I missed academic top by one, two, three points. I trained with ladders, hoses. We did a couple of live burns.

Freese: Our class was thirty-four guys. I went through the old Academy on Jersey Street. That used to be the Newark Fire Department Academy. If I recall correctly, it was like eight weeks.

They started with a bunch of paperwork first, obviously. That's important, but they started with your basic fire science and basic firefighting tactics and stuff like that. And then we got some practical and hands-on evolutions. Stretching lines, pumping, putting ladders up, and eventually we graduated to live burns which is probably the most exciting part. Where you actually gear up completely and they light up a couple of pallets for you and you go in there with a couple of lines and put the fire out. That was it. After that they assigned you and you went out to the field.

Carr: I went to the Academy on Jersey Street. I had this interesting gentleman as my safety officer in the Academy for the Academy class. His name happened to be Captain Stoffers I believe.

We were in the Academy I think for about ten to twelve weeks. Because we left and went in the field for a while and then came back. Then we resumed and then we went to our graduation. I remember having twisted dread locks in my hair when I came on. And we went out into the field, and I saw what the guys have. So, when I came back, prior to us having to have the graduation ceremony, I had to cut them off. So, basically what I did was I did cut them off, but I cut them off all around the side. So, when I had my bell cap on, you couldn't really see them. In all the pictures of the Academy whenever there was a graduation, they never had to take their bell caps off. They always kept them on, but ours we had to take them off. When I went up to get the certificate, Sharpe James touched my hair. "Oh, I like this." Chief Connelly was pissed. He was looking for me after that, but I was gone. I was already assigned to roving on the third tour.

In the Academy, first we had First Responders' training. We had Firefighter One, the Essentials. We were told leaving the Academy that we weren't going to be trained firefighters. We were going to be trainable. That was the goal for us. To make sure we had the skills necessary to be competent and to be able to accept and understand once we got out in the field. You guys did a great job in giving us everything we needed. You were the good cop. You made sure that we were safe. You overlooked our safety when we did drills. I remember we had a drill over by West Bigelow. I think we had to do the roof ladder drill. Chief Nasta was the training officer for the drill. And I thought you looked like, "Oh my God, just please let everybody do their one round and get off this roof." But it was fun. It was good because I tell people all the time when it comes to heights, you don't have to be afraid of heights. Just have a lot of respect for them and you'll be fine.

Rosario: We were the last class, the class of thirty-five, to go through the Newark Fire Academy on Jersey Street. We were there for fourteen weeks. It was one of the longest classes. It was a bigger class and they wanted to make sure everything was on the up. So, when the guys were ready to take the written test for the State to be certified as Firefighter One, everybody was prepared. I didn't have to take it for Newark because I already had my Firefighter One and Two from Harrison. So, they wanted to make sure that they were prepared for that. Plus, it's such a large class, to get all the practicals, working the ladders, working the engines, doing the searches, actual fires. It took a little longer because it was such a big class. I'd say it was like thirteen, fourteen weeks. And then everybody's pretty much prepared, ready to go to the field by then.

They first started off with your basic fire sciences, your tetrahedron, just explain it to you. When you come in there, most people don't understand what the fire service really is. It's just a job they applied for and got called for and now they get in and they have to learn the actual job. So, it starts off very basic with the uniforms, what they're there for, what they protect, how to don your equipment, how to properly use it, especially in an emergency situation. Then they teach you exactly what's fire, the behavior of fire, how it travels, how more effectively to fight it. Then they expect you to use all the equipment you will be using. Your hose lines, your hooks, your axes, how to effectively use those. How effectively to sit on a roof and operate to do vertical ventilation. And why you ventilate. So, all that is just layers and layers and layers until you get to the point where you can go on to the fire ground and not get hurt. Because you're not going to know anything. You're pretty much a baby out of the mother's womb when you're first come out of the Academy and into the field. You start learning from mostly the firemen that have been there for a while. But at least it gets you a foundation so you can start building your career from there.

Kupko: We had forty-eight in my class. They taught us pretty much everything we needed to know. They went over the Newark way as opposed to the book way. There were certain things you would read in the book that weren't necessarily how it would go in the real world. So, it was a matter of drawing conclusions and pulling information from both of the things that you could and use it as a practical application going forward.

I don't recall exactly how many weeks we were in the Academy. I know we had to spend an extra week or two because we had people that had a hard time passing Firefighter One. I remember doing donning and doffing drills for time with turnout gear and everything like that, anything to keep us busy at the end. Until they got everybody up to speed, up to code sort of speak.

Mickels: I went to the Academy. I'm going to guess it was twelve weeks. I believe it was about twelve weeks. They taught us all the basics and fundamentals of firefighting. The five types of building constructions, how fire starts, the methods of extinguish, extinguishing agents along with water and other different forms of foam, things like that. Practical exercises when it comes to ladders, extrication tools, meters. We learned how to be very respectful to senior officers. That this was a para-military organization, so we had to learn to respect our superiors, even when it came to our dressing, our shaving, our face, things like that. So, we learned how to be polished. The Academy taught us how to be that way. And one of the things that I remember too from you, personally from you was gloves. You kept saying, "Leave your gloves on. You're going to have to work with your gloves. Stop taking your gloves off because you're going to have to work with them. And still today your words echo in my mind when sometimes I want to take off my gloves. I'll leave them on because I remember you always said leave your gloves on, you're going to have to work with them. Even if they're wet, you have to leave them on. So those are some of the things that I learned how to do in the Fire Academy.

Gaddy: We went to Morris County. We pretty much outsourced at the time. I came on in Mayor Booker's first class. So, we had everything outsourced at that time. We didn't have what they have now with Newark being the head of the firefighters. We were in Morris County. We had Chief Sereico as the Newark representative and he was pretty much in charge. But the guys that ran the Morris County Fire Academy, they oversaw all the criteria. We went to the Bergen County Fire Academy for live burns. Pretty much that's all we did at Bergen that one day. That was our only class trip. And after that it was graduation.

We ran every day. I believe it was like three miles a day. Nothing compared to the troopers. We had troopers with us. That was pretty much it. It was nothing like Newark. They were more military there. Newark is now starting to get up to par, from the last two classes up there they're getting better as time goes on, but nothing like Morris County and Bergen. They had things a little bit more incorporated. We did two and a half months at least. They taught us Firefighter One and Two. Stretching lines, throwing ladders, simple, just fire one, fire two. We did propane, burnings. We did search and rescue. We did safety. Breathing techniques, how to skip breathe, how to conserve your air, how not to allow your tank to freeze on you from overexerting yourself and breathing too fast. Learning ranks.

Jenkins: My class was thirty-five, thirty-six in the class and we were in the Academy for eight weeks. They taught us about fire, how to fight fires through live burns. They taught us how to tie knots to hoist tools from the ground to different levels. They taught us also how to prepare for the day when you come into the firehouse, how to check the equipment to see everything's in order. How to check that your SCBA works, and you're protected. And they also taught you how to intertwine with the company.

Figuereq: We had about forty-eight. So, they split us into two classes. They sent half of us to Morris, The other half to Bergen. We had two months, about eight weeks in the Academy. They went through Firefighter One every day, but they had hands-on training. During the morning we pretty much hit the books, went over some scenarios and then in the afternoon we went out. They had an academy in the back with propane tanks and everything. We were there for about eight weeks. I think the Newark Academy, the new one, the last two classes they're doing here right on Orange Street, have done training at night. We did not. Back in oh six when I went, we only had day training.

Medina: My class was originally fifty and only forty-six guys are on the job now. We got to forty-seven, three dropped out. Two dropped out of the Academy. Actually, they were here on Springfield Avenue. Six Engine was on Ninth Street then. One of them was here a week and left. He never came back the second week. But this kid's actually on the job now. He took the test some years later and is on the job a year and a half, two years. He was one of them. There was a guy in our class, a month in he didn't like the mask. He dropped out in the Academy. And then probably two months after we graduated one of the guys, he was actually a Newark cop, he didn't like going into a fire so he dropped out. So, let me rephrase that, forty-eight graduated out of fifty, then one dropped out after we got on.

We went to Bergen County. They split the class. Twenty-five went to Bergen, the other twenty-five went to Morris County. And I believe we were the first class to ever go out. We had Bergen County instructors. But Chief Nasta also taught us there, so we saw him regularly. So, they did it sort of the book way and then they threw some Newark stuff in there. We'd do class work and then we'd go outside. We'd do search and rescue, stretch lines. We also did flashover, the pan, we did that. We did smokehouse. We did a lot of that.

Coming from Bergen County into Newark, it's different. It's totally different and they tell you that it's Academy stuff. We'll teach you, our way. And then when you're there, you're ruled by their rules. I guess we were the first class. There was a class that was hired four and a half, five years before us, so there were a lot of empty spots.

Dugan: My class started at fifty and ended at forty-seven. It was the first year that they sent people out. There was no more Newark Academy. So, I went to Morris County, twenty-five of us went to Morris County, twenty-five went to Bergen County's Academy for eight weeks. While I was there one kid felt he would rather go back to working his City Hall job. So, he went to his City Hall job. When we first got together, we all had to go to Six Engine on Springfield Avenue. It was an empty firehouse at the time. While we were there, the first few days they had senior captains and firemen come and talk to us. And I believe it was Fire Chief Centanni who came by with his helmet was all burnt up. One of the kids in the class got second thoughts about being a fireman and he quit. But he actually just came on the job again because he realized the mistake he made. He came on two classes ago maybe. So that's how we lost those two people. And then when we graduated the Academy the one kid went back to the police department after one day and went out on stress leave. He was able to do that because just before he got into the fire academy, he got into a shootout. He wasn't able to go out on stress leave because he went to the fire academy. Then he maybe did two shifts in the firehouse, wanted to go back to the police department and then was able to go out on disability.

At Morris County we did have Chief Sereico. He was one of the instructors. We had a few, but he was the one Newark instructor that we did have. Surprisingly, we didn't get any specialized training for the airport or the Port Newark. Even when we came into the field, they're asking me what's a signal ten and all this. They didn't really go over all the signals or how Newark operates. It was all Firefighter One, Firefighter Two, by the book type stuff. It wasn't until I got to South Ninth Street that I started to learn all the different calls and what they meant. It was more by the book and not the Newark way.

K. Alfano: Well, we had a total of fifty in my class at the beginning. We went to Engine Six on Springfield Avenue. It wasn't opened up yet, but that's where we went. They had a few chiefs come in and give the spiel about the job. A few other guys came in and told us how it was that you could get burned. One of the chiefs brought in a helmet from when they were first doing the flashover simulator in Bergen County. The first guys who did it didn't know how close they were, and I guess their helmets melted a little bit. One of the kids after hearing that quit. Another guy we had from the police department came over and he said it wasn't busy enough. But I think he had other issues going on too.

I went to Morris County Academy with Morris County instructors. We had Chief Lee with us. He was a captain at the time. They sent over a few captains; they had to be in the class. We had Captains Lee and Magnusson there with us. I guess there were other captains that went to Bergen because they split our class in half. Half went to Morris County, twenty-five of us went up there and then the other went to Bergen County. I forget how many weeks I was in the Academy, somewhere around twelve weeks.

We learned everything about the book. They taught us Firefighter One. We did a lot of classroom work. We just learned about the books, about firefighting, the type of structures you would be going into, the different stuff with the fire truck, different hose that you're going to be doing. They showed us things we would see out in the field the last couple of weeks and then they were like, "Alright, you're going back to your city. They'll teach you the rest there." They just gave us most of the book work, made sure we passed the test. Compared to what I'm hearing from the kids that are in our Academy, they still got to learn the books here, but up at the Morris County Academy, they're more concerned with the books than actually getting out in the field and doing hose stretches. We had very few live burns up there. We went to Bergen County with the flashover simulator. At the time the live burn house they had in Morris County, after having all the live burns in there, the concrete was spalling. They were supposed to be getting a new one. The place was in shambles, but at the end we had a few in there. Not too many, probably like you could count on my hand.

M. Bellina: We had nineteen people in my class and went to Morris County. Everything was in Morris. We didn't have any instructors from Newark. We just had a Newark captain monitor us, but like he didn't teach any classes. I'm not sure how many weeks. I just know when we were there, there was a police class in the academy. We got out before them and it annoyed them. But I don't know. I don't remember how many weeks it was, to be honest with you. It didn't seem that long. It was at least two or three months.

They taught you the basics like Firefighter One. Honestly it was a different world once we got out of the academy. So, you learn the facts, the foundation, but once we got out into the field you learned what everything meant. You can't really visualize in the academy or experience it, so it was tough. It wasn't because of the Morris County instructors. It's like anything else. You can learn as much as you want, even if you went to college, in a specific field, but you get in that field and you're actually doing it hands-on it's a different way.

B. Maresca: I think we had thirty guys in my class. We went to the Academy on Orange Street in Newark; I want to say about twelve weeks. We did live burns, a lot of practical, and a lot of stuff in the classroom. Practical meaning hose, ladders, putting on SCBAs, we had a lot of stretching lines. The live burns we did in Linden with Newark instructors.

G. Centanni: I went to the Academy on Orange Street for twelve weeks. We had forty-two people in our class. We had two veterans and the rest were just regular Joes. That was because the vet class was before us and they got all them in.

We learned all the basics, all the book work and then they gave us the Newark way to do things. And we learned all the Newark way when we got out of the Academy. We had a live burn. We went to Linden, in their burn house. We did a couple of live burn scenarios. They had a four story. We cut the roof, cut power, stuff like that.

G. Pierre: In my class we had about twenty-six people at the end of it. I think we started off with like twenty-nine. The first guy that fell off, I don't know who he was. I don't remember seeing him. I was in front of the class, first in class, pencil, pen, and paper. We had a second guy. I do remember the second guy. I don't remember his name, but there were two guys that were out the first three weeks in the Academy. The first guy was out maybe the first week, week and a half in the Academy. He was out. The second guy got kicked out like maybe a week after that. And I think it was more focused on the matter of getting to class on time, don't be tardy. Firefighting is really serious, so don't be tardy. Make sure you had your stuff; make sure you're in your uniform, etcetera. I don't think the guys met the mark early on. The next guy he got real mouthy with the chief. His mom was like a council woman or something. He was talking like I'm already in. And the bad part about it was he was a big guy. He's obese, always talking about working out. Always talking about how he does Pilates, but he was a big boy. And I'm like, Dude, you didn't know this stuff was coming? You didn't know you're running five miles? I think he took like an ownership to the point where he's giving chiefs high fives and acting like they're chummy. I'm looking at the chiefs and they're like, "Who is this dude?" He didn't make it. He's actually a firefighter in the city of Clifton right now. So, God bless him.

I was really focused on forcible entry, search and rescue, on ladder raises, stretching lines, putting out fires, reading smoke, rehabilitation, hot zone, warm zone. raising ladders. Weapons of mass destruction was really good. Actually, we were one of the first classes; I want to say maybe the second class in the city of Newark that used the weapons of mass destruction section of the Academy. It was a whole section by itself where they actually brought guys from Trenton to train us in weapons of mass destruction. The crazy part about it is that after I knew all that, I got on the fire ground, it was like I was a baby all over again.

Rawa: I did twelve weeks at the Orange Street Academy. For live burns we went to Morris County. We did our live burns there, but a large chunk of it was on Orange Street. For me, the very first day into the Academy was my very first introduction into the fire service. I had zero experience, zero knowledge about what I was getting myself into, so it kind of took me by surprise. Basically, it was a chapter in our books every day. Go home, study the entire chapter, come in. We do physical training in the morning for an hour. As soon as you're done with your PT, you get your quiz for the day based on the chapter you studied the day before and then you move on to the next chapter. Then just get your hands-on a physical activity. If you were studying extrications, they'd have cars outside for us to cut up. We did a lot of the practicals down there. We had the Borden's building in the back. They would have little scenarios set up for us. There were forty-one of us, so we were broken into two battalions and three companies within each battalion.

So, we were basically our own firehouse within the academy. And that's how we would work. We would do our drills as if we were a functioning fire company.

J. Centanni: I went to the Academy on Orange Street for twelve weeks. We did Firefighter One and Two. They taught us how to act in the house, how to stretch hose, truck stuff, rescue, how you use your gear, CPR, first aid. The live burn was at the Morris County Academy. They split the class two times. Then the last time we went, they did it all together.

Garay: The Academy was on Orange Street in Newark. I believe we were there for fourteen weeks. We definitely got exposed. Me being a teacher, it was really beneficial for me because I learned the terminology. I was exposed to live fires. We participated in drills. It was in the transitional period because all the people that were in charge of the Academy had just changed there. They had no experience. We missed out on certain things. But it was still very good for me because I was able to learn a lot of the terminology, a lot of the procedures, how to size up and everything else. Things that you don't actually learn until you're in the field, but you need to know. I did my live burn in Morristown. Half the class went one day then the other half went the other day because there was too many of us. Then we went to one live fire with the entire class. The instructors were there and some ladder companies and some engine companies went with us.

Fortunato: I want to say we were in the Academy eleven or twelve weeks. They taught us a lot of classroom stuff. Did Haz-mat stuff, we had to pass the two-suit test. Then we did hose stretching, going up the aerial, cut up a couple cars. We did the simulated fires, the flashover simulation and all that. I think one we went to Bergen County; one we went to Morris. The Newark instructors went with us.

Earp: We went to the Academy for twelve weeks. They taught us a lot. We learned about the basics of firefighting when we first entered the Academy. How to don our PPE, mask up, learning the importance of our protective gear. Learning we must wear it at all times when we're fighting fires. We learned the different stages of fire, how fire reacts. We dragged hose. We did reduced profile. We did searches in boarded buildings. We had live burns. We did the flash over simulator in Morris County which was pretty cool. The classroom was done at Orange Street, One Ninety Orange Street.

Corales: We were there for three months, March seventh and June first we graduated and guys that came out of the class are thirty-six. We learned the job as we went forward, but they applied discipline on us a lot. I didn't think I was going to go into it learning paramilitary ways of going about it. I did learn a lot of discipline which I was kind of happy about. I think they went about it the right way. They actually caught my attention when I first walked through the door. We had to speak in military terminology. We had to have the same mannerisms that the military had to a certain degree. And I kind of liked that. I'm not a military background type of guy. And I thought that was pretty cool that they had us go through that. I actually have a lot of respect for a lot of that.

We did our live burns in Morris County. We had a couple of Newark guys. We had some captains from our department. Then we had the Academy instructors there with us and we also had some firefighters from Newark that assisted the trainers that they had over there at the Academy. For the most part they were great. Very aggressive and I get it because that's where they mold you. That's what they want you to become when you work for the city of Newark. They want you to be aggressive. So, they were pushing us. At first, I didn't understand why we are rushing. I don't know what I'm doing, what's going on. Where do you want me to hook up at? I get it because there are going to be situations where you just got to think on the go. And they were preparing us. They were great. They made it kind of more than it was supposed to. They made it seem like you were going to be cooking in there. And once you got in there, you realized it was alright. It wasn't as bad as what they make you think. It looks worse from the outside.

Alexander II: The Academy was tough. They instituted a military style training. You had to, yes sir and no sir. They wanted to instill more discipline. So, yes sir, no sir, we had to line up in formation every morning. We had a drill instructor for our physical training. We sang cadences when we ran. It was an interesting experience. They taught me how to be a firefighter, how to fight fires.

We were on Orange Street every day and then when we had live burns, we would go to Morris County. That's where we got our live burn fire experience. They had a building in the back of the Academy on Orange Street, the Borden Building. We did some smokehouse drills there. They smoked it out. Let us crawl around, do some searches, hose line stretches back there. We were in the Academy twelve weeks. It's about the standard now.

Cruz: We were in the Academy thirteen weeks. It should have been twelve weeks, but they extended it one more week. They taught us firefighting. They taught us about the job, how to use the machines. We did evolutions. We actually did live fires as well. We did a lot of physical training. Half of the day was physical training. We probably had about two hours of lecture and every day we took a test. Every day we had an exam. We were in Newark. We would just go to our live burns in Morris County. They would use their instructors as well as our instructors as well as captains that were from the city. They would come.

Hours and Salary

Conville: It was two days on, twenty-four on, two nights and then twenty-four off. It was eighty-four hours a week. And it paid something like twenty dollars a week. I had just left a job where I was in charge of an IBM department which was the new thing. No one knew IBM. I knew IBM. I left a job that was paying me ninety-eight dollars a week for maybe thirty-five hours to come in on this stupid job, but it was a future. I think the salary came to around a couple thousand dollars a year. One time I was detailed to Six Truck and there was a man there that had a Packard automobile, a captain. I questioned him, "Where the hell you get the money to get a Packard?" But his wife wrote books and that's where he got the money. He said to me, "When you retire, you'll most likely be getting maybe a ten-thousand-dollar pension. I was looking for three thousand. I wanted to make a bet with him that I would not get ten thousand dollars in pension. In fact, I said to my wife, if we could only save ten thousand dollars by the time I retire when I was fifty-two, we could go down to Florida and buy a house for five thousand dollars. And then we would have five thousand dollars cash and we would have the pension. We would live like a king and a queen.

Conover: In July of '48 when I went in the fire department, they started you off at twenty-four hundred dollars a year. Top pay was thirty-three, nine hundred dollars more. It took you about three years to get there. But two hundred dollars a month, even back in those days didn't go to darn far. Almost every fireman that I ever knew was doing something on the side to earn a few bucks. When I went in we worked seventy-two hours a week. You worked three days and two nights then you worked two nights and three days. But that only lasted for a year, maybe a year and a half, then we went to the fifty-six-hour week.

Ryan: You worked too many hours in them days. You had meal trick babies then. The old timers used to call them meal trick babies. You were in the firehouse, thirty days in a row. You got a couple of days off. Working night and day, night and day. You worked those twenty-four and forty-eight hours, you only got a meal trick off for four hours. With the fifty-six hours, you worked two days followed by two nights with two days off.

But don't tell me about the hours before the war or during the war. They were long hours, that's all I know. I used to see the schedule on the calendar. They were in the firehouse more days than they were home, whereas the cops were working forty hours. The cops were working forty hours a week, during the war and all. The firemen were working like eighty-four. It took a long time, but it came. It should have been there long ago, but it was the way the city was saving money to have us working all those long hours. You had to put a whole shift on to improve it.

J. Doherty: We were working fifty-six hours. It was three tours, so you worked two days, two nights, two days off. Monday and Tuesday days, Wednesday and Thursday nights, Friday and Saturday off.

I'm pretty sure the salary was twenty-six hundred dollars. Within maybe six months, they got a raise. It went to three thousand dollars. The one thing that stuck in my mind was the salary of a chief engineer when I went on, sixty-five hundred dollars. Honest to God.

Gibson: In the beginning they had the fifty-six hours and then they switched over to the forty-two. The salary, well, see that was the funny thing. I started in the cops in '48 and they made twenty-four to thirty-three hundred dollars a year. And when I went on the fire department, the pay was the same and I had to go back to twenty-four. I had a friend of the family's, he was a corporation counsel for the city and he went all through the archives and everything looking for any way of getting me to get that money, nothing. They eventually did change the law because of McDonaugh, Dick McDonaugh, but it didn't relate to me.

A fireman didn't make nearly the same as a schoolteacher. My father was a cop, but was a gentle man and people liked him. He worked Down Neck in the Third Precinct and there were a lot of union people down there and he got to know them all. But my father wouldn't do you a favor if he didn't think you would stick to the job after he recommended you. You know, if you quit six months later, he took that as a personal affront. But he wouldn't get me a job. And in those days in the labor, you got a hundred bucks a week. You didn't get that much in the fire or in the police departments. But I was glad I got the fire department because I can do a lot of other things. I drove trailers. I sold real estate. I had my own businesses.

G. Alfano: The salary at that time, I started with three thousand dollars. I took a cut in pay from my other job because I was making over five. That's why I said I got to be crazy. I was in the Teamsters. I had my own route and '47-'48 the Teamsters were making at least a couple of thousand more than the firemen. And not working as long. The work schedule just went to fifty-six. It went from seventy-two to fifty-six maybe a few weeks before I came on, so I worked fifty-six. It was two tens and then you were off and then you got two fourteen nights and then you were off two days, forty-eight.

D.C. Griggs: It was actually two days, two nights, two days off. That's the way it was. No swing in the middle, not in those days. I can tell you exactly what the salary was. Four thousand dollars and after four years we got forty-nine, four steps. I really didn't know how that compared to other jobs. I knew I would be doing better with the fire department than where I was working with the paint company.

Duerr: The pay wasn't that good because we were working fifty-six hours. I started at forty-two hundred a year. I had been making five thousand with Public Service. But I just liked the job. I thought it was going to be beneficial to me.

Schoemer: We worked two days. You were off a day. You worked two nights, then you were off three days. You worked an eight-day week, forty-two hours. The salary was forty-five hundred dollars a year. You got paid the first and the fifteenth. It didn't matter what that was on, that's when you got paid. So, it made up twenty-six pay days. That's how they paid you. I made more money working for a new car dealer, but the combination of the two salaries was even nicer.

You make about five grand working for the dealership, then you come in do forty-two hours a week and you're getting forty-five hundred a year. Back in those days you got maybe a hundred dollars a year or two hundred dollars for a pay raise.

A. Prachar: I came on in 1959 when the forty-two-hour week started. We would work two fourteen-hour nights, from six at night until eight in the morning, come back the following night, six at night until eight the following morning. Then be off seventy-two hours. Then work two ten-hour days eight A.M. to six P.M. Come back the next day, eight A.M to six P.M. Then be off for forty-eight hours. Then we'd start the night schedule.

I can tell you my salary because we just found my W-2. My first-year salary was two thousand four hundred fifty dollars from March to December; that was with a wife and two children. I learned right away that I had to get a part time job to supplement my income. I had taken a fifty dollar a week pay cut leaving Public Service to come on the fire department, but it didn't matter to me because the fire department was to be my life. It was what I wanted and what I always wanted. Well, fifty dollars a week pay cut was a big hurt back then.

After my first year of making under three thousand, our pay was forty-five hundred dollars a year which with a wife and two kids didn't go far. We were fortunate in that area that we had a dairy and a bakery that used to give us the old breads and cakes to take home to the family. It saved us money and Dairy Lee was on Elizabeth Avenue. They would send a case of milk down to the firehouse which everybody would share because we all had young kids. But it certainly helped. I don't know that it was legal, but you know, it certainly helped. You get a couple loaves of bread and a couple quarts of milk. I don't remember what the prices of them were then. It couldn't have been too much, but it certainly helped.

Bitter: I had four kids and at the time I lived on McGraw Avenue on the third floor. Four kids, on the fire department, starting out at forty-five hundred dollars. Before that I was driving a truck. My first paycheck, two weeks, I brought home a hundred and twenty-two dollars. And my wife says, "What in the hell am I supposed to do with that? You should have stayed driving a truck." A couple of months before I went on the fire department I bought cab, a taxicab. I was driving one for a few years. Life was good then because I would be on unemployment and driving a cab. Working the cab, if my wife said she needed a hundred dollars. I'd go out to work. She'd ask, "When you coming home?" I'd say, "As soon as I get a hundred dollars." Sometimes it was two and three days later. You'd work the streets all day driving a cab and then at night go down to the airport because you can wait in line and take some shut eye.

Cardillo: Hours were eight to six and six to eight in the morning. The salary was terrible. I'll just give you an idea. They use to come around to give the checks out. So, we're in the alarm room; the checks are given out; and I'm standing next to Paul Hauser. I look at my check and I says to Paul, "You know what? I think I'm going put a volunteer fireman's light in my grill." Looking at my check, it was like eighty dollars for two weeks.

Elward: Oh God, the salary? I'm trying to think. I was making money in the trucks. I'm going to say fifty-seven. That puts us around teachers, I would say. I know that our pension was so solvent because that was a selling point, you're going to have to think about it. What these guys were getting as a pension was a joke. We were paying about nine percent of our pay, maybe seven percent into our pension. The retired guys were getting five, six hundred a month. I think so. I know for a fact that it was all based on fifty percent of their final salary, not the sixty-five to seventy percent we got when I retired.

Schofield: You used to work two ten-hour days; you were off two days; then you worked two fourteen-hour nights; then you were off for three days. And it was based on an eight-day schedule so every eight weeks it would go back. If you were working Monday and Tuesday days this week, eight weeks from now you'd be working Monday and Tuesday again. And any time somebody asked you to a party or a special occasion, you had to take out your little Bible there to tell you what days you were working, whether you could make it or not.

We didn't really have personal days when I started. After a while we negotiated, in the contract I think we had three personal days, but it was up to the manpower. Your captain or your battalion chief, usually had to give time off before that. But you couldn't count on personal days. One New Year's Eve there had been a lot of sick time taken by certain individuals, so the chief decided that you had to cancel all days off, all personal days just in case of a conflagration. Some guys had put out a lot of money for the New Year's Eve parties. They were all cancelled. We worked New Year's Eve night; there wasn't even a fire. So, a lot of people were bent out of shape.

We had the hospitalization and when you first came on you weren't really thinking about benefits as far as medicals. We didn't have contracts at the time. It was negotiating and you were thinking about give me the money. They're going to give you a thousand dollars more. It was fifty-one hundred dollars when I went on the job. I was twenty-two when I went on the job. It was "give me that money", but then you start thinking. Wait a minute I've got a couple of kids here and I need benefits. Even so, after you're on the job a few years and you start getting the benefits, when we used to do the votes, the young guys would stand up, "No I want that money." But the older guys who were on for a while and had families said, "Wait, take it easy kid. Get the money, but get some benefits, too." That's the way that worked out.

Cosby: I worked the forty-two-hour schedule my whole career. And when I came on it was forty-five hundred or five thousand something like that.

Dalton: Ten-hour days and fourteen hours nights. The salary wasn't a lot. I worked part-time for most of my time on the job. Before that I worked at Westinghouse as a mail boy. It was pretty comparable.

Gaynor: The forty-two was in place when I came on the job. My starting salary was one hundred and eleven dollars per week and that was until the next year. And the top salary I think it was seven thousand dollars for the senior men. The following year it was eight thousand. And then it turned out it held for a while because the next time I recall it may have been ten five. At the time it wasn't a bad salary.

Perez: I was a cop before coming on and the work week wasn't an improvement over the police work week. Two different schedules, the cops were four days on, two days off and were a rotating shift. It came out to thirty-six hours, but in the long run it came out to the same thing as a fireman. So, there was no difference. I preferred the fire schedule, you could sleep. I used to go to police roll call at the midnight shift with my blanket and pillow. That's what we did, First Precinct on Washington Court, unbelievable.

I started with four thousand dollars as a cop. Then Addonizio with that big raise he gave us from six thousand to ten thousand. That really, really, really was a big raise. But then until the '67 riots we were only making six thousand dollars a year. Then the '67 riots, that's when Addonizio brought it up to ten thousand which was good.

Calvetti: I took a cut in pay. I was driving a bus making good money. I took a cut in pay to go to the Post Office then I took another cut in pay to come on the fire department. I think my starting pay was like fifty-nine hundred when I came on the job for a fireman. Top pay was maybe seven thousand. Back then it was three or four steps. Right after I came on the job, we had a meeting. I was one of the guys at the meeting. And I bitched and moaned. I says, "Not for nothing. I'm doing the same job as the other guy. I'm in a busy house. These guys are in slow houses. I got to wait all these years to make top pay. That doesn't make any sense. From the day you come on the job, you should be at top pay. They should do away with a lot of these steps." They did away with some of them. I don't know if they did away with all of them. We did get a raise.

Lawless: When I came on it was sixty-six hundred. A hundred and twenty-eight dollars every two weeks is what I took home. We also got clothing allowance; we got fifty dollars or something ridiculous, no holiday pay.

Benderoth: Four thousand eight hundred and two dollars and fifty cents a year. I make more than that in my pension cost of living now. That's the starting salary, like a hundred and twenty dollars a week, a hundred and fifteen dollars a week. Teachers were above us, probably two thousand dollars or more a year. They only worked ten months, but we weren't quote skilled.

Miller: I was making eight thousand dollars a year. I know there were steps at the time, but they came pretty quick if I remember. I didn't care after a while because I was having such a good time. They could have asked me to do it for free. I think I would have done that. But eight thousand a year and then in '72, that's when we had the strike, and we went to ten five. We got a twenty-five hundred dollar raise. At that time, I was thinking, "Who's making more money than me." I mean all my peers, nobody's making ten thousand dollars. But that's what it was, eight thousand. I can't even think what we used to take home. But it seemed fair. With what I was doing, and I was having such a good time at it. I used to be like the major league baseball player or football player who was doing something they loved and was getting paid plenty of money for it.

We worked two days on, two days off, or the second day you're off. That night you worked in the firehouse, and you worked two nights on. Then you're off for three days. It was a great schedule for somebody that had hobbies or wanted to work a little part time job or something. It was a great schedule for that. It was a bad schedule in the way of when holidays come up and you're scheduled to work. You had to be there. Later on, we were able to work out switches and as you get up on the seniority list you get vacation picks. You can start picking the holidays. I spent many Christmas Eves which also seemed to translate into a New Year's Eve, in the firehouse. But looking back at it, it wasn't so bad because you were with people you enjoyed being with.

Weber: Forty-two-hour work week, two ten-hour days, forty-eight hours off, two fourteen-hour nights followed by seventy-two. They remained the same for me, unfortunately. If they changed to the twenty-four on, seventy-two off, I might still be there. My starting salary was six thousand nine hundred dollars. Top pay at that time was eight thousand and I believe two, eight thousand and two dollars. Part of the incentive for taking the job to begin with was my father told me that shortly after appointment we were expecting a major raise. That was when the cop salary went to ten thousand five hundred dollars. It was almost a twenty-five percent raise. It did happen shortly after. I was appointed in January; that summer the raises came through as predicted.

There was a strike and I didn't show up. I was a rookie without protection and was informed that I don't have union support, so it be a good idea if I got my butt back to work. But it was a short-lived situation, so no harm, no foul.

Saccone: Okay, when I first started on the job, the salary at that time was sixty-five hundred dollars in the '60s, the late '60s which was a lot of money at that time. The mayor was Mayor Addonizio. And he was sympathetic to our cause. If it wasn't for him giving us a twenty-five hundred dollar raise, I think we would have been the lowest paid fire department in the state of New Jersey. That really brought us up to par. And at that time Atlantic City was the lowest paid. Gas was only twenty-three cents then.

P. Doherty: When I started it was nine five. There were three steps. You went from nine five to ten five.

Daudelin: When I took the test for the police department, I think fifty-four hundred was the starting pay and the top pay was eight thousand and two dollars. In the meantime, that was right at the end of Mayor Addonizio's term. As a matter of fact, my police class got backed up about five months. I would have gone on actually in '69. But they wound up getting a twenty-five hundred dollar raise. So, I started at eighty-five hundred dollars a year. The fire department was the same. The salary in those days was exactly the same. They had parity, even all the ranks were the same.

Marcell: My tour was two days on, one day off, two nights on three days off. So, Monday and Tuesday ten hours each in the daytime. And then I would report on Thursday night and Friday night at six o'clock. We'd work from six to eight in the morning. The day tricks were eight to six and the night tricks were six to eight, six to eight. Fourteen hours, two fourteen hours and two ten hours tricks. And then you'd have the three days off.

When I first came on, I started at nine-five. When I was in the American Can Company working nights when I was in school, I was making about fifty-five hundred dollars a year. I was a porter, in the wintertime, I was a porter. I had some bathrooms and stuff to clean and this kind of thing. And I had a little extra time to read. As quickly as I would do the cleaning, I'd have extra time. But in the summertime in the can company, I could bid on another job. I would bid on a forklift operator. I would be able to get overtime in the summer. But as soon as I went onto the fire department, it started at nine five and the top pay was ten five.

I remember my uncle telling me, it's a great job and you have all these different benefits. We're very shortly we're going to get eyeglasses which we never got. We never got eyeglasses in thirty-eight years that I was on the job. But it was a great job. I always thank my uncle for that, putting me onto the idea of this job.

The pay was comparable to a teacher's job. Teachers were making about ten-five, eleven. So, we were about the same as teachers at the time. It was good. It was really good. Then about a year later, I finished my last year at Seton Hall while I was a fireman. I got a degree in psychology.

Kelly: It was, go in at eight in the morning and you get off at six for two days. Then you're off a day, then you go in at night from six at night to eight in the morning. So, that's two tens, off one, two fourteens nights and off three. The salary was nine five. At that time, it was pretty decent. I think my older brother was only making about seven grand driving a truck. So, it was good money and then one year later it went up to ten five.

Romano: The tour schedule at the time was the two ten-hour days and the two fourteen-hour nights. It took quite a while to get used to it. The sleeping in the day and sleeping at night and then trying to sleep at home, that took a while to get used to. I don't know if I ever really got a solid night's sleep in the firehouse. I never had the ability, like some of the other fellows to fall asleep between alarms. The bells would wake me up and I'd be awake most of the night. I think I went through most of my adult life suffering from sleep deprivation. Between the fires and the alarms, I just never had the ability to get into bed and fall asleep. So, I was constantly tired. For thirty, thirty-one years I was tired. I didn't realize how tired I was until I retired.

The salary wasn't much more than the Post Office. In 1972 I think we might have been making ten thousand. I could be wrong on that, but it wasn't much more than I was getting in the Post Office. But comparing the fire department job to the Post Office, it was like a difference between night and day. To me it was just the greatest thing in the world to be with a group of guys that you worked with. You ate with, you slept with them. I don't think I made one friend in the Post Office in four years. The fire department was a completely different atmosphere.

Rosamilia: Well, the cadet schedule was different because of the college. When you went to college, they didn't put out a schedule for you to go to the firehouse. You had three components that controlled your schedule. You had some firehouse duty. They would send you to different firehouses and you would be under the direction of the captain. They sent us all over the city. So that would be part of your week. Then you would have school and then you would have Training Academy classes, either classes or drills. They would schedule it and it would come out to roughly thirty, forty hours a week. I guess they figured in some study time for you.

The firehouse was a standard ten and fourteen schedule. It was two ten-hour days, started at eight in the morning until six at night and two fourteen-hour nights from six at night to eight in the morning. And then you would have three days off. It's an eight-day cycle. That's how they covered the twenty-four hours a day seven days a week. As cadets we were mainly in the firehouse at night. They never let us stay too late. We would do two nights. You would work with the same crew for two nights in a row. But it would be from six until eleven in the evening.

At that time ten five was the salary that they got through the strike and state funding trying to rescue city firefighters. They weren't making much. I think they were making like eight thousand. They went up to ten five and that was what they were making I think when I got on, when I became a cadet. They were still at ten five. And then when I started on the fire department, maybe eleven five or twelve thousand. Cadet pay was exactly a hundred dollars a week. By the time a year and nine months went by, it had gone up. We were getting half of the annual salary. That was fifty-two hundred a year, fifty-two fifty I guess, a hundred dollars a week. Good money.

Burkhardt: When we came on the pension didn't know what to do with the guys under twenty-one. In fact, it took about a year for the pension to catch up with us. They really weren't quite sure. I was probably one of the younger guys at the time. I was right out of high school; in five months I was on the fire department. You still had to be twenty-one. Civil Service adapted. Of course, our pension rates because we were so young, I think we were paying maybe six-point seven eight percent of the pension, compared to the eight and a half now. They moved the age when you could retire, but they adapted only because change was mandated. But we were young kids getting fifty-five hundred dollars as cadets and then when we came on the fire department, we got ten-five. We thought we hit the lotto.

They had our schedule all planned. You worked different tours. You constantly met different people. Up to probably about twelve, thirteen years, I probably knew everybody on the fire department. Because they wouldn't let you detail a cadet out. They'd send a fireman out. That's the other thing. Like at Six

Engine there were two cadets. There was Harry Kapinowski and me; we were the team. We'd go there. Six Engine's back step had no room. They'd have to send a guy down to Twelve Engine/Five Truck. The trucks are no problem because you can stack a lot of guys on a truck, but the back step of the engine, there's no room. And you always had to stay in the house with the chief. They found out there weren't many chiefs, so they started putting them in busy companies, put you in Five Truck, put you in Twelve Engine. A couple of times Twelve Engine was crowded, so they put four cadets on Five Truck. They'd almost strap them to the aerial because you rode the turntable back then. It worked out pretty well. Some companies were a little miffed, Now I got to go on detail, but we were only there for four hours.

Stoffers: And it was five thousand dollars a year, sounds about right. That was the pay for the cadets.

Morgan: We've come a long way. A few years on the job, after I got married, I was making seventeen thousand three hundred dollars a year as a fireman in Six Engine doing forty-three hundred runs a year, averaging two-three fires a day as a company.

Brownlee: We did tens and fourteens, two ten-hour days, one day off, two fourteen-hour nights, three days off. My starting salary was eight thousand five hundred dollars. But the good thing was I came on in November. I got my first step in January, and I was full grade the next January.

That was ten five. I was like king of the world. We were somewhere between teachers and stockbrokers. I could buy a house which was a big improvement.

Coale: I think the salary was ten thousand five hundred. They'd just gotten a big raise and they were all happy about that. You had time to get a part-time job with your schedule and most of us did have two jobs and it worked out fine. We always had food on the table and the roof never leaked. So, it was great.

When we first came on it was fourteen-hour nights and ten- hour days, so you'd work for two days, off a day. You'd work two nightshifts and be off for seventy-two hours or three days.

Killeen: The salary was better than what I was making outside, because I went in the Marines. Between the time I got discharged and the time I got on the fire department I was working back at the tire place where I was working as a kid at school. That money was just a little bit better than horseshit and the fire department was just a little bit better than that. The fire department bumped it up a little. I was able to do better with the fire department.

We worked a forty-two-hour week, but it's based on eight days. We worked two ten-hour days, we're off the nights. Then we did the swing which was twenty-four hours. You were off forty-eight hours after your days. You came back on. You did two fourteen-hour nights then you're off for three days. Before that they had the fifty-six-hour work week, three tours. Now we work the twenty-four-hour shifts which is you work twenty-four hours on then you're off for three days. Then you come back and you do twenty-four hours again. So, you kind of miss a whole shift of guys. When you worked the tens and fourteens, you would see guys in between. There seemed to be more camaraderie because there were more fire department type parties. They would have parties. They would have events. Guys would do things together because no matter where you lived, you could work in the firehouse in the daytime and then the night in between the two days you'd go out to dinner with your friends. You'd go out, do whatever you wanted to do with your friends and then come back the next day. You'd be in the firehouse. The nights the same thing, but nowadays you work in the firehouse, the next day everybody's gone. You don't see anybody for three days. We've lost that part in the middle.

Banta: We worked the ten- and fourteen-hour schedule at that time. I believe the salary on the certification that I got was ten thousand two-fifty to twelve thousand two-fifty at that time.

It was two steps. You went to the second step on January first of the second year and you went full grade I believe January first of the third year. So, in my case, I came on February of '74. I went to the second step in January of '75 and then I was full grade January of '76. I was single, so it wasn't too bad. I had a lot of money in my pocket at that time. When I got married later in '74, it wasn't the greatest, but it was still more than a lot of people were making, I guess, at the time. I paid all my bills. I didn't have any debt collectors, so I guess I was doing okay at that time.

Straile: We were doing ten-hour days; you'd work two ten-hour days. You'd be off a day then do two fourteen-hour nights and you're off three days. It was a good schedule, but things changed.

The starting salary, everybody thought I was crazy because I was taking a cut in pay for what I was doing, the job started at eleven thousand eighty-four dollars a year. I remember that distinctly because they said, "Are you nuts? You're going to lose like five thousand dollars a year. But I took it anyway. At the time, we were making about the same as teachers. I would think. It wasn't that much different at that time.

Partridge: We worked two ten-hour days and we were off for a day and a half. And then we worked two fourteen-hour nights and then we were off for three days, seventy-two hours. It was a forty-two-hour week. That's how they broke it up. There were no twenty-fours in those days.

I think I started around twelve thousand if I remember correctly. I think it was about twelve, twelve-five, something like that. They had just gotten a couple of raises. Within the previous couple of years before I came on the job there was a big bump. They went from something like eight all the way up to twelve or something like that in a period of a couple of years.

That probably put me equivalent to teachers and other civil service type people. For me I was rolling in dough, young and single. I had gotten out of high school. I had to wait I think almost three years to get appointed from taking the test. So, in the meantime, I was doing things like working in gas stations and driving the school bus, working for a surveyor. All transient jobs for probably little more than minimum wage. So, when I came on the fire department and all of the sudden, I had a regular salary with benefits and everything that was quite a jump up.

J. Prachar: Something tells me we were making about fourteen thousand dollars, thirteen seven twenty-eight is the figure that floats around in my head. For a nineteen-year-old kid living at home in Newark, that was a lot of cash. I had to pay room and board after that. I guess it was okay because there were guys that I came on the job with that were already married with kids and they seemed to be making a living before working their second job. The hours for probably ninety to ninety-five percent of my career was the old forty-two-hour work schedule with two ten-hour days, eight A.M. to six P.M., with forty-eight hours off. You'd come back after two days and work two fourteen-hour shifts, six at night until eight in the morning and off for seventy-two hours. It wasn't bad until a few years before retirement they kicked in the twenty-four shift which was pleasant. It started out with twenty-four on, forty-eight off, twenty-four on ninety-six off because the firemen were still working tens and fourteens. That schedule allowed us to see our regular crews for a day trick and a night trick every week. Worked out nice. Then the firemen went to twenty-fours, but they went to the standard twenty-four, twenty-four on seventy-two off. We had an opportunity to adopt that as the officers. We liked what we had. The firemen like what they had and that's how I retired. I got to see my guys for a twenty-four hour shift every eight days and then

I worked with the second tour twenty-four hours every eight days. I preferred my guys.

Daly: I didn't mind the hours. We did fourteen-hour nights, we did one night, had ten hours off, did fourteen the next night, had three days off. Ten hours from eight to six, have the night off, come back and work to six at night. So, the hours weren't bad. They were pretty good. If you wanted a part time job you could get one and my wife was my part time job. I hung out with my friends. I loved it. But it was tough because of the weekends. That was tough for my wife to get used to, but it wasn't tough for me. It's easier if you're single because you wouldn't mind it that much.

The salary was twelve, fourteen, it wasn't much, let me tell you. It wasn't much. My wife's an RN. She was working at Mountainside Hospital. I'd be working in the firehouse and on my days off, she would go work at the hospital so we could make ends meet. We always tried to save some money so we could buy a house someday. But it was minimal. It was maybe close to fourteen thousand. It was tough. It was tough, especially if you wanted to buy a house. We didn't reach full grade until three years. Five years longevity kicks in at five. When I first came on my wife made more. You'd think RNs make a lot. They don't make a lot of money. If she worked, she worked in Newark she would get combat pay. That's what they call it. Teachers get combat pay too. She made close to twenty-five and I was at fourteen. And so, I said something is wrong there. But it eventually worked out.

Sandella: We worked two ten-hour days and two fourteen-hour nights. Your shift began on the days. It would start at eight in the morning, work ten hours until six. Return the next day for the same shift. Then you would be off a full day and return the following night at six until eight and the again the next night from six to eight. Then you would be off for three days. And the cycle would repeat. In my particular personal experience, I never worked the twenty-four-hour shift. The twenty-four-hour shift changed in I think it was around two thousand two. We went to the twenty-four-hour shift. I was president of the officers' union at the time. And the city of Newark was probably the last fire department in New Jersey to go to the twenty-four-hour shift. If we were not the last, we were pretty close to being the last. The twenty-four-hour shift now is more or less the recognized shift for fire departments around the country. So, we were one of the last ones to do it and it's funny because I went to the union office in 1995 as vice president and I worked tens and fourteens. We were able to get it in 2002. And it was funny because the firemen didn't have it. It was a big deal with the contracts. We worked different shifts actually. The fire officers worked the twenty-four-hour shift, and the firefighters work a ten and fourteen shift which caused some confusion. We worked it out, but it wasn't the ideal way to operate and there were some issues. Eventually everybody went to the twenty-four. When we worked different shifts, the officers worked one on, one off, one on, four off.

I don't think we were making as much as some of the others. I know the trade unions were doing better than us. Back then we were trying to get raises and binding arbitration was fairly new when we came in. It came in around 1978. So, we didn't have arbitration up to that point. And after we came on in '78, that's when we started negotiating through arbitration and we made some gains. But when we came on, I think we were very low compared to the others, especially the trade unions. Nowadays it seems that they've taken a position against us unfortunately. The firefighters today from the media and the politicians the public workers seem to be villainized. We always just wanted to get to where they were because they deserved it and we thought we did. But it doesn't work the opposite way, unfortunately. So, I think we were below teachers. We were equal to cops pretty much. But I think the teachers and some of the trades were a little ahead of us.

Zieser: It was ten-hour days, and it was fourteen-hour nights. So, we worked two ten-hour days. We were off for one day. You would come in the following day and you did two nights in a row. And then you'd be off for seventy-two hours and then you'd go back to the same schedule. So that was always a good schedule because it always progressed one day each week. So, if I worked days Saturday and Sunday this week, the following week would be Sunday and Monday and so on. Everybody had the same number of weekends off. If you hit the holidays, you hit the holidays. It was luck of the draw. But no particular tour had more weekends off or more certain nights off, so in that respect it was always a very fair schedule. And it was a good schedule. I always said, when you were tired of being home, you had to be in the firehouse. When you were tired of being in the firehouse, it was time to go home. So, whoever set up that schedule, I think they did a good job. Especially for the married guys, they always said the same thing. When I was married it was the same thing. When you were tired of being home, "I got to go to work, honey."

Then we went to the twenty-four-hour shift. You work twenty-four hours then you're off for seventy-two. I was an officer at the time and the officers made that switch first, we were working the twenty-four-hour shift. The firemen were still on the ten- and fourteen-hour schedule. So, the way it worked, we would work with two different tours. You'd be a captain of one tour during the day and then at night you'd be a captain of a different shift. It worked out well. I think there were some benefits to that because the crews experienced different captains and the captains experienced different guys. So, for most of us it made you appreciate your normal guys more than you might have if you didn't work with the two tours. Then they all got onto the twenty-four-hour shift. I love the twenty-four-hour shift. I think it's great. But how busy we were years ago, I don't think we could have in a busy house, I don't know if you could have survived the twenty-four-hour shift in those days with the number of fires and workload we had. Obviously, the workload has come down over the years so you can do it now, but it wouldn't have worked back in the '70's.

The officers' schedule wasn't twenty-four seventy-two. You worked one day. Then you were off two days. Then you came in a day, and you were off four days. Now we work a twenty-four-hour shift, off for three days, a twenty-four shift off for three days. Back then you worked a twenty-four-hour shift, off for two days, a twenty-four hour shift off for four days. So obviously the hours stayed the same, but that kept it consistent that you always worked with the same two crews all the time. That was the best shift for that.

The salary when I came on was thirteen eight. But at that time, if you talked to guys in the firehouse there would be about three or four different salaries that they made because it would be the salary plus your longevity. But nobody was at different rates except for the four different categories. Now you sit at the table, everybody makes a different amount of money. It depends on when they came on, where the longevity is. Yeah, it's totally different, the amount that everyone makes at the table. It's probably the biggest difference from the brand-new guys to a senior firefighter. It comes from the contracts over the years.

I was twenty-one when I came on and I knew a lot of cops and firemen. The salary was about the same at that time if you wanted to be a postal worker, a cop, fireman, correction officer, all were in that same ballpark. Us and the cops, kind of stayed the same over the years, but the postal workers fell way behind us by today's standards. At that time, it was a great job because I was single living at home. So anytime you're thinking of living at home, whatever you have goes a long way.

Hopkins: We had two ten-hour days. Then we were off a day and a half, and we worked two fourteen-hour nights. So, we worked from eight in the morning to six at night for days and then from six at night to eight in the morning for nights. Then we were off seventy-two hours.

The salary, thirteen thousand, I think it was one year, but I'm not a hundred percent. Comparing it to teachers, well the teachers are off in the summer, that's why we sort of liked it, me and Rickie, but for the most part I guess it was all right. We were single so, burned every dime.

Witte: It was the tens and fourteens. Salary was twelve five. When we were hired, we didn't have a contract. So, then it jumped up I think to fourteen.

Kormash: We worked two ten-hour days, off, and then two fourteen-hour nights. Salary might have been around fifteen grand a year. I think that actually was a little decrease from what I would have made if I had stayed in Corrections.

Reiss: We were on the tens and fourteens which was two ten-hour days followed by one day off then two fourteen-hour nights and then three days off. So, it moved up a day every week.

The salary was around fifteen thousand, fifteen thousand six hundred because I actually took a pay cut from where I was working. I was making like twenty thousand where I was working as an EMT for Record Ambulance in Orange which did the emergency work for Orange and East Orange and the Pabst Brewery in Newark. But that was with thirty hours overtime every week. Fifteen six was just the straight salary, that didn't include overtime.

Caufield: My job title was Fire Alarm Operator. That was the equivalent in pay, in structure, in everything to a firefighter. And where, as a firefighter you were promoted to captain, we were promoted to Chief Fire Alarm Operator.

My work schedule at the beginning, we started our shift at four P.M. and worked until midnight. We were off at midnight until eight A.M. We worked eight A.M. until four P.M. Got off at four P.M. and came in that midnight and worked until eight A.M. Then we were off three days. So, it was eight on, eight off, eight on, eight off, eight on, three days off. Just terrible, just terrible. And that could be terrible on a marriage, doing eight-hour shifts, take my word for it. The one thing good about working the eight-hour shifts and it's the only thing that was good about it was you dealt with every company in the field at one time or another.

Our schedule changed; we got twenty-fours. I was on the first tour. I think the firefighters in the field were closer then with the fourteens and tens than with the twenty-fours. I definitely do. I think there was more of a camaraderie then than there is today. The guys by today's standards and the workload that they have, they probably swear by the twenty-fours, and I wouldn't blame them. Especially if you have something on the side. It afforded people to live further out because they're only travelling one time, but it ruined the camaraderie.

Almaguer: They were the greatest hours in the world. We had four tours and we worked two days, ten-hour shifts. And then we worked two nights, fourteen-hour shifts. And between the days we would have forty-eight hours off. Beautiful, a beautiful schedule. That was our schedule back then. Back in the beginning. Yes, it was two days, two nights. With our hours off it was great because I was a fulltime fireman. I did not hold a second job at the time. As far as I was concerned, that was my number one job first. And the time off that I was blessed with at the time, I used to be with my children. Because I had just gone through a divorce, a separation from my family that April. Easter Sunday of 1980 my wife walked out on me, separated me and my boys. And then the following year I used that time to spend with my children. I used to pick them up and spend that time with them and go to the firehouse. So, that was a blessing. So, I didn't work another job. That was my job.

I went from Saint James Hospital to work for the Newark Fire Department, It did make a big difference. I think it was like a dollar fifty more an hour. It was like a dollar fifty more an hour and the benefits were just as good. I wish I knew what I was getting into because I didn't know anybody in the Newark Fire Department.

I didn't have a cousin. I didn't have a brother. I didn't have an uncle. I didn't have a third cousin. I didn't have my mother. So, I came on the fire department brand spanking new. I wish somebody would have told me because I would have never left Saint James Hospital. I would have held onto that job. In the beginning at least. In the beginning I would have kept working at Saint James because I was a veteran already. And I made my own time anyway, so I could have worked around my schedule. But within the first year and a half I paid off all my debts. I was debt free. All of the sudden I was paying off debts. And for the first time since 1975 when I got married, things were going my way financially. I was also working in Newark Beth Israel in the emergency room orthopedics department and I worked there for about a year or two.

F. Bellina: You would go to work at eight o'clock in the morning and work until six o'clock at night. Then you go back the next day and do the same thing, eight until six. And then you were off two days. Then you would work the nights. You worked from six at night to eight in the morning. You would do that, two nights and then you were off three. I did that until we changed to twenty-fours. I caught the twenty-fours.

Wapples: When I first came in the door, we were making approximately nineteen thousand dollars a year. And to look at it from the time I started and up until present, it has more than doubled. Now you're talking security. It definitely brings security to you. When I look at the salaries now, I see guys starting off with thirty-one thirty-two thousand dollars, basically two hundred dollars away from it. It just makes me wonder, where will the salaries be if it has more than doubled for me, I guess soon it will be around sixty something thousand dollars. A guy who's starting out today, ten years, nine years from now, would probably be around sixty thousand dollars. So, and that is just something that is just hard to turn down. In '80 when I filed for my application it was like nineteen thousand. It might have been lower than that. It had to be lower because when I came on, I was at nineteen thousand. So back then that particular salary wasn't a salary at which you would turn your nose up against and just say, "Ah, I wouldn't want to do that." Because it was a pretty good salary. Prior to me working on the fire department, I didn't dream of starting at a nineteen-thousand-dollar salary because I didn't have a profession nor the education that would have substantiated me in a position such as that, so it paid off coming this way.

Griffith: You worked two days, two ten-hour days. That's supposedly the start of it. Then forty-eight off and then you worked two fourteen-hour nights and then you were off three days. Looking back at it now after doing the twenty-four-hour shifts, the camaraderie then was tremendous. A lot of that has to be attributed to you seeing every tour. In between nights there would be things where you could do things together. On certain occasions you could get together, go out to a dinner with the guys or even with the wives and families, that type of thing. In between your nights I worked. I did some landscaping, but then you could also get together, maybe get some golf in or do something. I remember going with the guys from Eleven on the third tour. We actually went to New York City, went to mass over in the cathedral and then had brunch over there and kind of walked around, ended up in McSorley's Ale House. But those were the type of things that you could do.

Mostly it was working. During the week you worked, so you really didn't see your family when you were working nights because you'd go to work. You'd go to the firehouse, go back to work, and then go back to the firehouse and then come home on those three days. And even then, you went to work, you were home nights. So, in the beginning, probably wasn't great for family life, because you got home, you were tired, especially if you worked part time. You made time on weekends and so forth, but then there were a lot of holidays missed. There were a lot of different things that you missed with the kids. So, the twenty-four-hour shift now, looking back, I would say is more beneficial to family. But as far as camaraderie, you see guys leave, they don't come back. They're gone for three days. So, I'm really happy that I got to work when I did with that schedule because you got to know everybody. Every house had its own identity which was really sharp then.

The salary when I came on was sixteen thousand when I started as a dispatcher/lineman. It was sixteen thousand, but again I started in November. Then it was three steps. The steps were not as they are today. The steps were if you came on in November, January you went to the second step. And the following January I was at third step. Even for the guys I knew from college, I was making money. I had cash. I had money. Looking back, it's not a lot of money and it wasn't as much as say my father was making, but as a twenty-two-year-old kid making sixteen grand. I mean I had a car. I was paying for my stuff. I was living at home, so you know.

It took me fifteen minutes to get over to Central and Ninth once I got on the fire department. And even down to Prince Street when I went down to the line division. I mean I got up in the morning and I was at work in no time. So, I had money, especially compared to the guys from high school. We'd go to dinner or we're going out for drinks, I was happy tip, buy a round or two, bought dinner and so forth. Buddies of mine graduated from college. One of my buddies does my taxes now and I said, "Well you guys all passed me." And in some of the cases that happened. But with the decline there are guys that lost their jobs. He says, "Ed, think of the money you were making before we started. You were making really good money. You had medical. You had everything before we had work on the outside." I was truly blessed.

Arce: I think my starting salary was twenty-two thousand dollars. The hours were tens and fourteens. One day you would be on ten hours. The following day you would be on ten hours. You had a day off and then you worked fourteen hours twice, then you have three days off. Then as officers, we had a weird schedule because some weeks you would have four days off. And now we're on twenty-four hours, one day on three days off which is probably the best thing. That other schedule we had as officers we worked a different tour. You were the same battalion but different group of men.

Nasta: Tens and fourteens were our original shift when I started. We worked two ten-hour days then you were off for forty-eight hours. Then you worked two fourteen-hour nights and you're off for seventy-two hours. Which kind of appealed to me, so it was one of the things I liked about it.

When I started the salary was around twenty-four thousand dollars a year which I thought was good money. Back then it was. I said, I was fortunate to have it. I was just getting married and now I had the best job in the world in my opinion. I'm sure you've heard that before. I had a steady salary, retirement plan, medical benefits; it was great.

Weidele: Tens and fourteens. You worked ten hours, then you're off. You're off, come back and do the fourteen-hour nights. The salary was twenty-six. But from what I was making, that was huge. Before I came on the job, I was working in a gas station being a mechanic and pumping gas in Irvington on Clinton and Cummings Street.

O. Johnson: We were working with ten-hour shifts and fourteen-hour shifts. That was different for me because I came literally right after high school, a year after high school and I adjusted to it. The shifts were pretty good. I enjoyed it. I think the tour schedule changed if I'm not mistaken, it was in the nineties. It was the nineties where everybody was talking about twenty-four-hour shifts. And everybody was looking at it. They wanted that really bad, but to me personally, when they did the twenty-four hour shifts it took away from the connections with other tours and guys getting to see each other. Once you did your twenty-four hours, you were gone for like three days. It took away from the job. I kind of like the ten and fourteen hours because you always had a chance to change your schedule or to move with different companies. The twenty-four-hour shift is sometimes long, especially if you're busy in a ten-hour shift and you've got fourteen more hours to go. But a lot of guys wanted it I guess because some guys live farther away, and they got it. But I tend to like the ten and fourteens.

I think the salary was around twenty-seven thousand when I came on. We were in the middle of a contract, so me being like nineteen years old, twenty-seven thousand that was a lot of money in my pocket. Plus, after a few years you got the overtime. There was overtime for everyone. I went from twenty-seven to up to thirty-five thousand. Back then, after three years, you were full grade salary. The union fought for the benefits which was good. A lot of guys had part time jobs and when your income increased, you moved up the economic ladder.

DeCeuster: When I came on the schedule was the tens and fourteens. Two ten-hour days, off forty-eight hours and then two fourteen-hour nights and off three. Which wasn't bad at all. I got to spend a lot of time with my family. My ex-wife always worked. She worked in Newark at Mutual Benefit Life at that time. And so, I spent a lot of time with my kids. I probably changed more diapers than her. I fed them more. So that was a credit; that was a good thing.

I took a hit going from Wall Street to the fire department. I forgot what it was, to be honest with you. I don't know what I got paid. In the thirties probably, thirty-six. I'm guessing. I really don't remember.

Giordano: When I first came on it was four tours and traditionally days and nights. Two ten-hour days, off a day, two fourteen-hour nights, you're off three days. That was the shift primarily used pretty much everywhere. And then somewhere in the early '90s people started negotiating for the twenty-four-hour shift. It actually went to the State Supreme Court to say it was a negotiable item. That was very interesting. It was a good win.

How we got the twenty-fours was interesting. It was in the campaign with Cory Booker and Sharpe James. The Fire Officers went in there as they were supporting the mayor. They got the twenty-four-hour shift. And the firemen remained on the old shift, ten hours on, fourteen hours off, and the men were very upset. It was not a good situation at all to have your officer only working with you fifty percent of the time. It was very bad for the morale of the department in many ways. So, at that time we were on different shifts. Following the election, myself, all the members of the firemen's union negotiating team, we wind up bargaining and we actually hammered out a good contract and we got the twenty-four-hour shift. I'm thinking in 2003.

After Sharpe James' election, we got it then. And the interesting story is when the union supported Cory Booker for mayor against the incumbent, I went on the famous *schmooze* cruise as some of my adversaries and friends call it. I went there and took our licks for the fire department and told him we're going to build him a beautiful monument next to City Hall with his name on it, beautiful black granite that will have all the firemen that died in the line of duty on it, the police had one for years. We never had any, so it was about time we got our share. And between that and going on the *schmooze* cruise, the *schmooze* cruise was a small token, but that monument was sixteen thousand dollars for a multi-million-dollar contract and the twenty-four-hour shift. It was the best sixteen thousand dollars the union ever spent. People go by City Hall Newark; I like telling the story of the monument. The guys all wanted the twenty-four-hour shift. It has its ups, and it has its downs, but the guys really like the shift.

The salary started at twenty-three. Twenty-three to twenty-six thousand was the spread of year one, two, and three to reach the max. Imagine a fireman making twenty-six thousand dollars 1985. Full grade fireman in 1985 got twenty-six thousand dollars. The three salary steps soon went to five, six, and now it's many, many combinations.

I couldn't wait to get my first check for five hundred dollars. I kid you not. I still have that check stub, five hundred and twenty-five dollars. And I couldn't wait to get it. In 1986 we were protesting for a new contract, I got interviewed at our first protest march with Sharpe James, who was counsel president running for mayor, and John Gerow. And I was interviewed by a Star Ledger reporter. I said we can't even make enough money to qualify for a home mortgage in the city of Newark. And we couldn't. You couldn't qualify for a loan with twenty-six thousand dollars. The lady was amazed.

At the time teachers were probably even doing better than us salary wise. Not much though. Newark always held its ground with police, fire, and teachers' salary wise, but that was the kind of salary going on in those professional services.

Throughout my tenure in the union, we went from thirty-two thousand to close to eighty thousand dollars which now nine-year guys are making. On the other end they're losing that fifteen, eighteen thousand on health benefits. And the problem is that you can only get a two percent raise and the health care is up ten percent, your take home pay could be less. We did spread sheets. Any pay you plug in, the spread sheet does the math, the employees are going to take home less money. This law they changed is horrible against the public employees, against police and fire. It was unbelievable that we had not one person vote with us. The Assembly was eighty to zero. The Senate was thirty-nine to zero and one person abstained. And it happened to be a friend of ours who we didn't support on his first election for mayor. We endorsed Cory Booker, but he was always a friend of ours, a friend of mine. Senator Ron Rice, he abstained, but you look around. They went in and bullshitted the municipalities, the Democrats, the Republicans. "Oh no, this is the best for all the municipalities." I don't think it's the best to see police and fire making a lower salary each year and even when they retire, they're not getting a cost of living. They're going to pay a percentage of that health insurance, and everyone knows health insurance does not go down.

I think working for any of the bigger cities, with the exception of Edison, Newark, Jersey City, Elizabeth, Edison their contracts are pretty much second to none. Anybody else who makes near our money, they're working fifty-six hours where we're working forty-two. And they're working EMS. Anything west of Delaware, those people all work one day on two days off. We're one day on three days off. Well, geographically I know it plays a part. I know it's cheaper to live in those places, but everyone's risking their lives.

The conversation to get the twenty-four-hour shift. How are guys going to do it if they get two, three fires in a shift? We used it through the union as we made our pitch that you would need seventy-two hours to get all the carcinogens out of your system. We made our point in power points after negotiations. Actually, it went to the Supreme Court of New Jersey, and they ruled that the shift is a negotiable item. Working shifts for labor has always been a mandatory part of negotiations, employees' shifts. And cities are saying, no they can't negotiate this. It went to the Supreme Court in New Jersey. We prevailed. And our lawyer at that time was David Fox and he was one of the great ones. We always say when they change all these new rules in interest arbitration to where you pick and choose, they changed the rules because they couldn't beat David Fox. They represented all the big fire departments throughout the state.

Lee: My salary when I came on was roughly twenty-two thousand and some change. It was only two steps, so when January first came, I went from the bottom step to the top step which was twenty-five-five. A lot of guys I graduated from high school went into either police or fire. So, we were all in the same category. I graduated from East Side Down Neck in the city of Newark and a lot of the guys became police officers and firefighters and teachers and such, so in the same salary range.

I worked tens and fourteens. We were working two ten-hour days and then we would be off one day and then we would come back, and we would work two fourteen-hour nights and we'd be off three days. One of the reasons why we did tens and fourteens was the idea of rehab. With ten and fourteens you had the opportunity to rehab. If you caught a fire at eight o'clock in the morning and that fire went all day, you knew you were getting off at eighteen hundred hours. So those fires were common then, when you would get a fire where it would last like that. Once the fire load decreased and the guys were not working those long shifts, the union proposed that we go to twenty-fours. So, the union put the proposal out to the membership and the membership voted on it. Some guys were against it. They really didn't want to go to the twenty-fours and some guys voiced their opinion. I was sort of neutral to it. If it stayed tens and fourteens, I was okay with it. If it switched over to twenty-fours, I was okay with it. But after it came into effect, I really liked the twenty-fours better. Because with the twenty-fours, once you're in the firehouse, you do what needs to be done and then when you get off you off for three days. I actually grew to like it a lot better than the tens and fourteens. But it had an adverse effect on the camaraderie. With every good thing there's bad thing, some bad things occur too. What happened with the tens and fourteens was we had a better outside relationship with each other. Tens and fourteens if, for example, I want to put a deck on my house, we would be around the kitchen table eating dinner and go, "Yeah, I'm thinking about putting a deck on my house." The guys would say. "Oh, I'm in. I'm in." So, the guys on that tour, you would get off that morning, come back that night. Those guys would come with you, and they would help you build the deck. We would tear roofs off. We would put roofs on. We had better camaraderie. And then when we did the ten hours, we would go out and have dinner that night. We would socialize a little bit. We would socialize outside the job more. So, you know, we would stay in the city. We would do things together.

But then after the twenty-fours came into play, all that went to the wayside. You rarely, rarely would hear of a group of guys go on to build a deck for a guy. A group of guys go on to help somebody put a roof on to their house. And a group of guys just going out to play golf or go to a football game, because we used to go to football games and baseball games. We'd get off that night at eighteen hundred and go see a baseball game or go see a basketball game or go see a football game. But now you lost that when the twenty-fours came into play.

Sorace: When I got hired in '86 we worked ten-hour days which was from eight o'clock in the morning to six at night or fourteen hours from six at night until eight o'clock the following morning. We worked two days then we were we off forty-eight. Then we worked two nights and we were off three days.

I think the salary was like maybe twenty-seven thousand. I'm not sure, but that put me probably about equal with the guys I went to high school with at the time.

Masters: My work schedule back then was the old schedule, which was two days, eight to six, eight to six. Then you were off forty-eight hours. Then you go in for your two nights which was six to eight, six to eight, fourteen-hour nights. Then you were off three. That was it for years until maybe fifteen years ago. Then we switched over to the twenty-four-hour schedule where you work one twenty-four-hour period and then you are off for the three days and that was it. You can map out your whole timetable on the calendar for the whole year. I mean it was good.

The twenty-four hours had its pluses I'm going to say for certain guys on the job which is the far away guys and being away from the family twenty-four hours wasn't too bad. But with the twenty-four hours it was like you come in in the morning; you punch in; then twenty-four hours later you punch out. That's the end of it. But with the older shift, in between our days, we used to go at night when we got off to a baseball game, basketball game. We used to have a ski trip twice a year. It's a completely different thing and we got to see every tour. Now you're limited to maybe three tours. The guys got to know each other better with the older shift. A lot of stuff did decline over the years with this new shift, with the camaraderie. Like our first night in the firehouse, we would meet somewhere specifically then we would go to work at six o'clock. They don't do that anymore. It's totally different.

My first salary my first year was twenty-two thousand five hundred. Back then in the '80's I was working for my father-in-law and that was about comparable.

Goetchius: I believe that first year I grossed eighteen because I came on in April towards the end.

I happen to hit the contract just right. When I came on it happened that in less than two years, I was up to full grade fireman's salary. So, I was very grateful and happy I hit the contract just right.

N. Bellina: Tens and fourteens, you worked two ten-hour days. You had a day and a half off. Then you went to work two nights, fourteen hours and then you had three days off. We went to twenty-fours in the early 2000s maybe. You have twenty-four hours on, three days off.

A lot of guys didn't like that because it interfered with their part time believe it or not. I thought they got more part time with the three days off. One of the guys I worked with didn't like it right off the bat because of that change at that point with his part time. He had to redo things; but I always thought it was more time off. It changed the firehouse because you weren't with the guys that much anymore. You only worked eight days a month. So, you weren't as close as you were on the tens and fourteens. You still were close. I don't think it really did that much, but it was a change. You don't see one tour.

The salary? I'd have to say top pay at the time had to be in the fifties. I think I was around twenty, maybe twenty-one when I started. That's comparable to maybe a teacher, what they were making.

Ch. Centanni: Tens and fourteens, two days, off a day, two nights off three days. The salary? My wife and I were just talking about this. When we got engaged my wife was working as a secretary and she was making more money than me. So, I took the test. On the application it said nineteen thousand dollars. When I took the job, I believe it was just making under twenty-four thousand. So, that was the starting salary when I came on in '86.

Growing up in Newark, the salary I don't think was as important as the security of having a real job, having the benefits and all. So, I didn't pay much attention to it at the time. I think my group was a fortunate group because shortly into my young experience on the job, maybe two, two or three years into it, we experienced a couple of real good raises. We were into like the thirty-five, thirty-seven-thousand-dollar area pretty quick.

Ziyad: At that time our hours were, we were working two days in, one day off, two nights in three days off. The two day shifts consisted of eight to six, ten hour shifts, so two straight days ten hour shifts eight to six, eight to six. We'd have off a day. We had to come in the following day, from six to eight. So, we're working two days in, one night off, two nights in. Then we'd have three days off. So, we're working tens and fourteens as they would call them, ten-hour days and fourteen-hour nights.

Eventually, they did change. We were advocating for twenty-four-hour shifts. The unions were, the firefighters were for years. Most of the fire departments throughout the country were on some type of twenty-four-hour shifts. New Jersey was one of the few states that was holding onto days and nights , the split shifts. So, eventually we went to twenty-four-hour shifts. We weren't on a twenty-four seventy-two initially. The officers were the first given the twenty-four-hour shift. The firefighters stayed on a ten and fourteen-hour shift. But it wasn't twenty-fours/seventy-twos. It was a twenty-four/forty-eight. Then a twenty-four/ ninety-six. So, initially we had that shift and then when the firefighters were given the twenty-four-hour-shift, everybody went to a twenty-four, seventy-two. It was confusing. Especially me being a captain at the time because fifty percent of the time I had my crew, but then twenty-five percent of the time I'd have another tour and the other twenty-five percent of the time another tour. Basically, you're dealing with three companies. It was a very, very strange time, but we loved the fact that we got the twenty-four-hour shift.

I actually don't remember my starting salary. I doubt it was thirty-thousand dollars. It may have been close to that. Maybe thirty-one if I was lucky. For me, I came out of a background of administration. I was in management for private sector. So, I was used to making decent money. Making at that time, 1986, I might have been making close to fifty thousand dollars. I took a pay cut literally to come to the fire department. But I loved the schedule. I loved the camaraderie and the benefits were much better. The benefits for my family and myself particularly were much better. And that's what really encouraged me, not just the money. I always worked a part time job. It gave me the opportunity to work my second job to make up for whatever lost wages. When we came on the job, I believe the fire department actually hadn't had a contract in a number of years. They had been in a contract dispute with the city. So, we actually came on in 1986 and the contract was settled. One of the advantages was even though my starting salary may have been low, we didn't have to wait. After one year we went right up to the top level of the firefighter's salary. Because part of the settlement of the contract was that everybody would start at the same salary. So, that was the advantage. Even though we came in the door as probies, within a year we were at top salary as a firefighter. Then I think they negotiated five steps and then seven and eleven or something like that.

I was doing much better than most of the people I went to high school with. Most of the people I went to school with literally, if they didn't have a civil service job in the police or fire or corrections, they were struggling in the private sector. So, I was considered middle-class, doing relatively well for a guy from Newark.

But I wasn't really a young guy. That's always relative. I actually didn't come on the job until I was twenty-nine years old. So, I had a wife and family. I worked the private sector in management for a number of years at different career directions.

Alexander I: I started out making thirty thousand a year. In the minds of my friends, I was rich. I left a job as a warehouse manager for Levitt's Furniture and at that time I was making about twenty-one annually. I went right from twenty-one right up to thirty.

Work schedule, we would do two ten-hour days, eight A.M. to six P.M. And then we would get one full day off, come back that third day and do two fourteen-hour nights which consisted of six P.M. to eight A.M. the next morning. We would do that, back-to-back nights and then we would have the next seventy-two hours off. That schedule went to the twenty-four shifts.

I think that affected the camaraderie because with the twenty-fours it was like, okay we're just here for the day and then everybody went their own way after that. You didn't see that person again until the next twenty-four. With the tens and fourteens, it was like, we would get off that evening, a couple of guys might say, "Hey let's go hang out or something." The next day we were right back together. We spent more time together although when you average it out it was kind of the same, but the way the time was you did a lot together. That's why I thought the camaraderie was better then than it is now. Now I see guys and it's like they don't even have a clue of who the next guy is that they're putting their life on the line with.

Maresca: When I first came on, we were doing two days, off a day, two nights which were fourteen-hour nights, and then off three days. I believe the salary was twenty-eight thousand, with the benefits it was like thirty-two. It was a pay increase though. I was a computer programmer before I got on the job.

DeLeon: We did ten and fourteens. Ten and fourteens is two ten-hour days followed by a day off. And then you go into the nightshift from six until eight o'clock the next morning. In the beginning, I used to get there about a quarter to six. I'm used to my old job. Fifteen, ten before and you're good. Until I learned that, no that's not good enough, try to get there an hour before. Get to know what happened, what's broken, what you need to do. Get your equipment, check your stuff, get yourself ready. Because if you walk in so late, it's going to happen that you're caught off guard. That fire's going to come in.

Twenty-five thousand was my starting salary. I left my job that I was making twenty-six thousand five hundred. Because I was a warehouse manager. They called me a week before to go to the Academy and being inexperienced I said, "Well, I got to give my job two weeks' notice because I'm going to lose money." Mr. Whalen goes to me, "You want the job or not?" "Yeah, I want it. I want it. I'm not saying I don't want it. I just don't want to lose the money." So, I went back to my old job and told them I'm going on vacation, emergency vacation for that week. When I was supposed to go back, I said "Oh by the way, I quit." They got upset, but what are they going to do? I found a new thing here. Whatever you want to call it and I wasn't going back. So, it was twenty-five thousand dollars.

I remember my first couple of months in the firehouse, what they told me, "Oh, kid you're lucky. You're going to be making sixty thousand." That number didn't make any sense to me. Sixty? No way I'm going to be making sixty. On this job? I'm lucky if I make fifty when I retire. It was crazy. I can't believe that. And you know when I retired, I was making a hundred and sixty. So, that goes to show you. You learn things as you go along.

I had a little one-bedroom apartment. My daughter was only six months when I went to the Academy. Four hundred dollars was my rent and it's hard to believe. Like I can never afford a house. I'm not going to be able to buy it. The following year I bought a house.

As far as other people's salaries, I didn't recognize anybody where I worked, people that met there made like twenty, twenty-two thousand. It wasn't a bad field. It was very demanding though. I worked almost seven days a week, ten hours plus. And I had a pager. I would be on call. We would take turns being on call. So, if it was ten o'clock at night or midnight and they call because they have problems, the equipment failed or something, I would have to get in my truck and go. Put it on the sheet to get paid. So, that probably helped with how I made more money at that time. But I was starting to hate the job. I was hoping that I caught a break. The same day that Mr. Whalen called me, UPS called. "You start Monday." Because I applied for them too at that same time. I was simply worn out. I had to call them up and say I don't want it. I didn't know. I had no idea, but I'm not taking that job. I'm not taking that job. Now, I'm sounding selfish because I'm lucky where I'm at. I'm willing to take the pay cut. I know that the medicals and the benefits and the pension and the chance to move up the ladder were there. I had some insight as to its potential. So, this is what I want to do.

Taylor: We were working tens and fourteens when I came on. Days, you worked two days from eight A.M. to six P.M. Then you're off a day. You work two nights from six P.M. to eight in the morning. Then you're off three days. But I don't know if you remember, personally for me, I didn't like twenty-fours, but my wife died in 2000 and my guys were two and five. When my days off were Monday through Friday, it gave me time to see them off to school every day. So, I went from a non-advocate of twenty-fours to a firm endorser of twenty-four-hour shifts. That's a personal side. It ended up working out better for me.

I don't remember my starting salary, but it got sweeter in the years. Compared to the guys I went to college with, I was way ahead of it. Let's say it like this, Neal. When I left Elizabeth teaching and came to this department my annual earnings jumped fifty thousand dollars. So, that should give you a bit of perspective on those numbers.

Griggs: When I first came on, I think the salary was twenty-five thousand five hundred dollars. That was the most money I ever made in my life, so I was happy. I was ready to buy a Corvette, but that didn't happen either. After we finished the Training Academy, then we were assigned to the tours and it was two ten-hour dayshifts, a day and a half off and then two fourteen-hour nightshifts.

Greene: Salary was, I'm going to say it was maybe twenty-six, twenty-eight thousand, somewhere around there. I think it might have put us slightly below I would say a teacher.

Sperli: I started at twenty-five thousand five hundred dollars. That was the starting salary when I came on. I think there were only like three steps at that time, but now I believe they're up to seven or eight steps for top salary. I think twenty-five five was maybe the lower middle class or middle class at that time.

Alvarez: We had what we called tens and fourteens, two ten-hour days, a day off, two fourteen-hour nights and three days off. I did that for probably the first fourteen, fifteen years that I was on the job. Until we switched over to the twenty-four-hour shift. My salary was twenty-nine five when I first came on. And I believe the top salary at the time was like forty-nine thousand. There were four steps to top salary.

Cordasco: The longevity was a four percent difference in my salary because we had to wait for a fifth year to get it on the police, when Wayne and I switched over we actually got a thousand more a year. I guess just because of the forty-two-hour schedule. Whatever it was, we got like a thousand dollars more on the fire department than we did on the police department. We didn't get the over time, but we didn't have to go to court on our days off. We didn't have to work sixteen-hour shifts and stuff like that. I think it was close to forty because I was at steps. What happened was switching over at that time police to the fire you stayed at whatever salary you had. So, when we went on the police there were only three steps to the top pay and since we got on the police in July, it took us a year and a half to get to top pay. So, when we came over to the fire it stayed at top pay but then we also got a four percent increase on longevity and like a thousand dollars more a year on the base salary.

The tour schedule on the fire department was two ten-hour days, eight to six, day and a half off, and then two fourteen-hour nights followed by three days off. And it was like an eight-day schedule, so you always shifted up a day how you worked. So, Monday, Tuesday this week, Tuesday, Wednesday next week and so on.

Daniels: Oh, wow, we were on tens and fourteens when I came on. And you had the twenty-four hours in the middle, so getting used to that. That eventually changed. Now it's twenty-fours and we're off seventy-two and we work another twenty-four and that consists of a week.

When I started, I must have started with maybe twenty-eight, maybe thirty. I was just happy to be making that money. I was twenty-five exactly when I got the job. Cause it took two years for that whole process. I was still looking for a job and I didn't find anything really that I had a passion for. When they started looking for me for this job it was great. This was the first opportunity at a career job. It just opened up my world to me. I was just really grateful.

LaPenta: The work schedule was tens and fourteens. What we would do is we would come in and work two dayshifts in a row. We'd work from eight in the morning to six at night. Then we would be off for forty-eight hours. And then we would come into work two nightshifts from six at night until eight in the morning and then we would be off for seventy-two hours. So, it was the old two on one off two on three off. You know guys liked it a lot because it gave you the in-between day which was good. Guys worked a lot of part-time jobs. So, some guys to this day miss it, but I love the twenty-fours. Actually, when I got promoted, they switched the schedule. The officers had the twenty-fours and the firefighters' union didn't. They weren't playing nice with the mayor at the time, so the mayor gave us twenty-fours. I think it was a twenty-four on, a two off, and twenty-four and four off or something. It was great. It was one of those schedules. Then the firemen eventually got twenty-fours and they wanted us all to be on the same page. Twenty-fours is a great schedule.

My salary, I want to say my salary was like twenty-three thousand, twenty-four thousand or something like that. I think half of the guys I graduated high school with weren't even working to be honest with you. I stayed in touch with a bunch of guys, but guys weren't making as much. I remember I had a piece of crap car and as soon as I got my check I went out and I leased a new car. I needed a car. I got a real job now; I need to get to work back and forth. Even though I'm coming from Bloomfield Avenue to Summer Avenue I still needed to have a car. What was nice was I got hired in August. At the time there were three steps to top pay for firefighter, so I got hired in August and I went to the second step January. And then the following January I was at top pay. Now I know there's a multitude of steps. I don't know how long it takes, but the guys coming on the job are making like fifty. So, it's all relative.

Tarantino: My salary was twenty-five thousand five hundred dollars. I actually took a pay cut to come here. I was doing pretty good at Shoprite stocking shelves. Probably took a ten thousand dollar pay cut at the time. Best move I ever made though. Other than that, everything kind of stayed the same for me. I had moved out of my mother's house when I was like eighteen years old. I used to live on High Street in the frat house in the basement. So, I was going to school. I continued to go to school after I came on the fire department. I went part time. Captain Haran was my first captain, and he would allow me to take a radio. I had a little white pickup. I put all my gear in the back. I used to park on the sidewalk in front of the frat house and go to class and bring the radio, the roof radio, to class. He says, "If we get something, go there." He was awesome. I was able to finish my degree going there.

West: Tens and fourteens are the schedule that most people used back then. You worked two ten-hour days, eight in the morning to six at night and you had a swing day in the middle, then two fourteen-hour nights, six at night to eight in the morning. And then after those two nightshifts you would have three days off and then start the cycle over again. I believe my starting salary was twenty-eight or thirty-two, somewhere in that area. Wasn't bad, I wasn't complaining.

When I came on at twenty-three years old, I wasn't really sure where that put me. I think it was more than I was making in the Post Office. I was a mailman prior to. So, anything more than that, well I was pretty happy with. I'm not really sure on the economic scale where it ranked, but certainly I was okay with it.

Pierson: Salary was thirty-one eight to start out. I was young. My friends were mostly all still finishing up college, starting new jobs. So, I was doing pretty good for the first couple of years.

We had two ten-hour days, a day off, and two fourteen-hour nights and then three days off. Now we work the twenty-four-hour schedule. You lost a lot of the in-house camaraderie with the other tours. It used to be you saw everybody and you got to have laughs with all of them. Now you're down to two that you see and you know. When you're showing up now-a-days, it's not a lot of people hang and have coffee anymore. That was a real treat in the morning, to have all the guys there. You have to get to work, but I think you lose a lot there. I like the schedule because it's a little more flexible, but I kind of wish these younger guys would have experienced the old one. You could go have fun, a lot of excuses to get out. Years ago, went out with the guys from work and that made it fun. That made you a little tighter because you meet before work, for a nightshift. You could go out after the days.

Petrone: We worked ten/fourteens which was two ten-hour days, a day off, then two fourteen-hour nights followed by three days off. Now we just work a twenty-four-hour shift. We have three days off in between. I preferred the old shift myself. I remember when we had the vote, for the firemen's union and I think there were maybe five guys who voted against going to the twenty-four-hour shift. My biggest concern was that you were going to lose all the camaraderie that you had over the years on the fire department and that's exactly what happened. But now if you talk to guys, everybody voted against the twenty-four-hour shift. Even though there were only five guys that voted against it, now everybody was one of those five guys.

I believe we started at thirty thousand eight hundred dollars even. It improved dramatically. Last year I think I made a hundred and seventeen and change. I think back then it was only five steps or six steps. And I think now there are seven or eight to get to top salary. So, it takes you a little bit longer.

When I started, we were offered a choice between three different companies for our medicals, and you had the open enrollment every year. Whatever was given to us when we came on, I just stayed with that because I was single so, I wasn't too concerned with it, but the medical benefits were good. They were better than most people get. And they still are good now. You're just paying a little bit more for it. But I was single for all those years, so I didn't really concern myself with that. I was just more worried about money going into my pocket.

Castellucio: Tour schedule was the ten and fourteens when I came on. You'd work two dayshifts in a row, ten-hour days. You would start at eight and get off at six. Then you would get a full day off and then you'd be off the daytime the next day and come in that night at six o'clock until eight in the morning. And you would do that for two shifts in a row and then you would have three days off.

My starting salary I believe was twenty-six thousand dollars, in that range. At the time I was in the carpenters' union making about fifty thousand dollars a year. So, I took almost a fifty percent cut in pay for the job.

Snyder: We worked tens and fourteens which I loved. Guys worked during the day or even at night, they would do the two fourteen hours. You would work the night, and everyone would go on the boat for the day, go golfing for the day, and then go back to work. Then those three days that you're off, you kind of did your own thing and then you'd be back. But it was a great schedule. I was still a fireman when we got the twenty-fours. We were still on the tens and fourteens when the captains went to the twenty-fours. So, the captains were working a different tour than us. If you were on the first tour, they would do the first tour, second tour.

A lot of guys too were actually trying to work with their captain so they would do a lot of swaps. So, they would like swap with their sister tour so the captain and the guys would stay together. It all worked out.

Unfortunately, I think we did lose our fire department because of that. It's a great schedule and it does the guys good to go home and regroup, but you don't hang out, don't help each other like they once did. Once you leave that tour you don't hang out as much, not like we used to.

I was paid twenty-nine thousand when I first came on and there were five steps. I think that puts us pretty close to par with the guys I went to high school with. Probably a little bit behind, but at top step at seventy grand or whatever at the time some of these guys were making a little bit more, but I was happy. You had a little money. You had a little time.

Bartelloni: We were working tens and fourteens when I came on the job. You would work two ten-hour days back-to-back eight to six eight to six. Then you would have one day off. The following evening you came in for two six at night to eight in the morning in a row and then you had three days off. You begin that same pattern of eight to six, eight to six, a day off. Six to eight six to eight three days off. So, you can look at the whole year. You can look at years and see where you'd be if you were on a certain tour.

Gail: We worked ten-hour days, fourteen-hour nights. So, it was a good schedule. You worked two days in a row, two dayshifts, two ten-hour days, eight in the morning to six at night. Then you would have one full day off. The next day you would come in at night starting at six o'clock and you'd work until eight in the morning. Following day was the same thing, six at night until eight in the morning and then three days off. It was an eight-day cycle.

I don't remember the starting salary. I want to say it was about thirty-one thousand maybe. I don't know how that compared to the rest of the world. The biggest thing was it is a steady paycheck. Now don't forget I just came out of college, so I had nothing. I was working two days a week roofing. So, I was making two hundred dollars a week. That was my salary. It was enough to pay rent, pay my car, and I had some extra money, so it wasn't bad money. But it wasn't good money either. So, when I got a steady paycheck. You knew what that paycheck was going to be week after week, it was a big difference. Even though it wasn't a lot of money it was still a steady paycheck. It was pretty cool.

Ostertag: We worked tens and fourteens which I think is the greatest shift. We'd come in, work two ten-hour days, one day off, two fourteen-hour nights, three off. I liked it because you get to see everybody. You got more chances for a fire because then you're here four days a week compared to now, you're here twice a week. So, you got to see more, I think, than you do in a twenty-four-hour shift.

You were here in the city more. And also, I like the camaraderie. I mean we did things in between our nights and in between our days as a crew. Now, I'll be honest with you, after the twenty-four-hour shift we work now, you just want to go home. There's no hanging out anymore. You're done. You're tired. You're in the same building for twenty-four hours. You just want to go. It was a great shift. I loved it.

I started at twenty-seven thousand. The starting pay was probably a little bit more than average, but not much more. But the security was here. I didn't expect to make what I'm making now. I think over the past few years, salaries went higher in the fire department. But starting it was about the same, maybe a little bit more. It depends; some of my friends made more, others made less. It's kind of in the middle. I'd have to say I was in the middle.

Ramos: When I first started, we worked tens and fourteens, ten hours during the day, fourteen-hour nights. It was a great shift. We had a good time with that shift. We'd work a ten-hour day then we're off that night. We come back the next morning, another ten hours. Then we'd be off two days, come back for the fourteen-hour shift that night. Come in at six in the evening until eight in the morning. Did that again, then we're off three days. Today's hours have changed. Today we work the twenty-four-hour shift which means we come in at eight in the morning we leave at eight in the morning the next morning and you're off for three days.

When I first came on the salary was thirty-five thousand. Compared to the people I went to high school and college with, it put me up there. I was making probably more than some of them were. It improved my salary from the three jobs that I had at one point. They didn't compare to the fire department without benefits.

Richardson: It was tens and fourteens when we first came on. And that was pretty good because I never worked shift schedule like that. So, it kind of broke you into it. The camaraderie was a lot better I think with that. I did a lot of part time work, but you had a lot of time where if a guy needs your help, that short day was perfect for that. You could go and help other people. The twenty-fours have kind of wiped that out. But the part time going from firehouse to part time to firehouse to part time, it kind of was a little strain on the family life because it was days basically before you got home. But we managed. I enjoyed the tens and fourteens. I liked the twenty-fours, but it changed the job. Really did.

The tens and fourteens, your tens you were drilling, you were going to the Academy. You were making sure that the guys at night didn't have to worry about the rig breaking down or stuff around the firehouse not being done. You made sure that things were done for them just like you were hoping that they were done for you. The night, you came in, it was more of a social routine. Somebody would bring in dinner. You would cook, hang around watch some TV, go to bed and you got up. If it was your final night, you would pack up your bed. You could leave your bed on that first night. You would leave your bed made up then you would come in that second night and that was all done. You didn't have to worry about it. But for me, especially for being on Five Truck, it was learning the job. You really did all that during the day, those ten-hour shifts. And they went by pretty quick, but you did a lot. The nights were really more relaxed because you knew no matter what, for some reason back in the '90s and I only caught the very end of it, you almost knew that one of those two nights you were catching a job. So, you kind of like waited for that.

I don't think I really lost money when I left my previous job. I think I made maybe a little bit more. But it wasn't a lot. I was a kid in an office in an aerospace division. I was supplying parts for an assembly puller. If I was making forty thousand; I guess I was doing good. So, this kind of kicked me up a few notches. You got to remember I only had a high school education. I didn't have college. I didn't have any prospects in the works. So, anything was better than where I was. Economically it did help, and it was really more about benefits. I had a young son at the time and my wife. We needed benefits and we needed a future. This department gave that. This job brought me up. We were thinking about moving to a different area of the country. Figuring out what we were going to do. This job kept me here which kind of is a blessing and a curse. But economically I never could have made the money that I'm making and had the opportunities that I've had, not only for myself, but for my family if I didn't have this job. No doubt about it.

Jackson: My salary was twenty-eight thousand. That put me ahead of the game because my job prior to that, coming out of high school I worked for Federal Express. I did that part-time. And I really didn't like the job too much and it was only part-time. It really wasn't doing anything for me. A lot of my friends worked for the airline. At the time they had just completed the construction of Northern State jail. Some of my close friends, they applied for that job and got it because at the time they were hiring a lot of Newark residents.

We worked ten-hour days for two days straight, from oh eight hundred hours to eighteen hundred hours. Then I would have one day off. And then I would work two fourteen-hour shifts from eighteen hundred hours to oh eight hundred hours the next day. You would do that for two days and then you would have seventy-two hours off. It was a great schedule and I kind of miss that schedule. Now we have twenty-four hours. If you never worked the old schedule, it did a lot for the department because the camaraderie was a lot better. We were an extended family.

Y. Pierre: I think I was making forty-two thousand dollars a year when I first came on. That's including vacation, shift differential all those combined together. I think it was about forty-two thousand. But at the beginning when I first started it was a different schedule. We worked ten hours and then one day off and you work fourteen hours. But the schedule now, as far as I'm concerned, is the best schedule ever. I love it. You get more time to play with your kids, enjoy your family. It's just wonderful.

Farrell: Tens and fourteens, two ten-hour days, a day off, two fourteen-hour nights, three days off. Tremendous.

The salary started at thirty-one. I think it was thirty-one we started. But contractually we were still doing okay. We were still getting those raises. Now you don't get them. So, you were able to bump up in the first couple of years. It took the sting out of leaving the job that I was making good money. I know I'm not the first to say that. There are guys in the FDNY they had to go on food stamps in the Academy. You don't come on this job for the money anyway. You make good money once you hit senior step fireman, once you get promoted. Yes, you're making decent money. But that's another thing, with the civilians and the public that those numbers keep getting thrown out there. "You make that kind of money?" Yeah, but let me show you my paystub. I stunned a judge one time in a hearing. She looked at my paycheck and said, "That's your gross pay and that's what you take home? What's this figure here?" I said, "That's what we pay into our pension." She goes, "You guys pay that kind of money into your pension every month?" I said, "No, that's what we pay into our pension every two weeks." She said, "You're kidding me." "No, I'm not kidding you." So, people would be stunned by our gross and our net. That's why ninety percent of firemen have second jobs because you kind of sort of have to.

Roberson: Our schedule was tens and fourteens. We worked two ten-hour days; we're off a day; we worked two fourteen-hour nights; then you're off three days. That was the shift back then. We negotiated a contract to change the shift to twenty-four hours. So now it's twenty-four hours on, seventy-two hours off. Base salary for a basic firefighter was about thirty-eight thousand dollars when I first came on and for a senior fireman, I think it was like sixty-eight thousand.

Most of my friends were policemen and firemen and military guys. I really had very few guys that were corporate that came out of school with me. We had a few, but most of us were public servants. They started a lot earlier than I did.

Meier: We worked tens and fourteens, two ten-hour days, then a day off, and then two fourteen-hour nights and then three days off. Salary was twenty-eight nine twenty-two. I never went to college, so some of the guys I went to high school with went into trades and some of them went to college. I would say it was an average salary. It was average. It wasn't upper. It was at the lower area.

Rodrigues: Back in the day it was tens and fourteens. It was two days, ten hours a day, a day off, then two nights fourteen hours a night, then three days off. Salary, I believe, was twenty-eight thousand five hundred. Back then I was making close to fifty at the Manor Hotel, so I took a little cut there. But I knew that down the road I would be getting what I'm getting these days. Compared to college guys back then, I would say, and you know what? I've seen this for the last twenty years. Including myself, a lot of guys like myself go to college. Unfortunately, some of us ended up at the mall for the minimum. So, twenty-eight thousand five hundred back in the day was decent.

Montalvo: When I came on, we were working tens and fourteens, come in the morning, work from eight until six, go home, come back the next morning work eight until six again. Then we would get a day off in between and come back and work our two nightshifts. So, we worked a fourteen-hour shift from six at night to eight in the morning. And we would do that for two days and then we would get three days off. When I first came on the starting salary was like twenty-eight thousand. That was a pretty decent salary back then. Twenty-eight thousand to start with, that was decent.

Willis: We worked two ten-hour shifts and then we were off for forty-eight hours. And then we came back and worked two fourteen-hour shifts and we were off for seventy-two hours. I liked that shift. When I was on the twenty-four hours, I thought it would be a good thing, but as I got older, I realized that I might have made a mistake pulling that hammer for that vote. Because when we were on the tens and fourteens the camaraderie was very high. We were always challenging each other in baseball. We always met for drinks, lunch, dinner depending on which shift the guys wanted to meet. We had swing night with the guys in the Burg in the beginning, when I started up in the Burg. I was at Twenty-one Engine. The twenty-four-hour shift I think took all that away. Guys don't even know each other on the job anymore on the first, second, third, or fourth tour. You only see them at change of shift and that's it. When it was the tens and fourteens, you saw everyone. One way or another you knew everyone. And I think the twenty-fours did a lot of damage to the morale of the department.

Leaving Port Newark to come on the job was a hell of a drop in salary. I took a sixty thousand dollar pay cut to take this job. I think it was twenty-eight thousand when I came on. We went through six steps. At that time there really was no fuss about how it was structured. If you came on in October on the first step, when you reached January, you went to your second step. Now these guys play games and make you go a whole year before you get your second shift if you're hired after August thirty-first. I would have made more as a longshoreman, but the time with my family is very important. That's what my father was talking about. Things are going to change. He was there forty-five years, in Port Newark and he turned around and said, "Jimmy, you've got to find something different. This job is going to ruin you." Coming on this department changed my life dramatically. I was a wild horse. It took a couple of years to calm down. And I wind up raising a beautiful family and here I am. My base salary is ninety-six thousand. That's my base. At the end of the year, I'm making a hundred and fifteen plus. I mean I never thought that I would ever find a job making that kind of money for these hours. I think the men should appreciate it more.

Highsmith: We worked tens and fourteens. Tens and fourteens, starts eight in the morning to six at night; let's say that's a Sunday morning. Then after you get off at six at night you have to come back in eight in the morning the next day to six at night. Then you have a day off in between; then you come in at night for fourteen hours the day after the day off. And that's a fourteen-hour shift. Then you come in the night after that and that's another fourteen-hour shift. And then you get three days off in between that and it starts all over again.

I came on in my fourth step since I was already hired as a mechanic for the City of Newark. I worked on apparatus on overtime most of the time, but I was in the police shop where I worked on police cars. So, when I came across, I was on my fourth step which was around fifty thousand dollars or forty-seven thousand dollars. It was an increase. The city policy is if you make a lateral transfer from department to department your pay would never go down. It would either stay even or go higher to reach the next step. It took me a little bit higher than my pay was already. Compared to guys I went to high school with, some are college educated. Me being a mechanic, when I first came out of the army, I made more money than them, but over time they passed me. Now, I go to the fire department. I probably make more than them now.

Freese: We had tens and fourteens. We worked two ten-hour days; we had one day off; then we worked two fourteen-hour nights; and then we'd be off three days, seventy-two hours.

I believe my starting salary was twenty-eight thousand. That put me a little above the guys I went to school with. Obviously, I had some smart friends, some really smart friends. They became lawyers and stuff like that, so they were doing pretty well. Everyone else was more the blue collar, nine to five in a factory. So, yeah, it kind of put me a little above.

Carr: The hours were tens and fourteens. It was eight to six and the six to eight. You'll do two ten-hour shifts and then one day off. Then you'll do two consecutive fourteen hour shifts with seventy-two hours off. It changed after my fifth or sixth year on the job. Then we went to twenty-fours. And the crazy thing about that was there's no way in your time that you got through would they have been successful with twenty-four hours. There's no way, no way, nooo way. There would have been a lot of divorces and a lot of angry men during that time. A lot of injured firefighters, imagine that, twenty-four hours.

When I came on my salary was about twenty-eight, twenty-nine thousand. And you really don't get to top pay until after your seventh step. That put me in the higher medium scale of salaries at that time as far as entry level is concerned. I mean for the most part, it was one of the best paying jobs entry level wise. I worked for UPS. I worked for the Post Office. I worked for Verizon. So, I was quite pleased. But it was okay until you start getting that double pension payment. You got to pay that back. It was a little rough but, a lot of us did what we had to do. We took part time jobs and everything like that. We made the ends meet. So, I was still bumming off my parents a little bit. But it was cool. I mean actually that May of 2000 I got married. It was a step up. What we got basically was we came on with less vacation days as per the contract negotiations prior to us coming on. They took two vacation days coming in. We had to earn them later.

Rosario: My salary, I remember very well. I started at twenty-seven five. I was making over fifty or sixty thousand with the post office at the time. I took a big pay cut, but I knew it was coming, so I prepared for it. I always saved money and you sacrifice for your dream.

We worked the tens and fourteens, I remember. I actually came from another fire department, the Harrison Fire Department, before coming here. They had the twenty-four-hour shift there. So, I come to Newark, after going through the extensive Academy they put us through, going to tens and fourteen was a little shock to me. Since I pretty much got spoiled doing the twenty-four-hour shift with three days off. When you do a ten and fourteen, what that means is you come in for a ten-hour shift at eight o'clock in the morning. You get off at eighteen hundred hours. You have the night off. At zero eight the next morning you have to come back in. And then you work to eighteen hundred hours again. Then you have that night off, the next full day off, the next half day off, and then you come in at eighteen hundred hours. That starts your nightshift. So, you come in for your nightshift at eighteen hundred to zero eight. Then you'll leave for the day, for your ten hours, rest, and then you'll come back at eighteen hundred to zero eight. Then you have three full days off. It keeps going in that manner. You have four tours doing the same thing. That's how everything is covered twenty-four hours a day.

Kupko: It was still tens and fourteens. Two ten-hour dayshifts, a day off, two fourteen-hour nights, and three days off I believe is how it went. And it was eight to six for the dayshifts and six P.M. to eight A.M. for the evening shift.

Starting salary was right around thirty thousand I would say. Since I was a teacher, it was rough. I took a pay cut initially, but one of the deciding factors taking this job was the salary was going to advance at a much more rapid rate than if I stayed in the teaching profession. The hours were better too, obviously.

Mickels: Ten and fourteens was a schedule that was like a split shift type schedule. That was very temporary. We did that for about a year. We were the last class that came on with the old school. My class was the last of the old school, the last class to have a class on Jersey Street downtown. So anyway, going back to the scheduling, I remember doing two ten-hour days, a forty-eight hour, two fourteen-hour nights, and then three days off. Most of my career was the twenty-four-hour schedule.

The twenty-fours for myself personally, worked pretty well. I liked it. It gave me a chance to do a lot more on my own personal side. And it was nice. For some guys it wasn't good because it decreased the camaraderie with the guys. A lot of guys spent a lot of time together during that forty-eight and went right back to the firehouse together, so a lot of the camaraderie went away with the change of the shifts. But on a personal level, it was nice. I liked it and I still like it. I like working two days a week, seven, eight days a month. So, on a personal level it worked well for me. There are four tours. I'm on the fourth tour. I just got off this morning, so today is my first complete day off. So, we have a twenty-four-hour shift on then we seventy-two hours off which is three days. So, I worked yesterday, Thursday. I got off today. Today is my first of the seventy-two, three days off. So, I'll be returning back to work Monday.

The salary was right around thirty thousand. We started off at about thirty, twenty-nine, thirty thousand, wasn't quite thirty. Six steps, the fourth step was a nice big step. That was a big jump in pay. And then we had the fifth step which was a small step and then you had the sixth step. I actually drove tracker-trailers before I came on and at the time with the overtime, I was making well over fifty thousand dollars a year. I think my last year was fifty-two thousand. I worked for a freight company driving tracker-trailers. And so, it was a hit. It was a pay cut.

All of us knew what the senior step was going to be and the benefits, the medicals, the promotional opportunities, and the scheduling. Back then we knew that they were working on the twenty-fours. So, we knew what the benefit of that was. More time to get another job, go back to school. So even with the pay cut it was well worth it because of what we were looking forward to coming on.

Jenkins: The tour schedule was tens and fourteens. Tens and fourteens were where you worked two ten-hour shifts on two days. You're off one day and we worked two nightshifts. The two ten-hour shifts were, you worked from oh eight hundred to eighteen hundred hours. That would be your ten-hour day. Then you're off that night and you come back the next morning. Then you would be off a day. Then you would come back for the fourteen-hour shift. It would start at eighteen hundred hours to zero eight hundred. I was making twenty-six thousand. I took a substantial pay cut. At the Post Office I was making forty-eight thousand dollars a year. I left the Post Office, came to the fire department to make twenty-eight thousand. People thought I was crazy, but I was good. I understood what you can get from being on the job.

Gaddy: My salary when I came on was thirty-five thousand and the work schedule was the twenty-fours. I come from the environment of the south ward. So, you can imagine the struggles that everybody else was dealing with compared to what I was dealing with. It was me getting on with new money. I had a steady income. Where other people were working for twenty dollars an hour, but not making the money that I was making. So, the hardship was looked at kind of differently from my point of view because I was still there for eight years. Anybody that was in my circle, I was helping out. My inner circle, I don't think they felt any hardship on my end because if I did something, they did something. I grew and got my family. Now is more of family helping out. Instead of your friends that are leaching off of you, those that like to see things coming their way, but not on the other end where they give you. So, you had to cut leaches off and grow new stems and pretty much I'm more surrounded with people of my statue now.

Figuereq: I think the salary was at thirty-three starting. I actually left a job where I was making a lot more, but it was a career for a career, so I think ahead. I was making eighty plus in the IT field. It's not a decision I regret at all. I love the job, so I'm happy I made the decision. When I came on, they were already on the twenty-fours and three days off.

Medina: I was working the twenty-four hours. We didn't do the tens and fourteens. The salary was pretty good. It was thirty-two thousand. I was a mechanic. It kind of evened out.

I had time off, a few days off. Over there I was working sixty hours, five days a week. The people I went to school with actually a lot of them are military and a lot of them are cops. A couple are firemen as well, on the job. I grew up in a neighborhood where everybody did something like that.

Dugan: Yeah, they were working twenty-fours when I came on. We still had the gongs for about a year and then they switched over to no more gongs and the Locution stuff. It could have been close to two years when they switched it. The salary was mid-thirties.

K. Alfano: Twenty-four-hour shift, that's the only shift I know. When I first came on the salary was thirty-four thousand a year. I was doing a lot better than most of my friends because I was twenty turning twenty-one when I came on. I had a job before most of the kids I went to school with had one.

M. Bellina: It was the twenty-four-hour shift. I'm not really sure what my salary was when I came on. It was tough. It might have been thirties or forty something. I think there's seven or eight steps now. Without those other things they add into it like the time. Compared to my friends I guess it depends. There's a wide range of people. Two of my closest friends are engineers. They do well for themselves and then one is actually the assistant district attorney in New York City. A couple of them work doing trading, so they're making good money. My one friend sells insurance and he makes a killing. But the time that they put in, the time that I'm here, it's a totally different world.

B. Maresca: Twenty-four hours on, three days off. I think the salary was about forty-three thousand.

G. Centanni: The twenty-four hours on, seventy-two off. Starting I think the salary was forty-two. When I started step one was forty-two. I didn't have any college or anything like that. A lot of people I know started around that, maybe fifty, so a little bit under maybe.

G. Pierre: I was informed at how you guys used to do the half on and half off. But we've been on a twenty-four-hour schedule, twenty-four on seventy-two off. I do a lot of swaps. For me it's good because it's a good way for me to meet and see all the guys. Via swaps, via details, I work a lot of other tours between looking out for guys and details for guys.

The starting salary was so low it didn't even matter. I'm a working bee. I worked two jobs, so I don't even know what my salary was. But my check, I did the math. When I first came on, I was running into burning buildings for sixteen bucks an hour. There are like five steps. I'm currently on my second step, going to my third step. Twice a year I go down to the union and I'll approach somebody who is in my step.

How did that compare to my peers? That's the one thing about me. I thank my mother and for instilling it in me. I thank my family as a whole. I've always been kind of like that worker bee that stays busy, go get a job. You want more, go get another job. You want more. You go to school. If you've got two firefighters in your family, you see somebody with a nice little car. We had a model, you want more, go get more. You got to work for what you want. So, I paid my school loans off on my own. I always had two jobs, so compared to my peers I always tipped the bar. I was never one I could compare to my peers. I would definitely say I was well off. I got what I worked for.

Prior to getting the fire department, I made sixty-eight thousand dollars a year before I got laid off. And that kind of hurt. And then after that I was making like thirty-one thousand dollars a year prior to becoming a firefighter. To this day I still have that same job. I'm on call at a nursery hospital for kids. I work on call and if I have a free day or two, I go there. I do the work. They pay me like fifteen bucks an hour. Every now and then if I wanted something nice, I put the work in and go get something nice. That's kind of how I live.

Rawa: My salary's not so good right now. Every two weeks we get paid. My paycheck is about a thousand eighty-two after everything is taken out. I think I'm at twenty an hour. The gross would have to be like what fourteen, before everything's taken out. Then your insurance and union dues and all those associations. There are six or seven steps.

You look at my friends who I grew up with here in Newark and it's hard to compare. I feel like I'm more stable now because I have a steady career going for me. I might not be more financially stable, but the money is going to catch up. So, I'm going to have that stability as long as I do the right thing. Even friends who have graduated, it doesn't mean anything to them. One of my best friends is a college graduate. Right now, he is completely unemployed. No job, no income, he's collecting unemployment.

I work twenty-four hours, one full day, three full days off. Every four days we work.

J. Centanni: We worked twenty-four hours on and three days off. I think forty-one thousand we started with when I came on. That was relatively normal. I think most of my friends are cops or construction guys. So, I think we're all around the same.

Garay: The salary was forty-three I believe. I had to take a pay cut because I used to be a teacher. So, I took a tremendous pay cut. But it was worth the while because I realized I can't be a good teacher and a good mom. I was just burnt out of the whole situation with the teaching. So, since my husband and I came together on the job, it balanced us out financially. We were pretty much making the same amount of money because he was a substitute while I was a fulltime teacher. And now that we both came on the job, we're pretty much making the same amount of money. Our schedule is three days off, one day twenty-four hours then another three days off.

Fortunato: Kind of low starting off, but I think it ends up pretty good. I think after all the holiday pay and all that it was forty-two. I took a big pay cut to come here. I was a lineman for PSE&G before this. But it was what I always wanted to do so it's worth the sacrifice. A lot of kids I went to high school with, even though they got college degrees, don't have jobs that pay that high.

Earp: Forty-five thousand, is the salary. Compared to my peers it's definitely above where my peers are at this point. It's a step back from where I was working, but sometimes you have to take a step back to do something you really like. So, that was my situation. For me to take a cut from my other job to come to this job because this was something I wanted to do. So, I took the sacrifice and I'm enjoying what I'm doing.

Corales: My salary is forty-two thousand two hundred and some change. It puts me there on average with the guys from high school. Some are doing good. They're working in Port Newark. I have other friends who are working in the insurance industry. We're making all about the same thing. We're all at about the same level, for the most part. My work schedule is twenty-four hours on, three days off.

Alexander II: My salary is forty-five. The economy isn't terrific right now, so besides doctors and lawyers and guys that work on Wall Street I'm doing pretty well. As far as my other peers, I'm doing pretty well.

Cruz: I make between forty and forty-five. I took a pay cut at the moment, but I know it's going, absolutely it's going up. So, it's perfectly fine. I don't have a problem with that.

Interviewees

Alexander I, Captain Donald, 2 September, 2016, transcript. (appointed 1987)

Alexander II, Firefighter Donald, 23 July, 2016, transcript. (appointed 2016)

Alfano, Firefighter George, 19 December, 2005, transcript. (appointed 1953)

Almaguer, Firefighter Arnold, 22 September, 2022, transcript. (appointed 1980)

Alfano, Captain Kevin, 9 August, 2016, transcript. (appointed 2006)

Alvarez, Captain Orlando, 26 July, 16 August, 2016, transcript. (appointed 1989)

Arce, Battalion Chief Orlando, 9 October, 2016, transcript. (appointed 1984)

Banta, Captain Robert, 6 July, 2000, transcript. (appointed 1974)

Bartelloni, Battalion Chief Paul, 9 July, 2019, transcript. (appointed 1993)

Bellina, Deputy Director of OEM Frank, 17 August, 2016, transcript. (appointed 1981)

Bellina, Firefighter Norman, 5 September, 2020, transcript. (appointed 1986)

Bellina, Firefighter Michael, 18 August, 2016, transcript. (appointed 2008)

Benderoth, Captain John, 15 November, 2005, transcript. (appointed 1967)

Bitter, Deputy Chief Richard, 27 December, 2002, transcript. (appointed 1959)

Brown, Firefighter Anthony, 14 July, 1991, transcript. (appointed 1979)

Brownlee, Battalion Chief Walter, 4 September, 2019, transcript. (appointed 1973)

Burkhardt, Captain Kevin, 9 February, 2004, transcript. (appointed 1973)

Calvetti, Battalion Chief Francis, 8 July, 2005, transcript. (appointed 1966)

Camasta, Captain Joseph, 23 July, 1991, transcript. (appointed 1974)

Cardillo, Firefighter Felix, 5 October, 2008, transcript. (appointed 1959)

Carr, Captain Delwin, 30 April, 2021, transcript. (appointed 2000)

Castelluccio, Deputy Chief Anthony, 23 August, 2016, transcript. (appointed 1993)

Centanni, Fire Chief John, 9 November, 2016, transcript. (appointed 1986)

Centanni, Firefighter Gerard, 31 October, 2016, transcript. (appointed 2013)

Centanni, Firefighter John, 31 October, 2016, transcript. (appointed 2014)

Coale, Captain Michael, 12 October, 2005, transcript. (appointed 1973)

Conover, Firefighter William, 24 April, 2005, transcript. (appointed 1948)

Conville, Captain Francis, 20 November, 2009, transcript. (appointed 1940)

Corales, Firefighter Joel, 8 August, 2016, transcript. (appointed 2016)

Cordasco, Battalion Chief Matthew, 20 June, 2016, transcript. (appointed 1989)

Cosby, Firefighter Boisy, 17 June, 2003, transcript. (appointed 1963)

Cruz, Firefighter Mellisa, 24 July, 2016, transcript. (appointed 2016)

Dainty, Battalion Chief Cliff, 6 September, 2016, 21 June, 2019, transcript. (appointed 1970)

Dalton, Captain Francis, 13 October, 2008, transcript. (appointed 1963)

Daly, Captain Phillip, 4 December, 2008, transcript. (appointed 1978)

Daniels, Battalion Chief Christopher, 22 July, 2016, transcript. (appointed 1989)

Daudelin, Captain George, 24 February, 2000, transcript. (appointed 1970)

DeCuester, Battalion Chief Steven, 22 May, 2019, transcript. (appointed 1984)

DeLeon, Battalion Chief Albert, 20 February, 2021, transcript. (appointed 1988)

Doherty, Captain John, 18 April, 2006, transcript. (appointed 1949)

Doherty, Captain Patrick, 18 September, 20 September, 2000, transcript. (appointed 1970)

Duerr, Chief of Apparatus Carl, 24 February, 2008, transcript. (appointed 1958)

Dugan, Captain Kevin, 23 July, 2016, transcript. (appointed 2006)

Earp, Firefighter Marky, 1 August, 2016, transcript. (appointed 2016)

Elward, Firefighter James, 9 July, 2005, transcript. (appointed 1962)

Farrell, Captain Daniel, 30 July, 3 August, 2016, transcript. (appointed 1996)

Figuereq, Captain Julio, 22 August, 2016, transcript. (appointed 2006)

Fortunato, Firefighter Michael, 20 August, 2016, transcript. (appointed 2014)

Freese, Captain Miguel, 11 August, 2016, transcript. (appointed 1998)

Gaddy, Firefighter Saadiq, 7, 19 August, 2016, transcript. (appointed 2006)

Gail, Deputy Chief Richard, 16 July, 2019, transcript. (appointed 1993)

Garay, Firefighter Veronica, 16 August, 2016, transcript. (appointed 2014)

Gaynor, Battalion Chief Robert, 22 October, 1999, transcript. (appointed 1965)

Gibson, Captain Richard, 22 April, 2005, transcript. (appointed 1953)

Giordano, Director David, 25 September, 10 October, 2020, transcript. (appointed 1984)

Goetchius, Captain Donald, 12 February, 1999, transcript. (appointed 1986)

Greene, Captain David, 29 July, 2019, transcript. (appointed 1988)

Griffith, Captain Edward, 29 September, 14 October, 2016, transcript. (appointed 1983)

Griggs, Deputy Chief John, 23 April, 2005, transcript. (appointed 1956)

Griggs, Captain John, 28 September, 2016, transcript. (appointed 1988)

Highsmith, Captain Gregory, 8 August, 2016, transcript. (appointed 2000)

Hopkins, Captain Mark, 23 October, 2019, transcript. (appointed 1978)

Jackson, Fire Chief Rufus, 6 August, 2016, transcript. (appointed 1995)

Jenkins, Captain Thomas, 14 November, 2019, transcript. (appointed 2002)

Johnson, Captain Otis, 21 July, 14 August, 2016, transcript. (appointed 1984)

Kelly, Captain Michael, 26 April, 15 September, 2005, transcript. (appointed 1971)

Killeen, Battalion Chief Kevin, 28 September, 2009, 12 March, 2019, transcript. (appointed 1974)

Kormash, Deputy Chief Michael, 24 October, 2016, transcript. (appointed 1979)

Kupko, Battalion Chief James, 25 August, 2 September, 2016, transcript. (appointed 2002)

LaPenta, Battalion Chief Steven, 30 September, 2016, transcript. (appointed 1989)

Lawless, Battalion Chief Michael, 1 March, 1999, transcript. (appointed 1966)

Lee, Battalion Chief Sylvester, 5 October, 2016, transcript. (appointed 1986)

Marcell, Deputy Chief Kenneth, 22 October, 2019, transcript. (appointed 1970)

Maresca, Battalion Chief Albert, 17 August, 2016, transcript. (appointed 1987)

Maresca, Firefighter Brett, 25 August, 2016, transcript. (appointed 2012)

Masters, Captain Alan, 20 August, 2016, transcript. (appointed 1986)

Medina, Captain Julio, 10 August, 2016, transcript. (appointed 2006)

Meier, Captain Donald, 9 August, 2016, transcript. (appointed 1996)

Mickels, Captain David, 18 September, 2020, transcript. (appointed 2002)

Miller, Battalion Chief Kenneth, 19 October, 2005, transcript. (appointed 1969)

Mitchell, Captain Michael, 20 October, 2004, transcript. (appointed 1978)

Montalvo, Firefighter Raymond, 5 August, 2016, transcript. (appointed 1996)

Morgan, Captain Bruce, 16 May, 2001, transcript. (appointed 1973)

Nasta, Deputy Chief Michael, 17 June, 2019, transcript. (appointed 1984)

Ostertag, Captain Steve, 29 July, 2016, transcript. (appointed 1994)

Partridge, Battalion Chief Peter, 26 July, 9 November, 2019, transcript. (appointed 1974)

Perez, Captain Joseph, 23 August, 2002, transcript. (appointed 1965)

Petrone, Firefighter Michael, 23 July, 2016, transcript. (appointed 1991)

Pierre, Captain Yves, 15 July, 2016, transcript. (appointed 1995)

Pierre, Firefighter Gregory, 14 August, 2016, transcript. (appointed 2013)

Pierson, Captain James, 28 August, 2016, transcript. (appointed 1991)

Prachar, Firefighter Andrew, 15 December, 2005, transcript. (appointed 1959)

Prachar, Captain John, 10 July, 20 September, 2005, transcript. (appointed 1978)

Ramos, Firefighter Juan, 12 August, 2016, transcript. (appointed 1994)

Rawa, Firefighter Adam, 7 August, 2016, transcript. (appointed 2013)

Reiss, Deputy Chief Thomas, 24 July, 2020, transcript. (appointed 1979)

Richardson, Battalion Chief Scott, 2 August, 2016, transcript. (appointed 1994)

Roberson, Firefighter Luther, 22 August, 2016, transcript. (appointed 1996)

Rodriguez, Battalion Chief Deblin, 21 August, 2016, transcript. (appointed 1996)

Romano, Captain Peter, 28 September, 2008, transcript. (appointed 1972)

Rosamilia, Battalion Chief Gerard, 21 August, 2020, transcript. (appointed 1973)

Rosario, Captain Angel, 5 August, 2016, transcript. (appointed 2002)

Ryan, Battalion Chief John, 6 July, 2005, transcript. (appointed 1948)

Saccone, Battalion Chief Thomas, 27 November, 2000, transcript. (appointed 1969)

Sandella, Captain John, 6 August, 2020, transcript. (appointed 1978)

Schoemer, Firefighter Richard, 1 July, 2005, transcript. (appointed 1959)

Schofield, Firefighter William, 27 March, 2015, transcript. (appointed 1963)

Snyder, Captain William, 1 August, 2016, transcript. (appointed 1993)

Sorace, Captain Michael, 18 August, 2016, transcript. (appointed 1986)

Sperli, Battalion Chief Joseph, 10 September, 2010, 21 August, 2016, transcript. (appointed 1989)

Stoffers, Firefighter Raymond, 8 July, 1997, transcript. (appointed 1973)

Straile, Battalion Chief Joseph, 31 July, 2018, transcript. (appointed 1974)

Tarantino, Captain Anthony, 27 June, 18 July, 2019, transcript. (appointed 1989)

Wapples, Battalion Chief Arnum, 5 August, 1991, transcript. (appointed 1982)

Weber, Battalion Chief William, 29 October, 2008, transcript. (appointed 1969)

Weidele, Battalion Chief William, 20 July, 2016, transcript. (appointed 1984)

West, Firefighter Charles, 12 July, 2019, transcript. (appointed 1989)

Willis, Firefighter James, 9 July, 2019, transcript. (appointed 1996)

Witte, Deputy Chief Michael, 13 August, 2016, transcript. (appointed 1978)

Zieser, Deputy Chief Richard, 25 July, 2016, transcript. (appointed 1978)

Ziyad, Director Fateem, 30 June, 2022, transcript (appointed 1986)